CHARLOTTESVILLE 2017

CHARLOTTESVILLE 2017

The Legacy of Race and Inequity

Edited by
LOUIS P. NELSON AND
CLAUDRENA N. HAROLD

UNIVERSITY OF VIRGINIA PRESS
Charlottesville and London

University of Virginia Press
© 2018 by the Rector and Visitors of the University of Virginia
All rights reserved
Printed in the United States of America on acid-free paper

First published 2018

ISBN 978-0-8139-4189-9 (cloth)
ISBN 978-0-8139-4190-5 (paperback)
ISBN 978-0-8139-4191-2 (e-book)

9 8 7 6 5 4 3 2 1

Library of Congress Cataloging-in-Publication Data is available for this title.

Cover photo: Alec R. Hosterman

CONTENTS

FOREWORD

Universities are complex networks of buildings and organizations that provide education and jobs and health care and cultural enrichment. They take form in classrooms, dorms, dining halls, and hospitals. They field sports teams and community volunteers. They possess histories that include shameful compromises with the inequalities and oppression of their times. And they nurture opposition to those moral and ethical errors. Most fundamentally, universities are students, professors, staff, and alumni who think together about what is needed—from food and computers and trust to books and ideas and evidence—for us to continue in this essential act of collective thought.

This book brings together University of Virginia professors thinking about and feeling their way through the events of August 11 and 12, 2017. When white nationalists and neo-Nazis marched through the University of Virginia, students staged a counterprotest in front of the Rotunda by standing in a small, brave circle around the statue of Jefferson. When white supremacists of all kinds rallied in Emancipation Park and fought in the streets of downtown Charlottesville, students, staff members, alumni, and professors stood among the counterprotesters and said no to hate in our town and our nation. Here, professors write about these events as scholars—as students of history, law, photography, literature, and music, yes—but also as humans, as parents and spouses and siblings, as colleagues and congregation members and citizens of a historical moment in which choices must be made and false equivalencies abolished.

I began my career as a professor of history researching how white Southerners created a culture that legitimated segregation: the system of violence, oppression, and discrimination they created to replace slavery. The question that animated my work was how white Southerners learned to live with what they had done, how they convinced themselves that their world was moral and good and true. Building Confederate statues in parks and in front of courthouses formed an essential part of that work. After twenty years of teaching at the University of Virginia and living in Charlottesville, I have become the rare academic who wishes her research was not quite so relevant.

Here, on a campus where slaves once labored and African American students were not welcomed until almost a century after emancipation, the right to speak freely is not an abstract concept. It is a material, grounded, and embodied act that has been defeated in the past by slavery, war, lynching, rape and other forms of assault, eugenics, and segregation. It has also at times been defended by brave students, faculty, and staff members. It is palpable. In this collection, UVA professors suggest answers to what this history means the next time the white supremacists come to this or another university campus. They turn the university's collective thinking to the prospect of creating a truly antiracist future.

Grace Elizabeth Hale

CHRONOLOGY

1607 The Virginia colony is founded.

1625 The census enumerates twenty-three blacks living in the Virginia colony.

1737 William Taylor receives a patent for the land that would become Charlottesville.

1743 Thomas Jefferson is born on April 13 in Shadwell, Virginia.

1774 The Virginia General Assembly establishes Albemarle County.

1784 Thomas Jefferson publishes *Notes on the State of Virginia*. In the text Jefferson argues that African Americans were inferior to whites in both body and mind. His racial theories elicited outrage and critical responses from a variety of African American intellectuals and leaders, including Benjamin Banneker and David Walker.

1800 This transformative year witnesses numerous events that reveal the tension between freedom and liberty in the American republic. Thomas Jefferson defeats the incumbent president, John Adams, in a highly contested election. Gabriel Prosser, a blacksmith owned by Thomas Prosser of Henrico County, Virginia, devises a plan to liberate his people and put an end to the brutal institution of slavery. Gabriel reads the Bible closely and sees himself as divinely chosen to deliver his people from bondage.

1807 Robert E. Lee is born at Stratford, Westmoreland County, Virginia.

1814 Thomas Jefferson proposes a bill for the establishment of Central College in Virginia.

1817 On October 6 Jefferson begins construction on what would become the University of Virginia, located on a rocky ridge one mile west of the City of Charlottesville. The laying of the cornerstone for the first building draws many dignitaries, including James Monroe and James Madison. Building the university relies on the labor of enslaved African Americans, as well as free blacks.

1818 Jefferson convenes a group in Rockfish Gap, located in the Blue Ridge Mountains and thirty miles west of Monticello. He presents a report on his vision for Central College and explains why Charlottesville is the ideal location. This report is known as the *Rockfish Gap Report*.

1825 On March 7 the University of Virginia officially opens its doors to students.

1826 Thomas Jefferson dies on July 4. He is buried at Monticello the next day.

1859   James Lawrence Cabel, an 1833 graduate of the University of Virginia who joined the faculty in 1837, publishes *The Testimony of Modern Science in the Unity of Mankind*. In this book he posits the inherent intellectual, physical, and emotional inferiority of African Americans. Though insisting that blacks could never be equal to whites, Cabel asserts that the "civilizing" influence of slavery has improved African Americans' condition.

1861   The start of the Civil War transforms both the City of Charlottesville and the University of Virginia. Ninety percent of the six hundred students enrolled at the university in 1860 would eventually fight on the side of the Confederacy.

1864   The Charlottesville African Church, now known as First Baptist Church, is organized. It remains an institutional cornerstone of the African American community in Charlottesville and surrounding counties to the present day.

1865   Robert E. Lee surrenders to Ulysses Grant at Appomattox Courthouse on April 9. A day later he issues his farewell address to the Army of Northern Virginia.

The Thirteenth Amendment to the Constitution abolishes slavery and involuntary servitude. The Senate passes the amendment on April 8, 1864, the House on January 31, 1865. It is ratified on December 6, 1865.

1869   The Jefferson Lodge of Charlottesville successfully petitions for membership in the Union Grand Lodge of Virginia.

1881   Virginia-born educator Booker T. Washington is named principal of the Tuskegee Institute in Alabama. The most powerful African American in the nation until his death in 1915, Washington would have a profound impact on the development of black education.

1892   A graduate of Hampton Institute and a friend of Booker T. Washington, J. F. Bell opens the J. F. Bell Funeral Home.

1901   The University of Virginia hospital opens. Under the leadership of Paul Barringer, who served as the chair of the faculty from 1897 to 1903, the hospital develops into an important intellectual hub of the eugenics movement.

1902   On July 10 the new Virginia Constitution becomes law. To reduce the black electorate and undermine African Americans' political power, the constitution implements requirements like the "understanding clause" and the payment of poll taxes in order to vote. The number of eligible black voters in the state declines from 147,000 in 1901 to 10,000 by 1905.

1907   Harvey Ernest Jordan joins the faculty of the medical school. A longtime member of the UVA community, he serves as the dean of the medical school from 1939 to 1949. A firm and unapologetic believer in the principles of white supremacy, Jordan promotes

sterilization laws that prevent procreation among those he deems
"unfit" for reproduction. To avoid
weakening the gene pool among
whites, he also advocates laws
restricting intermarriage among
whites and blacks.

1914   In the first of a series of attacks
on African Americans' property
rights, the Albemarle County
Board of Supervisors removes
African Americans from the
McKee Row section of Charlottesville by confiscating their land and
deeding it to the city. McKee Row,
a predominantly African American
neighborhood near downtown,
becomes the site of Jackson Park,
where the equestrian statue of
Stonewall Jackson is unveiled
in 1921.

1915   D. W. Griffith releases *The Birth
of a Nation*. Ivey Foreman Lewis
joins the faculty at the University of Virginia. As chair of the
biology department, he integrates
eugenics into the curriculum
and gains a reputation as an out-
spoken eugenicist.

1917   Philanthropist Paul Goodloe
McIntire commissions artist
Henry Shrady to create a statue
in honor of Robert E. Lee.

1920   On October 5 three African American women in Charlottesville,
Mrs. Maggie P. Burley, Mamie J.
Farwell, and Mrs. Alice Grady,
successfully register to vote.

1921   In June the Ku Klux Klan organizes
a local chapter in Charlottesville.
The City of Charlottesville unveils
the Stonewall Jackson monument.

1922   To expedite the process of "Negro
removal," Lily White Republicans in Virginia bar blacks from
participating at the Republican
state convention. Claiming to be
pragmatic rather than racist, white
strategists within the party defend
these moves as necessary steps in
improving the GOP's standing in
the South.

John Powell, a graduate of the
University of Virginia, forms the
Anglo-Saxon Clubs of America,
a white supremacist organization that promotes separation of
the races and the colonization of
black Americans to West Africa,
preferably Liberia.

1924   On May 21 the City of Charlottes-
ville unveils the statue of
Robert E. Lee as part of a two-day
event in which the Sons of the
Confederacy participate. The
Virginia Assembly passes the
Racial Integrity Act of 1924.

1926   Black Charlottesville celebrates
the opening of the city's first high
school for African Americans,
Jefferson High School.

1935   Alice Jackson, an alumnus of the
historically black Virginia Union
University in Richmond, applies
to the University of Virginia to
conduct graduate work in English.
The university rejects her application and does not admit an African
American until 1950.

1945   Under the leadership of Rev.
Benjamin F. Bunn, local activists
form the Charlottesville branch of
the NAACP. By 1954 the NAACP
chapter has 867 members.

1954   The U.S. Supreme Court issues its *Brown v. Board of Education* decision, which declares the separate but equal doctrine unconstitutional. Randolph Louis White founds the local black newspaper, the *Charlottesville Albemarle Tribune.*

1956   On February 25 U.S. Senator Harry F. Byrd Sr. (D-VA) calls for massive resistance against the Supreme Court's *Brown v. Board of Education* decision.

1956   Judge John Paul of the U.S. District Court for the Fourth Circuit issues an order for Venable Elementary School and Lane High School to integrate at the beginning of the school year. To delay the process the local school board appeals the decision for two years.

1958   After a federal court order to integrate several schools in Virginia immediately, Gov. J. Lindsay Almond Jr. orders the closing of public schools in Charlottesville, Alexandria, and Norfolk. In Charlottesville, Lane and Venable are closed until February 1959.

1960   The Charlottesville Redevelopment Housing Authority submits an application to the Charlottesville City Council calling for the redevelopment of Vinegar Hill, a central residential, business, intellectual, and cultural district for African Americans.

1964   Congress passes the Civil Rights Act of 1964, which bans discrimination on the basis of race, gender, religion, and national origin. This law plays a critical role in the desegregation of the City of Charlottesville and the University of Virginia. In addition, the Westhaven housing project is completed. It will house many of the city's black residents displaced by the razing and destruction of Vinegar Hill.

1967   Virginia Anne Scott, Nancy Jaffe, Nancy L. Anderson, and Jo Anne Kirstein file a lawsuit against the University of Virginia charging that the school discriminates against women in its admissions policies. The court mandates coeducation within three years. In the fall of 1970, 450 women undergraduates enter the university.

1968   African American student leaders organize the Black Students for Freedom, a precursor to the Black Student Alliance.

1969   On February 18 hundreds of progressive students march on the University of Virginia's historic Lawn, demanding an end to all vestiges of Jim Crow segregation, a living wage for workers, the creation of a Black Studies program, the integration of UVA's athletic department, and the appointment of an African American as assistant dean of admissions.

1970   In early May, following the murder of four students at Kent State University, student activists at UVA engage in a series of protests over the war in Vietnam, the slow pace of integration at the college, the status and working conditions of low-wage employees on grounds, and law enforcement officials' "invasion" of the Academical Village.

1972   Charles Lee Barbour becomes the first African American mayor of Charlottesville.

1974   UVA's student newspaper, the *Cavalier Daily,* publishes several articles on the large number of UVA administrators, including President Frank Hereford, who belong to the all-white Farmington Country Club, which at the time excluded Jews, African Americans, and other people of color. In addition to President Hereford, this list includes seventeen department chairs, seven deans, and eight Board of Visitors members.

1976   After protests over the Farmington Country Club membership issues, as well as other related incidents, the Office of Afro-American Affairs is created in 1976.

1977   The number of African American undergraduates enrolled at the University of Virginia reaches five hundred for the first time.

1978   In response to constant demand for affordable housing in Charlottesville, Friendship Courts is constructed on Garrett Street.

1979   The poverty rate among African Americans living in Albemarle County is 22.7 percent.

1980   The eleven-million-dollar Primary Care Center at UVA opens in January. The site displaces the former neighborhood Gospel Hill, which was predominantly black.

1982   The Office for Civil Rights finally approves the state's desegregation plan for higher education. This comes eighteen years after the passage of the Civil Rights Act of 1964.

1987   UVA releases the *Audacious Faith* report, a detailed account of race relations on Grounds, documenting the experiences of students, faculty, and workers. It began in 1986 when the university commenced its preparations for its decennial reaccreditation evaluation from the Southern Association of Colleges and Schools. University president Robert O'Neil appointed a steering committee for the self-study report. The committee had as one of its tasks the evaluation of the university's recruitment of black students and faculty. The committee suggested the formation of a separate task force that would focus solely on investigating the state of race relations on Grounds and recommending policies to achieve full integration at the university. President O'Neil impaneled a committee of sixteen faculty members, students, and administrators, who compile the *Audacious Faith* report.

1989   Virginians elect Lawrence Douglas Wilder as the sixty-sixth governor of Virginia.

1996   With strong support from the local chapter of the NAACP, the Office of Equal Opportunity releases *An Examination of the University's Minority Classified Staff (The Muddy Floor Report).* The report reveals "glaring disparities" in employment opportunities, performance evaluations, and disciplinary sanctions between white and black employees.

2001   Richard Spencer graduates from UVA with a bachelor of arts in English and music. About twelve hundred African American undergraduates attend the university in the 2000–01 academic year.

2003   A series of racial incidents on Grounds leads university president John Casteen to create the Commission on Diversity and Equity, which conducts a year-long study on race relations on Grounds. This leads to the creation of the position of vice president and chief officer of diversity and equity.

2006   On February 21 the Living Wage Campaign releases *Keeping Our Promises: Toward A Living Wage at the University*, a detailed report that encourages the administration to adopt a living wage ($10.72 per hour) for classified staff and contract employees. A month and a half later, on April 12, seventeen students affiliated with the campaign stage a sit-in at Madison Hall. For the next three days, the Living Wage Campaign captures the attention of students, administrators, faculty members, community leaders, and perhaps most importantly, the media.

2008   During a retreat the Charlottesville City Council identifies two issues deserving serious and immediate attention: the need to ease strained race relations between whites and African Americans and the necessity of promoting greater diversity within city government. A series of conversations leads to the creation of the Dialogue on Race project.

2010   In June Dialogue on Race creates working groups to tackle a variety of issues, including housing, employment, and education.

2010   Richard Spencer founds the publication alternativeright.com. In June 2011 Spencer becomes president and director of the National Policy Institute.

2013   UVA president Teresa A. Sullivan establishes the Commission on Slavery and the University.

2015   On March 18 Martese Johnson, then a third-year student at UVA, is brutally arrested by officers from Alcoholic Beverage Control (ABC) on "The Corner," a popular hangout near academic Grounds. His bloodied face circulates across the media and elicits a great deal of conversation about the politics of race and the treatment of African Americans on and beyond the Grounds of UVA. The following month the Black Student Alliance issues its report, *Toward a Better University*. In November, Wes Bellamy is elected to the Charlottesville City Council.

2016   In March Councilman Bellamy calls for the removal of the Robert E. Lee statue in Lee Park. On May 28 the Charlottesville City Council approves a resolution to create the Blue Ribbon Commission on Race, Memorials, and Public Spaces.

The Blue Ribbon Commission submits its report to the council in late December.

2017 February: The Charlottesville City Council votes to remove the Robert E. Lee statue and rename Lee Park.

March 20: Several groups, including the Sons of Confederate Veterans, file a lawsuit against the city council, noting that its decision to remove the Lee statue violates state law.

May 2: Judge Richard Moore rules that the statues cannot be moved for six months.

May 13: UVA alum and white nationalist activist Richard Spencer leads a nighttime rally in Lee Park to protest the city council's decision to remove the statue.

June 5: The city council votes unanimously to rename Lee and Jackson Parks. The former becomes Emancipation Park and the latter Justice Park.

July 8: President Teresa Sullivan issues statement to the UVA community encouraging its members to avoid conflict with white supremacists. That same day dozens of KKK members rally in protest of the city's plan to remove the Lee statue.

August 10: Jason Kessler—lead organizer of the Unite the Right rally, graduate of UVA, and resident of Charlottesville—files a federal suit against the City of Charlottesville with the support of the Virginia ACLU.

August 11: Federal Judge Glen Conrad rules that the Unite the Rally can be held in Emancipation Park. At approximately 8:45 p.m., a group of 250 white supremacists and nationalists assembles on Nameless Field, located in the back of Memorial Gymnasium at UVA. The group, led by Richard Spencer, then marches to the Thomas Jefferson statue near the Rotunda, where a small group of students have assembled to protest the white supremacists.

August 12: Early in the morning Unite the Right rally participants and counterprotesters assemble in various points in downtown Charlottesville, including the pedestrian mall and Emancipation Park. At approximately 11:32 a.m., law enforcement officials rule it an unlawful assembly as violence breaks out. At approximately 11:52 a.m., Gov. Terry McAuliffe declares a state of emergency. At 1:42 p.m., a car later identified as belonging to James Alex Fields plows into the downtown mall, killing counterprotester and Charlottesville resident Heather Heyer and injuring nineteen others.

August 20: The city council votes to shroud both the Jackson and Lee statues.

September 24: Thousands pack Scott Stadium for A Concert for Charlottesville, which features the Dave Matthews Band, the Roots, Brittany Howard (of Alabama Shakes), Stevie Wonder, and Pharrell Williams, among others.

October 7: Three UVA students are arrested for trespassing at the Bicentennial Launch celebration. At the event the students held up the banner "200 YEARS OF WHITE SUPREMACY" in front of a screen showing coverage of the event. That same night white supremacists hold a tiki-torch rally in Emancipation Park. Chants of "you will not replace us" pierce the air as the participants gather around the covered Robert E. Lee statue.

November: Charlottesville native and local activist Nikuyah Walker is elected to the city council. She is later appointed mayor. Walker is the first African American woman to hold the position of mayor.

CHARLOTTESVILLE 2017

INTRODUCTION

Dialogues on Race and Inequity at the
University of Virginia

In the spring of 2016, Charlottesville High School ninth-grader Zyhana Bryant petitioned her city council to remove the monumental equestrian statue of Robert E. Lee from one of our city's downtown public parks. Her cause was soon championed by Wes Bellamy, the only African American on the city council. Bryant's petition shone a spotlight on the material legacies of white supremacy that mark Charlottesville and hundreds of other towns in the South. In response to Bryant's activism, as well as the African American community's longstanding frustration with local politics, Bellamy began a very public conversation about past and present racism in a city that thinks of itself as highly progressive. Tensions escalated and as the conversation about the removal of the Lee statue gained currency, white nationalists and even the KKK came out to protest. The city council then expanded the conversation to include the "Stonewall" Jackson monument as well, the second of two large equestrian statues dominating Charlottesville's downtown parks. Then, in the summer of 2017, two white nationalists began planning a massive "invasion" of the city—with now-famous disastrous and murderous results.

Those arguing to protect the statues ground their rhetoric in constitutionally protected free speech, citing broad cultural claims about preserving heritage. And it is true that these events raise important questions about free speech, intimidation, citizenship, and other fundamentals of American political identity. For those eager to see the statues come down, the potential deinstallation of these works of public art symbolize a commitment to Charlottesville's African American community that the persistent structures of white supremacy will no longer be the default. What quickly becomes clear is that these monuments are potent symbols—flashpoints of the heated and polarized condition of contemporary America. These huge issues define our moment as a nation. That these events center on historical monuments confirms for us that Faulkner was right: "The past is never dead. It is not even past." In this utterance, Faulkner reminds us that our past is a part of us. We daily face the task of confronting or ignoring it.

When confronting these monuments, one of the first tasks is to recall that they are not a part of the immediate post–Civil War South, that era we generally call the Reconstruction, but of the era of the Jim Crow South, after the failure of Reconstruction. It is also important to understand the construction of these monuments within the regionally specific context of white anxiety over the growing political insurgency of the New Negro. The egalitarian rhetoric and political transformations engendered by World War I and its immediate aftermath had a profound impact on black Southerners, including those living in the town of Charlottesville. Convinced that the struggle for democracy extended beyond the bloody trenches of western Europe, African Americans across the South fought valiantly against the political, social, and economic manifestations of white supremacy. Operating in a variety of political arenas, southern New Negroes pushed hard to increase their presence in the electoral arena, formed independent labor bodies and trade unions, and lent their support to prominent political organizations like the National Association for the Advancement of Colored People (NAACP) and Marcus Garvey's Universal Negro Improvement Association. The growing militancy of black Southerners, particularly black Virginians, did not escape the notice of Garvey, who after a visit to the Old Dominion wrote: "The Southern Negro now feels that he has a part to play in the affairs of the world. A new light is burning for our brothers at this end. They are determined that they too shall enjoy a portion of that democracy for which many of their sons and brothers fought for and died for in France."[1]

This new light did not escape the town of Charlottesville. In fact, in 1921 the local black newspaper, the *Charlottesville Messenger,* published a provocative article entitled, "The New Negro: What He Wants." In that article the self-identified "New Negroes of Charlottesville" put forth the following demands:

1. Teacher salaries based on service not color
2. A four-year high school
3. Representation in the city council
4. Jim Crow streetcars abolished
5. Representation on the school board
6. Better street facilities in Negro districts

Identifying themselves as "tax payers and law abiding citizens," the letter writers noted their collective strength and vowed to "accept nothing short of justice!" The fiery article elicited a strong rebuke from white Charlottesvillians, including the editor of the local white newspaper, the *Daily Progress,* who dismissed the demands as "absurd tirades and impossible proposals."[2] The same year in which the local white community dismissed African Americans' calls for racial justice as "absurd," the Stonewall Jackson monument became a permanent fixture downtown.

STONEWALL JACKSON MONUMENT, 1921

On a night in late April 1917, a torch-bearing lynching mob centered their attention on an alley between residences that gave direct access to the county jail from the county courthouse. Hampton Crosby and Richard Jones, both black, had been caught stealing a ham by white policeman Meredith Thomas. After a struggle, Thomas was shot and killed by his own gun. Just days later Crosby and Jones found themselves detained in the old city jail, which still stands less than a block north of the courthouse. "Shouting and cat-calling" by the mob outside the jail persisted for hours. Authorities were alarmed when they learned that "a large delegation from the student body at the University was expected down to join them in the grand march to seize the men and carry out a spectacular lynching at a tree selected near the place of the killing [of Thomas]." The sheriff needed reinforcements and called in an additional one hundred men, half coming by train from Staunton. Just after midnight the fire department was called, "but the hose was not used against the crowd. It was reported that the men declined to shift their volunteered service from fire-fighting to mob chasing, and would not use the apparatus." The night was tense, but no one pulled the trigger. Into the early hours of the morning the crowd slowly dispersed, having "furnished no leader who could risk those glistening revolvers and shining bayonets seen dimly in the dusky night." On June 20 Crosby and Jones were electrocuted in Richmond.[3]

That mob in April filled High Street and the open spaces around Charlottesville's Thomas Jefferson–designed courthouse. They also spilled down McKee Street, which divided Courthouse Square from McKee Row, a row of rental tenements occupied largely by African Americans. Contemporary whites described the tenements as "ramshackle" and "an eyesore" (see fig. 1).[4] During the same period that the hooded mob gathered outside

FIGURE 1. McKee Row, a traditional black neighborhood near Courthouse Square, was torn down by the city and replaced with a white memorial. (Albert and Shirley Small Special Collections Library, University of Virginia)

the jail to threaten Crosby and Jones with lynching, Charlottesville's white community plotted to tear down McKee Row and replace it with a school for white children.[5] Just over four years after the lynch mob marched, on the spot previously occupied by McKee Row, Senator Pat Harrison of Mississippi offered a hagiographic celebration of Thomas Jonathan "Stonewall" Jackson at the unveiling of the new equestrian statue erected in his honor. The "eyesore" of McKee Row had been replaced not with a white school but with a white memorial (see fig. 2). The equestrian statue features Jackson with forward-focused attention sitting atop a horse approaching cantor. This duo is supported by a bold, pink granite pedestal dominated by spectacular allegorical figures of Faith and Valor. The two strong, strikingly Aryan youths carry a shield adorned with the stars and bars. Placed at what had formerly been street level, Faith and Valor replaced the "rowdy" residents of McKee Row. The unveiling was the capstone of three days of celebration that included a grand gala reunion of Confederate veterans and a five-thousand-person march through the city that concluded with white school children arranged as a living representation of the Confederate banner in Midway Plaza, which crowned the north slope of the city's largest African American neighborhood, Vinegar Hill.[6]

In the 1910s and '20s Courthouse Square—including the courthouse and its attendant jail (the site of the lynching mob) and McKee Row (eventually the site of the Jackson monument)—was the center of Charlottesville's political, legal, and civil authority.[7] Here the laws of the city, the state, and the nation shaped the lives of local citizens. Here, in the half century following the passage of the Fourteenth Amendment, black Charlottes-villians saw the legal and political recognition of their citizenship slowly recede. As early as 1900 the Virginia Conference of Colored Men met at the Oddfellows' Hall in Charlottesville to discuss methods of resisting Afri-can American political disenfranchisement. Within ten years black political power and legal authority had been so diminished as to erase their very presence from the landscape of citizenship. In his dedication speech for the Jackson monument, Senator Harrison noted that the Civil War tore

FIGURE 2. This equestrian statue of Stonewall Jackson sup-planted McKee Row. Jackson sits atop a granite pedestal featuring allegorical Aryan youths Faith and Valor. (Photo by Dell Upton)

a nation apart with "fratricidal strife." With no recognition of black presence, Harrison assumed his audience to be white. Such familial language is part and parcel of a reconstituted Southern identity that Dell Upton has described as "unambiguously white."[8] But what did "white" mean in the 1910s and 1920s? As recent scholarship on the KKK reinforces, "white" in this period was certainly constructed in opposition to "black," but white did not include all nonblacks. In this era of rising immigration, white also excluded immigrants, Jews, and Catholics, categories of individuals who were not considered part of the American historical and political project.[9] Like the Jackson monument, Harrison's speech was an act of both intimidation and erasure. So was the demolition of McKee Row. And so was the threat of lynching. Taken together, these urban rituals, public speeches, and the physical remaking of the city were the product of collective action by the city's population of white, Southern-born Protestants.

In the summer of 1921 the KKK organized a public address in the courthouse just feet from where the Jackson monument would be unveiled later in October. The public address was supported by bulletins posted around town that warned "LAW AND ORDER MUST PREVAIL." They announced that "all undesirables must leave town. The eye of the unknown has been and is constantly observing . . . We See All, We Hear All, We Know All." The bulletin ended with an invitation. Any "100 percent" white, native-born American man who "held to the tenets of the Christian religion, Free Schools, Free Speech, Free Press, Law Enforcement, Liberty, *and White Supremacy*" [italics added] was welcome to join.[10] The KKK spoke openly in the space of the courthouse about the enforcement of white supremacy as essential to the preservation of the ideals of the Confederacy. Charlottesville's nonwhite audience certainly got the message. When the echoes of the white supremacists' voices faded and the bulletins all melted in the rain, the monumental statue of Stonewall Jackson and its Aryan youth—erected just months after the KKK spoke in the courthouse—would serve to remind black and white Charlottesvillians of the unspoken requirements for full citizenship: "whiteness."[11]

THE ROBERT E. LEE MONUMENT, 1924

The monument to Robert E. Lee rose three years later (see fig. 3). As was the case with the Jackson monument, the week of its unveiling was filled with festivals and galas especially celebrating the last surviving Confederate veterans. One of the events was the ritual opening of the Grand Camp

FIGURE 3. Robert E. Lee, patriarch of the Confederacy. This statue was the flash-point of the August 12, 2017, white-nationalist riot. (Photo by Bill Emory)

of the Confederate Veterans of Virginia, which took place in the down-town Jefferson Theater, the center of white Charlottesville's social life. The ladies of the Confederacy were welcomed in the theater that evening. The most public spectacle, aside from the unveiling, was the grand parade of the KKK. "Thousands lined the sidewalks of Main Street from the C&O Station to the foot of Vinegar Hill," the newspaper reported. The nighttime "march of the white robed figures was impressive and directed attention to the presence of the organization in the community." The week culmi-nated in a grand Confederate ball to be held in UVA's Memorial Gymna-sium. Admission was limited to members of Confederate organizations, especially the Daughters and Sons of Confederate Veterans. The announce-ment of the ball also noted that the Sons of Confederate Veterans were now accepting applications from grandsons.[12] The KKK appears to have had a special relationship with Memorial Gym; just a decade earlier, the Klan offered a generous gift of $10,000 to UVA for the construction of that same facility. All for the celebration of Robert E. Lee.

If George Washington was the father of our country, Robert E. Lee was the patriarch of the Confederacy. So said Edwin Alderman, UVA's presi-dent, on the occasion of the unveiling of the Lee monument: "The South's great Chieftain had done even more than his great prototype, Washington."

Alderman continued, stating that Lee "was the embodiment of the best that there is in all the sincere and romantic history of the whole state. Its triumphs, its defeats, its joys, its sufferings, its rebirth, its pride, and its patience center in him."[13] By the opening decades of the twentieth century, the liturgies of the Cult of Lee were already deeply entrenched in the self-fashioning of white Southerners. Just months after the unveiling of the Lee statue, the pastor of the First Presbyterian Church (which at that time faced onto the park that was then called Lee Square) "described social life in the South before and during the war . . . with all that made it ideal and charming."[14] The unveiling of the Lee monument bound together the white supremacy of the KKK and the romanticized rebirth of the Old South. If the triumphs, defeats, and sufferings of the Old South centered on the person of Robert E. Lee, so too did its pride, charm, and glory through its rebirth in the 1920s. And the most explicit mark of the rebirth of the Old South would be the unveiling of the monument to Lee—the patriarch of the re-created Confederacy. When the Lee statue was unveiled in Richmond, one African American resident in that city noted its message: "The Southern white folks is on top."[15]

If the society and culture of the Old South were reimagined as charming, then black culture was recast as its antithesis. The Jefferson Theater, just two blocks away from the Lee monument, rescreened D. W. Griffith's *The Birth of a Nation* (1915) just months after the unveiling.[16] The *Daily Progress* touted the film as "the greatest picture of the age." The newspaper noted that the film's rescreening drew "as large crowds as it did originally." The Jefferson Theater offered multiple screenings a day as "thousands want to see it a second time."[17] The picture was notorious for its portrayal of African Americans as unintelligent and oversexed. The NAACP attempted to have the film banned. Just days later the *Daily Progress* ran a series of teaser ads exhibiting highly caricatured and stereotyped images of black men.[18] Ads announced the arrival of a minstrel show for charity in the Jefferson Theater. Composed largely of white men in blackface, the show openly mocked African Americans. The Grand Camp of the Confederates, the screening of *Birth of a Nation,* and the openly racist minstrel show were all part of the rebirth of the Old South in the imaginations of white Southerners.

This clear assertion of racial hierarchy depended on the education being offered at the University of Virginia. Paul Barringer, professor of physiology and eventually president of the faculty, spent his life researching white racial superiority through the study of eugenics.[19] In his 1900 publication, entitled "The American Negro: His Past and Future," Barringer professes the intrinsic racial inferiority of African Americans. He argues that

> the American negro is the resultant of a combination of forces, each one of which can be isolated and analysed. I will show from the study of his racial history (phylogeny) that his late tendency to return to barbarism is as natural as the return of the sow that is washed to her wallowing in the mire. I will show that the ages of degradation under which he was formed and the fifty centuries of historically recorded savagery with which he came to us cannot be permanently influenced by one or two centuries of enforced correction.[20]

Barringer's teachings were closely aligned with the convictions of the Virginia Grand Dragon of the KKK, who spoke at a 1922 meeting of the Charlottesville chapter: "The destinies of America shall remain with the white race; they shall never be entrusted to the black, the brown, or the yellow, or to the unclean hands of hybrids or mongrels." The newspaper article describing this speech concluded by noting that the Charlottesville chapter was not among the largest in the state but that it boasted "many of our able and influential citizens."[21] And strong support for the KKK's views appears also to have permeated the student body. That same year, the student yearbook pictured white-clad equestrians as the cover page to the section devoted to clubs and organizations (see fig. 4). The University of Virginia also had a connection to another important white supremacist group, the Anglo-Saxon Clubs of America, which was organized by John Powell, a graduate of the school. Though never enjoying a large membership, the Anglo-Saxon Clubs performed an important role in the passage of the Racial Integrity Act of 1924, which changed the statutory definition of white from anyone with less than one-quarter of "Negro blood" to anyone with a discernable trace of African ancestry. Under tremendous pressure from the Anglo-Saxon Clubs, legislators amended existing laws against intermarriage to correspond to this new racial configuration. Not completely satisfied with the new racial integrity laws, the organization also worked, albeit unsuccessfully, to secure legislation financing the colonization of blacks to the West African state of Liberia.[22] Much like the leaders of the alt-right, which includes UVA alums Richard Spencer and Jason Kessler, John Powell and other Anglo-Saxon Clubs leaders viewed themselves as the intellectual vanguard of white supremacy.

FIGURE 4. An illustration from the UVA student yearbook,
1922. White-clad equestrians adorn the cover page for
the section devoted to clubs and organizations. (Albert
and Shirley Small Special Collections Library, University
of Virginia)

Excavating the intellectual roots of white supremacy is important, as is
understanding the violence that undergirded the political culture of Jim
Crow. Far too often our focus on Virginia's tradition of gentlemanly, polite
racism blinds us to the racial terrorism blacks in the state experienced during the height of Jim Crow. In the months surrounding the rescreening of
Birth of a Nation and the staging of the minstrel show and other social spectacles in downtown Charlottesville, the KKK set off "heavy explosions from
three bombs," and then burned a cross in the yard of an African American
church just outside of town. The latter event was attended by fifty Klansmen, "only about six of them masked."[23] The notable choice of many
Klansmen to attend unmasked reveals their sense that the battle for public
opinion had been won. (This same confidence resurfaced in August 2017
when first the KKK paraded unmasked but otherwise in full regalia, and
then neo-Nazis stormed the streets of downtown.) It was no accident that

the Jefferson Theater was a focal point of the racist spectacles of the 1920s. The erection of the Lee monument was the culminating act in the remaking of a city as the *new* Old South, with all of the attendant political, racial, educational, and cultural implications.

Seen through the lens of history, these statues are more easily recognized as silent heralds of deeply entrenched systems of political disenfranchisement, educational injustice, health inequity, and neighborhood marginalization. The wounds from this history run deep. But this is not a history that correlates with Charlottesville's reputation as one of the happiest cities in America, nor does it align with the university's self-conception as smart and progressive, if genteel. Thus, this history has not been the subject of hard conversations about how our past is not even past.

Until August 11, 2017, the University of Virginia generally positioned itself as separate from the city. Faculty, staff, and some students understood themselves to be citizens of the city and participated in these conversations as individual activists, but the institution stood alongside the city disengaged. This policy of disengagement failed to safeguard the university from the rising tide of anti-Semitism, racism, and violence. In the dusk hours of August 11, hundreds of white nationalists gathered in a large open athletic field and prepared for a torch-lit march through Grounds to the iconic statue of Thomas Jefferson in the plaza in front of the university's Rotunda. The thin veil of distinction quickly dissolved.

Within UVA's expansive community, the tragic events of August 11 and 12 have occasioned critical and sober reflection on our individual and collective responsibility to advance the principles of democracy and justice, as well as to respond to the moral and ethical challenges of our times. Numerous faculty at the university teach and research issues of racism, public art, free speech, social ethics, and other related subjects, and many of these faculty have been actively involved in these public conversations. This volume is a collection of some of that work, catalyzed by these recent events but not bounded exclusively to them.

Grounded in our own convictions as historians (and in concert with Faulkner), we believe that to ignore the past is foolish, and we share a deep conviction espoused by professor of education and contributor Rachel Wahl that there are many very good reasons to engage in dialogue over difficult subjects. Thus, this volume is framed around truth telling, engaged listening, and ethical response. It opens with two sections on truth telling. John Mason, one of the co-chairs of the city's Blue Ribbon Commission on Race, Memorials, and Public Spaces, opens the first section, "Remembering," with a personal recounting of his experience through August and a reflection on the city's unseen histories. Civil War expert Elizabeth Varon then turns her attention to the complicated legacy of Robert E. Lee, responding to claims of equivalency in debates over remembering the Old South. Asher Beimann then offers a long view of anti-Semitism. Such a perspective is greatly needed, given the many ways in which anti-Semitism animates the politics of white supremacists within and beyond the alt-right.

The second section, "Speaking," again focuses on truth telling, but this time the discussions are grounded more in political action, policy, and law. Here, we invite readers to grapple with one of the greatest legal and public safety challenges confronting university presidents and administrators: white supremacists' use of free speech doctrine to expand their influence on college campuses. "The alt-right has figured out how to turn free speech, a cornerstone of liberal democracy, into a tool for dismantling that democracy," writes historian Nicole Hemmer. "It is able to do so because most Americans, even highly educated ones, have a fuzzy understanding of both free speech and democratic institutions and values. Now is the time, Hemmer argues, for institutions of higher learning to create a clear set of guidelines regarding white supremacists' "weaponizing" of free speech:

> Clarity cannot come quickly enough to institutions of higher education and the boards and politicians who govern them. The First Amendment gives Richard Spencer the right to shout on street corners (and even then within limits); it does not give him the right to set up shop in the student union and recruit disaffected white men to his cause. Until universities grasp this, and create a set of guidelines to govern their relationship to extremist, anti-liberal ideologies, they will continue to be the site where men like William Fears are radicalized.[24]

The essays in "Speaking" provide greater clarity and guidance on this critical issue. Renowned First Amendment lawyer Frederick Schauer offers a brief introduction to the First Amendment that helps to frame the next two essays.[25] Through her fascinating analysis of the "heckler's veto," Leslie Kendrick carefully considers several questions that have long been at the heart of free speech debate in this country: Under what circumstances can public speech be relegated? How much can local governments rely on the need for security and the enormous costs involved in hosting potentially violent groups as content-neutral reasons for regulation? Can a public institution consider the likely number of counterprotesters when deciding the appropriate time or venue for a protest or rally? With vivid clarity and great imagination, Risa Goluboff, legal historian and dean of the law school at UVA, closes the section with an exploration of the connections between the First and Second Amendments, the dangers of "protecting violence that presents itself in the guise of free speech," and the legal, moral, and intellectual challenges confronting American colleges and universities in our contemporary moment. Together with the other scholars in this section, Dean Goluboff offers us the opportunity to reflect on "what role the law has played in bringing us to this moment, and what role it can and must play in moving us forward once again."

But healthy dialogue and a vision for change require both speaking and "Listening," the frame for the third group of essays. This section brings together scholars in the fields of literature, critical race theory, history, and music. Literary scholar Lisa Woolfork listens well: her subject is the collective communications offered by the university administration. Through a close textual reading of a variety of documents, including the 1818 *Rockfish Gap Report,* which outlined UVA's educational and political mission, Woolfork provides us with a fascinating read on the long history of white supremacy at UVA. More provocatively, she forces us to consider whether the white supremacist marches and rallies of August 11 and 12, led by university graduates Richard Spencer and Jason Kessler, were invasions or homecomings. The theme of UVA's white supremacist legacies continues with Preston Reynolds's essay. Turning her attention to an important aspect of the university's legacy as both an academic and medical institution, Reynolds centers on the work of Paul Barringer and others to report the university's long involvement in the science of eugenics. Much like Reynolds and Woolfolk, Claudrena Harold engages the politics and history of the University of Virginia. With a focus on the post–civil rights era, she listens to the voices of black student activists and seeks to situate the recent demands of campus protesters within a broader historical context. In this essay, she also draws on her experiences as the faculty advisor to the Black Student Alliance, a group that in the aftermath of August 11 and 12 issued a set of demands to the university administration. Finally, ethnomusicologist Bonnie Gordon offers a critical interpretation of the words and theater of the white supremacists. By listening well to their theater, she opens windows into their use of deeper practices of oratory and performance. Here we can see the ways in which cultural analysis both deepens and complicates our understandings of the workings of white supremacy in theory and practice.

The collection closes with calls for response, but responses grounded in well-considered personal, social, and institutional ethics. Ethicist Willis Jenkins opens the section with an autoethnography of his own reconsiderations of sources of authority and responsibility. Rachel Wahl's essay on dialogue confronts the challenges and possibilities of public debate and exchange in a moment of crisis. Offering insights from her studies on human rights work in India, Wahl reminds us of the importance of *listening* to and engaging with the struggles of other communities that have also tackled complex political and social issues. Like John Mason's essay in the first section, Gregory Fairchild's essay is more personal, recounting his growing understanding of the troubling distinction between diversity and integration. Guian McKee closes the volume with a powerful assessment of the institutional responsibilities of the university and the medical center in the aftermath of the 2017 white supremacist riots. Fittingly, he provides us with suggestions and recommendations on how we can move forward not just in the aftermath of August 2017, but also in light of Charlottesville's and UVA's long history of racial slavery, Jim Crow segregation and exclusion, housing and employment discrimination, and medical apartheid and health disparities across racial lines.

We have worked hard to preserve the individual voices of the various authors, and we hope that through this volume you will hear them distinctly. Each of us experienced the terrible events of August 2017 in different ways, but they have affected us all. We come to this volume as individuals and as scholars, and through this publication we hope to catalyze individual reflection, yes, but more importantly we hope to provoke considered and responsible dialogue, a conversation that understands and owns our past and remembers that the past is part of our present.

NOTES

1. Marcus Garvey and Robert Hill, *The Marcus Garvey and Universal Negro Improvement Association Papers*, vol. 2, *August 1919–August 1920* (Berkeley: University of California Press, 1983), 121.

2. *Daily Progress*, Feb. 16 and 18, 1921.

3. This essay depends heavily on the excellent historical research published as "1917–1924: A Timeline: The McIntire Statues and Charlottesville's African American Community," an appendix to the mayor's Blue Ribbon Commission on Race, Memorials, and Public Spaces, www.charlottesville.org/departments-and -services/boards-and-commissions/blue-ribbon-commission-on-race-memorials -and-public-spaces. A deeper dive into the contexts outlined in this essay appears

also in the rich online project, The Illusion of Progress: Charlottesville's Roots in White Supremacy, available on the website of UVA's Carter G. Woodson Center, http://woodson.as.virginia.edu/woodson-projects. The author is grateful to the following readers who offered feedback on early drafts of this essay: Lisa Goff, Andrus Ashoo, Bill Wilder, Ian Stevenson, Marta Gutman, Claudrena Harold, and Dell Upton. The quote and the information on the executions are from the *Daily Progress*, April 17 and June 20, 1917.

4. This section depends heavily on research published by Daniel Bluestone, "A Virginia Courthouse Square," in *Buildings, Landscapes, and Memory: Case Studies in Historic Preservation* (New York: Norton, 2011), 220–26. *Daily Progress*, March 19, 1914.

5. *Daily Progress*, March 19, 1914.

6. Ibid., Oct. 19, 1921.

7. For more on the particular authority of courthouses in early Virginia, see Carl Lounsbury, *The Courthouses of Early Virginia: An Architectural History* (Charlottesville: University of Virginia Press, 2005).

8. Dell Upton, *What Can and Can't Be Said: Race, Uplift, and Monument Building in the Contemporary South* (New Haven, CT: Yale University Press, 2015), 33.

9. Linda Gordon, *The Second Coming of the KKK: The Ku Klux Klan of the 1920s and the American Political Tradition* (New York: Liveright Publishing, 2017).

10. *Daily Progress*, July 19, 1921.

11. For more on the activity of the KKK in Charlottesville in the 1920s and '30s, see "Chapter 1: Charlottesville's Confederate Past," from The Illusion of Progress website, http://woodson.as.virginia.edu/woodson-projects.

12. *Daily Progress*, May 19 and 15, 1924, respectively.

13. Ibid., May 21, 1924.

14. Ibid., Jan. 21, 1924.

15. From Kirk Savage, *Standing Soldiers, Kneeling Slaves: Race, War, and Monument in Nineteenth-Century America* (Princeton, NJ: Princeton University Press, 1997), 151.

16. Nancy Bishop Dessommes, "Hollywood in Hoods: The Portrayal of the Ku Klux Klan in Popular Film," *Journal of Popular Culture* 32, no. 4 (1999): 13–22.

17. *Daily Progress*, Jan. 25, 1924.

18. Ibid., Feb. 1, 1924.

19. Gregory Dorr, "Segregation's Science: The American Eugenics Movement and Virginia, 1900–1980," PhD diss., University of Virginia, Charlottesville, 2000.

20. Paul Barringer, *The American Negro: His Past and Future* (Raleigh, NC: Edwards & Broughton, 1900), 1.

21. *Daily Progress*, Aug. 23, 1922.

22. See Claudrena Harold, *The Rise and Fall of the Garvey Movement in the Urban South, 1918–1942* (New York: Routledge, 2007), 92, 101–02.

23. *Daily Progress*, June 21, 1924.

24. Extract and quote above are from Nicole Hemmer, "Weaponizing Free Speech: Alt-Right Activists Are Transforming College Campuses into Sites for Radicalization," *U.S. News and World Report*, Oct. 24, 2017, www.usnews.com/opinion/

thomas-jefferson-street/articles/2017-10-24/william-fears-and-the-alt-right
-weaponize-free-speech-on-college-campuses.

25. The First Amendment reads: "Congress shall make no law respecting an establishment of religion, or prohibiting the free exercise thereof; or abridging the
freedom of speech, or of the press; or the right of the people peaceably to
assemble, and to petition the Government for a redress of grievances."

REMEMBERING

Historical Considerations

HISTORY, MINE AND OURS

Charlottesville's Blue Ribbon Commission and the Terror Attacks of August 2017

JOHN EDWIN MASON

When I went grocery shopping that day, I already knew that Heather Heyer was dead. A white supremacist had run her down with his car on a street that's no more than a ten-minute walk from my house. Yet I read about it on Twitter.

I spent that afternoon—Saturday, August 12, 2017—at my desk, reading tweets from reporters and from friends who were at the scene. What they said followed an arc from concern to alarm and from defiance to dread. White supremacists terrorized Charlottesville, and I chose to stay at home.

By luck and by design, I avoided the violence of August 11 and 12. I have doubted the choices that I made ever since. I wonder if I had a moral obligation to physically oppose the presence of organized bands of violent white supremacists in my city and at my university. Many others—friends and strangers—put their bodies on the line to show their rejection of hatred and to prevent the white supremacists from seizing control of the city's streets. I did not, despite my role in creating the pretext that brought evil to Charlottesville.

The white supremacists came to town, they said, to protest the city council's decision to remove the statue of Confederate general Robert E. Lee from Emancipation Park (formerly Lee Park) in the center of Charlottesville.[1] Council acted in accord with a recommendation that was made by the city's Blue Ribbon Commission on Race, Memorials, and Public Spaces (BRC).[2] I served as vice chair of the commission, drafted parts of its report, and supported the recommendation.

Over seven months and seventeen public meetings, the commission listened to and learned from hundreds of people from Charlottesville and the region. They all offered opinions about what the city ought to do with its statues of Lee and of another Confederate general, Stonewall Jackson, that stands in a nearby park. Some defended the honor of the Confederacy; others urged us to preserve what they believed were civic objects of great beauty. Still others viewed the statues as emblems of racial oppression and spoke of the pain that their presence inflicted on them. Arguments about the statues and about the meaning of history sometimes turned into attacks on us, the commissioners. Public comments during our meetings tended to be polite, but I learned to avoid looking at references to our work on social media, where they often were not. Members of the subcommittee on which I served spent many hours in archives and libraries, asking what documents and scholarship could tell us about the intertwined histories of the men and the war that the statues memorialized, the Jim Crow era during which the white people of Charlottesville erected them, and the city's black community. Finally, we talked, debated, and sometimes argued among ourselves very publicly during our meetings.

Our final report reflected a consensus that we all supported, although with varying degrees of enthusiasm. (For the record, I am proud of our work.) We argued that the statues of Lee and Jackson symbolize white supremacy in two ways. First, they embody an interpretation of the Confederacy that sees it as an honorable "Lost Cause," a phrase that was coined in 1866 by Edward A. Pollard, a UVA graduate who was a proslavery propagandist before and during the Civil War. In its dismissal of slavery as the underlying cause of the war, its evocation of the notion of loyal, happy, and submissive slaves, and its emphasis on the honor of the Confederate cause, the Lost Cause interpretation of the war served to legitimate white supremacy.[3] The Lee statue particularly concerned us. As historian Kirk Savage has pointed out, Lee is the "key figure in the cult of the Lost Cause."[4]

Second, the statues memorialize more than the story of the Lost Cause. They also reflect the period in which they were erected—six decades after the end of slavery, when white Charlottesvillians, like whites throughout the South, had successfully reinvented white supremacy in the form of Jim Crow segregation. Black Charlottesvillians had no voice in the erection of the statues and were excluded from civic life in many other ways. By the early years of the twentieth century, African Americans in the city and throughout the South faced segregation and discrimination in virtually all walks of life, including employment, schooling, health care, housing, and public accommodations. Provisions in the 1902 Virginia Constitution had stripped the vote—the most fundamental of democratic rights—from the overwhelming majority (90 percent) of black men.[5] (At the time, no women voted in Virginia.)

Statues, we concluded, are a particular interpretation of history made visible. Massive figures of Lee and Jackson—cast in bronze and mounted on towering pedestals—speak without words. The statues announce to all who see them that these men are to be admired and that the cause for which they fought was honorable and just. Occupying central spaces in the city's landscape, they symbolize a white supremacy that will be as permanent as the metal and stone from which the statues were made. Little about the statues invites alternative readings, although such readings are possible, and nothing hints at the brutality of slavery or the remorselessness of Jim Crow. Yet they occupy two of the most prominent publics spaces in the city and, whether we like it or not, speak powerfully on its citizens' behalf.

Some viewers have historically rejected the statues' message, as we learned when listening to older members of the city's black community during our hearings. Scores of Charlottesvillians, both black and white, told us that the statues represent values that we should explicitly repudiate, today. We agreed. We offered council two alternative ways of addressing the problem that they presented. First, we suggested that the Lee statue should be removed from its central location and resituated at a more peripheral site where it could be viewed and interpreted as a historical artifact but would no longer occupy one of the city's most prominent public spaces.

Our second option more directly confronted the visual language in which the statues speak. We called for a physical transformation of the statues, opening them up to new and more complex interpretations. This would require, we argued, reconfiguring them "clearly, unambiguously, and on at least the same scale as the statue exists now, such as by lowering, covering, de-centering, or otherwise indicating the rejection of the Jim Crow–era narratives that dominated when the statue was erected."[6]

At the time, I favored the second option. I see the statues as historical documents that show us things about our collective past that we should acknowledge but prefer not to. We as a city and nation need to view statues like these as what they are: monuments that reflect the centrality of white supremacy throughout American history. But that is not all they can be. Transformed, they can also reveal history that has been denied and overlooked—for instance, the African American Union soldiers from Charlottesville and vicinity who fought for freedom during the Civil War.[7]

I understood the power and cogency of the arguments of those who wanted to remove the Lee statue from its park. Both options, I told myself, were good. One was better.

We delivered our report to city council in December 2016. In February 2017 council voted to remove the statue of Lee from what was then Lee Park and to change the park's name. (It has been renamed Emancipation Park.) It also voted to transform the statue of Jackson in place, while renaming the park in which it stands.[8]

The decision to remove the Lee statue disappointed me. Heyer's death changed my mind. The man who killed her and injured many others added another layer of meaning to the statue. It is now covered in blood. It always had been, of course, but the metaphor had been a distant one. Now the blood is that of women and men of our generation, our neighbors and friends. The terrorism of August 11 and 12 is forever attached to the statue, making it a continuing reminder of the trauma that white supremacists inflicted on the city. It cannot be allowed to remain in the heart of Charlottesville.

When I think about the role I played in creating the circumstances that brought death and violence to my city and ask myself if I did the right thing when they were here, I have only questions, no answers.

On the evening of August 11, I was one of several hundred people attending an interfaith service when the torch-carrying mob reached the statue of Thomas Jefferson, the university's founder, in front of the iconic Rotunda. There they surrounded a handful of counterprotesters who refused to let the presence of hatred at their university go unchallenged. Violence erupted and several counterprotesters were hurt.[9] No more than one hundred yards away, having come together in opposition to white supremacy and to pray for peace and justice, we were unaware of the evil so close by.[10]

Toward the end of the service, leaders asked us to remain in the church and told us that white supremacists had gathered at the Rotunda, but they provided no details. I did not sense any fear in the sanctuary. Whatever apprehension some of us might have experienced could not extinguish the feeling of solidarity that we had created during the service. We soon left the church by the back and side entrances, walked to our cars, and went home. All, I thought, was well. If I had known the details of what had just happened on Grounds—the size of the crowd, the nature of the racist and anti-Semitic chants, the violence at the statue of Jefferson, the power of the imagery that the mob and their torches had created—I would not have felt that way.

I began August 12, the day of the rally and of Heyer's death, in what had been Vinegar Hill, the heart of the African American community before the city bulldozed it in the name of urban renewal.[11] Early in the morning, one or two hundred of us met at the Jefferson School African American Heritage Center and, led by Black Lives Matter and clergy activists, marched to McGuffey Park downtown, proclaiming, in song and prayer, our opposition to everything that the terrorists stood for. We ended just as bands of white supremacists began to converge on Emancipation Park, only a block away, for their rally.

I did not know what would happen during the course of the day, but I understood the potential for violence. I am too old to fight and too fat to run. I went home. Most of the clergy and all of the activists stayed. Those who stayed, and the counterprotesters who joined them later, risked and endured the chaos of the day—beatings, tear gas, injury, and death. I was at home putting together a PowerPoint presentation. I was scheduled to speak, later in the day, about the history of African Americans in Charlottesville as part of a series of informal talks that UVA had organized on topics related to white supremacy. If I could not run, at least I could teach. In any event, the talks were cancelled when the governor declared a state of emergency in the city. It was just as well. I was already checking Twitter, already seeing reports of violence, already too distracted by what I was reading to think clearly.

Early in the evening on August 12, I walked over to an impromptu memorial vigil for Heyer in McGuffey Park. I saw a number of friends at the vigil. Some were photojournalists who had come to Charlottesville on assignment from all over the country. There were prayers and brief speeches. Otherwise we said little. My photographer friends were as shaken as anyone else. Cameras cannot ward off trauma. I invited them to stop by my house. They needed somewhere to eat and to decompress. Still working, they would come by later.

I walked home. The streets were nearly empty, except for a few cops and stragglers who may have been white supremacists or antifascist counterprotesters or simply the curious. Dusk, and it was almost silent in the city.

I drove to a grocery store and into another world. It was an ordinary Saturday night, and I was there to do ordinary things—pick up food and drink to offer my friends. Yet it felt surreal. No more than a mile and a half from my house, the vigil, and the place where Heyer died, no more than a mile and a half from people and places in mourning, everything was clean, bright, and relentlessly cheerful. As I pushed my cart out of the store, an employee, a perfectly nice young white man, gave me a smile and wished me a chipper good-evening. It felt like a provocation.

In the days and weeks to come, I thought a lot about trauma—about the anxiety, anger, depression, and distraction that I was feeling. I wondered about those who had suffered far more than I had. People who had risked injury, who had seen the violence and been hurt by it. I wondered about Heyer's family and friends. I also thought about the young man at the grocery store, even as I admitted that I could not know what he was feeling under that smile. I am sure, however, that trauma was not equally shared or earned.

Many of us asked where the city would go from here. The white supremacists were gone—most of them, anyway—but problems remained. The long BRC process had brought new attention to histories that had been too often ignored and racial inequalities that remained unaddressed. One of the most important steps that the city and its citizens can take is to accept the full challenge of the commission's report.

When city council summoned the BRC into being, it had more than Confederate statues on its mind. It asked us to think broadly and to provide "options . . . for specific ways in which our public spaces are used, or could be used, to address race."[12] "Race" is a slippery concept, of course, but what council was asking us to do was clear to all concerned. It wanted us to suggest ways that the city could use public spaces to address the historical practices that divided people into races, sorted those races into a hierarchy, and treated people differently according to that hierarchy. And it wanted us to recommend ways to honor the history of the black community.

To memorialize history in public spaces is to make it visible—that is, to make interpretations of history visible. The Lee and Jackson statues do this on a massive scale that gives them undeniable power. Public spaces that embody aspects of African American history and of the city's history of racial oppression are not hard to find, once you start looking, but they are not particularly visible. We wanted this history to be seen and made several recommendations about properly memorializing it.

One of the histories that we wanted to make more visible is the history of Vinegar Hill, once the heart of the city's black community. The city bulldozed the area in the 1960s in the name of "urban renewal." By the time the destruction was over, one church and thirty businesses had been leveled and 158 families (140 of which were black) had been displaced. Streets were paved over and the landscape utterly transformed. There is little left of Vinegar Hill to see. The largely disenfranchised black community had virtually no say in this act of historical erasure.[13] Even before the BRC began its work, the city had begun to draw up plans for a Vinegar Hill memorial park in which representations of what was lost would occupy public space.[14] Our report urged council to make the completion of the park a top priority. As of 2018, little progress has been made.

I was especially concerned with the almost total invisibility of the site of the Slave Auction Block. My interest is personal. I am descended from enslaved Virginians on both sides of my family, and I spent the first part of my academic career writing about a slave society very similar to Virginia's.[15] In the appendix that I wrote for the BRC's report, I pointed out that slavery

> was the foundation on which antebellum Virginia society was built. Slavery and its accompanying ideology of white supremacy shaped every aspect of life, from the law and the economy to politics and religion. Its economy depended on the labor of enslaved men, women, and children; the value enslaved people—who were legally chattel property—was its greatest form of wealth. Racist ideas that justified slavery on the basis of the supposed natural superiority of white people and inferiority of black people were enshrined in law and preached from pulpits.[16]

I went on to say that the "Slave Auction Block site is the symbol of the suffering of the enslaved people of Charlottesville and Albemarle. . . . Between 1820 and 1860, the sale of the enslaved from the upper South to the more dynamic economies of the lower South was a major economic enterprise. Over 1,000,000 people were forcibly sent to the lower South, about half of them from Virginia."[17] Hundreds, perhaps thousands, of those Virginians came from Charlottesville and the region. The Slave Auction Block and the courthouse square where it was located were public spaces of unimaginable sorrow and suffering, cruelty and greed. Yet the only memorials are a small bronze plaque, buried in the sidewalk, and a descriptive plaque, mounted on the side of a nearby building, that's eroded and virtually illegible. The plaques are grotesquely inadequate. Anyone could be forgiven for wondering if they were designed to suppress history, rather than to recognize it. Our report recommended a two-phased process for making this history visible. The result would be a substantial, somber memorial that would inscribe this history on the landscape.[18]

The commission didn't believe that the scale of new memorials to Vinegar Hill or the enslaved could match the size of the statues, but our recommendations did emphasize that they should be substantial. Substantial is right and proper, but it is also expensive and necessarily slow. Over the year since we submitted our report to city council, I have looked for quicker and less expensive ways to make Charlottesville's unseen histories visible. I have been thinking about this both as a citizen and as a historian of photography.

One answer may lie in the photographic archive of Rufus Holsinger, a white commercial photographer whose career in Charlottesville spanned the late nineteenth and early twentieth centuries. Holsinger's images—especially his portraits of African Americans from Charlottesville and vicinity—allow us to imagine a visual retelling of the city's history that is substantial, yet unburdened by the expense and difficulty of building memorials out of bronze and stone. Chronologically, this visual history coincides with the consolidation of Jim Crow segregation in the city and with the construction of the Confederate memorials.

The University of Virginia's Albert and Shirley Small Special Collections Library owns 9,500 of Holsinger's negatives. About 500 of the negatives are portraits of African Americans, and black people appear as secondary figures in many more.[19] The portraits and other photographs offer us a way to address a request that we heard repeatedly during our public hearings: that memorials be built to honor historically significant individuals from the black community. In part, this request reflects a longing for heroes. But it also stems from a desire to put a human face on the past, to see specific individuals from the past with whom one can identify.

Everyone who teaches history understands this dynamic. Our most effective lectures—or at least the ones that most capture students' attention—are those in which we make history personal. Those in which we tell stories about the things that people have said and done, the choices that they made, and the constraints under which they labored.

Holsinger's remarkably evocative portraits present us with images of highly individualized people—alone, as members of families, and with friends. Their potential for providing a window on Charlottesville's African American history is immense. They offer viewers insights into the lives of ordinary people that are otherwise unavailable, as historians have argued about other collections of African American portraits. Douglass Daniels, for instance, argues that "since most ordinary Americans leave few, if any, written records—diaries, autobiographical memoirs, or letters—historians and others must start taking seriously such seemingly inconsequential materials as family photographs. . . . For understanding the self-image of Blacks, photographs are especially useful when they are portraits approved by the subjects because they find the likenesses flattering."[20]

Holsinger's portraits, then, allow us to see black Charlottesvillians as they wished to be seen—as mothers and fathers, as friends and lovers, as women and men of dignity, style, and panache. But there is more to it than that. Given the widespread circulation of racist imagery at the time, Holsinger's portraits constituted small acts of resistance. The phenomenon wasn't confined to Charlottesville. Speaking about the country as a whole, bell hooks has argued that "though rarely articulated as such, the camera became in black life a political instrument, a way to resist misrepresentation as well as a means by which alternative images could be produced."[21]

Holsinger unconsciously helped African Americans in Charlottesville create political instruments. Although there is no evidence that he was a racial liberal—in fact, as a member of city council he supported an ordinance that segregated residential areas by race—he was a businessman who understood that his success depended on collaborating with his customers in creating a photographic image that pleased them.[22] What follows is a very preliminary assessment of the archive's potential, the barest beginnings of a curatorial project.

If Holsinger's archive can be seen as an unplanned library of resistance, it is also a repository of images that reinforce and naturalize the racial hierarchy. These photographs were commissioned by their subject's employers and show African Americans performing menial labor and working as domestic servants, defined by their labor and by the lowly position that white supremacy has assigned them. They are depicted as white people wished to see them. Such images are scattered liberally throughout the archive. This should be no surprise. A 1934 sociological study of the city found that "the majority of the Negroes are either servants or laborers, and therefore subject to irregular work with low pay. . . . Even when they have the same types of positions that are commonly held by Negroes, the whites usually get paid more, due to their race." The study also found that the percentage of working black women who were employed as domestic servants was a staggering 79 percent.[23]

In the photographs shown in figures 1, 2, and 3, for instance, black people are seen as cooks, stable hands, and manual laborers.[24] None of Holsinger's photographs of African Americans are explicitly racist. But the archive does

FIGURE 1 (*top*). Lyndall [*sic*] Apartments, Charlottesville, 1916. The Lyndhall opened in 1915 as a non-housekeeping apartment building. The kitchen and dining room served tenants and the white public. Both were closed in 1937.

FIGURE 2 (*bottom*). Mrs. G. F. Peter [employer], 1918.

FIGURE 3. Charlottesville and Albemarle Railway Company Machine, 1918.

contain a handful of examples of what Henry Louis Gates Jr. has referred to as "the astonishingly large storehouse of racist stereotypes that had been accumulated in the American archive of antiblack imagery."[25] These are not, in fact, images of black people. Instead they are portraits of white people in blackface makeup. A photograph (fig. 4) presents members of the University of Virginia Glee Club re-creating a scene from one of their minstrel shows. Minstrelsy, as Eric Lott contends in his book *Love and Theft: Blackface Minstrelsy and the American Working Class,* was a form of entertainment arising in the nineteenth century in which "white men caricatured black for sport and profit." It became one of the nation's favorite pastimes and flourished well into the twentieth century. Although its elements of "ridicule and racist lampoon" were not merely cultural anchors of white supremacy, as Lott convincingly argues, minstrelsy's implicit reinforcement of the racial status quo was indeed one of its most important functions.[26] Yet the photograph of a nanny with her young white charge (fig. 5) should remind us that black people were not solely defined by the labor they performed nor by the stereotypes through which whites saw them. Historian Jane Smith has identified her as Margaret Lewis, and she was much more than someone's nursemaid.

FIGURE 4 (*left*). Glee Club, University of Virginia, 1917.

FIGURE 5 (*right*). Mrs. Shepherd [employer], 1914. The woman holding the child has been identified as Margaret Lewis, one of the key figures in the operation of Charlottesville's Freedman's School.

Born into slavery, Lewis became one of the key figures in the opera-tion of the Charlottesville's Freedman's School, which educated former enslaved people in the years after the Civil War. Philena Carkin, a white New Englander who came to the city to teach in the school, described her as "quick bright, alert, and humorous. . . . She was of great assistance to us in ways outside her domestic duties, on account of her knowledge of the characters and needs of the people with whom we had to deal."[27] Lewis's husband, Paul, became one of the school's teachers and named his class after John Brown, the fiery abolitionist—a defiant move in post-war Charlottesville.[28]

Portraits that African Americans commissioned Holsinger to make for and of themselves, their families, and friends stand in stark contrast to the images of black people that we have seen thus far, none of which were made at their behest. These self-commissioned images show black Char-lottesvillians as they imagined themselves and as they wished to be seen by their community and by white people. While photography "offered

[all] Americans an unprecedented opportunity for self-representation," as Maurice O. Wallace and Shawn Michelle Smith note in *Pictures and Progress: Early Photography and the Making of African American Identity*, it is crucial to be attentive to the specific meanings and uses that photography—especially portraiture—had in the black community. Wallace and Smith point out that African Americans used photographs as a medium of self-representation at a time when they were claiming the rights of citizenship on the basis of new "legal, political, and socially recognized American identities."[29]

Holsinger's career coincided with an era of such new claims—the era of the New Negro. Alain Locke famously argued in 1925 that, across the nation, a "new spirit" was "awake in the masses." He described a generation that was "vibrant with a new psychology." New Negroes, he said, were breaking free from "the tyranny of social intimidation and . . . shaking off the psychology of imitation and implied inferiority."[30]

In 1921 the *Charlottesville Messenger*, the city's black newspaper, anticipated Locke's evocation of the "new spirit," publishing what amounted to a New Negro manifesto: "The New Negro the country over is coming to see that his salvation is in his own hands. . . . Thank God the pussy-footing, 'Me-too-boss' and hat in hand Negro is gone! That is why we are termed New Negroes."[31] The author, George W. Buckner, went on to demand, among other things, black representation on city council and the school board, the elimination of racial segregation on streetcars, and equal pay for black teachers. "We are taxpayers and law abiding citizens," he wrote. "We know our strength and will accept nothing short of justice!"[32]

I have, as yet, no direct evidence that the people in the portraits in figures 6–10 thought of themselves as New Negroes.[33] But it is difficult to view them and not think that they at least reflect the indirect influence of a new spirit in the African American community. Black people were well aware of the demeaning stereotypes that represented them all too often in American visual culture. They knew how they looked when seen through the eyes of white Charlottesvillians. The portraits that they commissioned were acts of self-determination and representations of truer, deeper selves. In some we see the profound simplicity of familial love. Others, such as the portrait of Viola Green holding her diploma, suggest the pride that accompanies accomplishment. In still others, black men challenged stereotypes that depicted them as weak and cowardly and, at the same time, staked a claim to the full rights citizenship—a claim that had been won in wartime service to the nation. Finally, we see romantic love, an elusive quality in

FIGURE 6 (*top left*). Mrs. Underwood with baby, 1914.

FIGURE 7 (*top right*). Dr. George Ferguson [with children], 1917. Dr. Ferguson was one of the first black physicians to open a practice in Charlottesville. His son, George Jr. (*above*), was president of the local branch of the NAACP in 1958 when it sued the city to force the integration of the public schools.

FIGURE 8 (*bottom left*). Viola Green, 1916.

FIGURE 9 (*bottom right*). Fayette Johnson, 1919.

FIGURE 10 (*left*). Henry MacMahan [and unidentified woman], 1916.
FIGURE 11 (*right*). Bill Hurley, 1909.

representations of African Americans. These portraits are quiet acts of resistance, confirming the resilience and dignity of Charlottesville's African Americans. And, in the portrait of Bill Hurley (fig. 11), we see something else—casual defiance and an unmistakable cool.

In Charlottesville, Rufus Holsinger's photographs are ubiquitous. They adorn the walls of restaurants and offices and appear in the pages of books and magazines, depicting people and places a century ago. Their popularity is rooted in their ability to give the city's past a nostalgic glow. When used selectively, they picture Charlottesville as a harmonious and homogeneous community, a place where conflict is unknown and where black people are seldom seen.

Yet Holsinger's archive can tell a different and more accurate story about Charlottesville's history, one in which the black community plays a vital role and in which white supremacy and black resistance to it are central themes. Holsinger's portraits of African Americans can be and should be as well known as his landscapes and portraits of white Charlottesvillians. In publications and public places, they can be used to tell the "new more comprehensive story of the city" that we called for in our BRC report.[34] We argued that Charlottesville, like the nation as a whole, has never "fully explored the truths and legacies of slavery, Jim Crow, and white supremacy."

The ways in which the city's history has been presented have done "more to hide these wrongs, to justify them, and even to glorify them, than to reveal them." The stakes, we said, were high. The results of our failure to fully understand our history can be seen in the "continuing systems and structures (cultural beliefs, institutionalized policies and practices) that disenfranchise, disempower, and devalue African Americans, Native Americans, and other people of color."[35]

We understood that the recommendations in our report were also a challenge. We were asking the citizens of Charlottesville and the students, faculty, and staff of UVA, its central institution, to acknowledge and confront a painful past.

Our challenge was similar to one that James Baldwin issued to the nation as a whole at several points during his career. I came across one of Baldwin's least known essays while I was serving on the commission. Published in 1976, it serves as the introduction to the third volume of the *Black Photographers Annual*. In it, he laments Americans' inability "to face the truth concerning themselves and [their] history which has made, and makes, the lives of all black and non-white people so dangerous and so hard." But he does not end on this note of despair. "Nothing lasts forever," he assures his readers, "not even our suffering, and we have everything to celebrate: ourselves."[36]

The portraits that African Americans commissioned from Rufus Holsinger are a celebration of themselves and integral parts of a larger struggle over self-determination and the rights of citizenship. Black Charlottesvillians rejected visual clichés and stereotypes even as they envisioned a city and nation free of racial oppression. One hundred years later, we can reclaim them in the same spirit and create a truer history of the city.

NOTES

Illustration credits: All photographs in this essay are by Rufus Holsinger; Holsinger Studio Collection, ca. 1890–1938, Accession #9862, Albert and Shirley Small Special Collections Library, University of Virginia.

1. Chris Suarez, "Unite the Right Rally Sparks First Amendment Questions," *Daily Progress*, July 29, 2017, http://infoweb.newsbank.com/resources/doc/nb/news/165FD0F6CA9682A0?p=WORLDNEWS.

2. Blue Ribbon Commission on Race, Memorials, and Public Spaces, *Report to City Council*, Dec. 19, 2016, www.charlottesville.org/departments-and-services/boards-and-commissions/blue-ribbon-commission-on-race-memorials-and-public-spaces.

3. BRC report, 7–12.

4. Kirk Savage, *Standing Soldiers, Kneeling Slaves: Race, War, and Monument in Nineteenth-Century America* (Princeton, NJ: Princeton University Press, 1997), 130.

5. BRC report, appendix C, 128–34.

6. BRC report, 7–12.

7. See, for instance, Matt Kelly's discussion of new research from UVA's John L. Nau III Center for Civil War History, in "The Circle of Liberators," *UVA Today,* Nov. 28, 2017, https://news.virginia.edu/illimitable/commonwealth/circle-liberators.

8. Chris Suarez, "Lee Park Statue Will Be Removed," *Daily Progress,* Feb. 7, 2017, http://infoweb.newsbank.com/resources/doc/nb/news/1626811A182FDD30?p=WORLDNEWS.

9. "Unite the Right Torch Rally Ends in Violence at the Rotunda," *Daily Progress,* Aug. 11, 2017, http://infoweb.newsbank.com/resources/doc/nb/news/16641D337B61EB68?p=WORLDNEWS.

10. Chris Suarez, "Faith Leaders Gather on the Eve of 'Hate-Driven' Unite the Right Rally," *Daily Progress,* Aug. 11, 2017, http://infoweb.newsbank.com/resources/doc/nb/news/16641D3386996460?p=WORLDNEWS.

11. See, for instance, the Vinegar Hill Project, www.vinegarhillproject.org/Welcome.html, accessed Dec. 18, 2017.

12. BRC report, appendix A.

13. BRC report, 15–16.

14. Josh Mandell, "Council Approves Plan for Vinegar Hill Park," *Daily Progress,* Dec. 6, 2016, http://infoweb.newsbank.com/resources/doc/nb/news/161260046E5724D8?p=WORLDNEWS.

15. See, for instance, John Edwin Mason, *Social Death and Resurrection: Slavery and Emancipation in South Africa* (Charlottesville: University of Virginia Press, 2003).

16. BRC report, appendix C, 129.

17. Ibid.

18. Council accepted our recommendation, but twelve months later, as I'm editing this essay, no signs of progress can be seen.

19. See the Holsinger Studio Collection, Albert and Shirley Small Special Collections Library, University of Virginia, http://small.library.virginia.edu/collections/featured/the-holsinger-studio-collection, accessed Dec. 18, 2017. (A decade and a half ago, the portraits were part of Race and Place: An African American Community in the Jim Crow South, a digital history initiative that was headed by Scot French and Reginald Butler, who were then colleagues at UVA's Carter G. Woodson Institute for African American and African Studies.)

20. Quoted in Deborah Willis, *Reflections in Black: A History of Black Photographers, 1849 to the Present* (New York: Norton, 2000), xvii.

21. bell hooks, "In Our Glory," in *Picturing Us: African American Identity in Photography,* ed. Deborah Willis (New York: New Press, 1996), 49.

22. Karen C. Waters-Wicks, "An Ordinance to Secure for White and Colored People a 'Separate Location of Residence for Each Race': A History of *dejure* Residential

Segregation in Charlottesville and Richmond, Virginia," *Magazine of Albemarle County History* 72 (2014): 125–26.

23. Robert Mitchell Lightfoot Jr., *Negro Crime in a Small Urban Community* (Charlottesville: Publications of the University of Virginia, Phelps-Stokes Fellowship Papers, 1934), 8, 61.

24. For information on figures 1 and 2, see Architectural and Historic Survey, Historic Landmarks Commission, Department of Community Development, City of Charlottesville, http://weblink.charlottesville.org/public/0/edoc/652682/64%20University%20Way_Historic%20Survey.pdf, accessed Feb. 4, 2018.

25. Henry Louis Gates Jr., "Frederick Douglass's Camera Obscura," *Aperture* 223 (Summer 2016): 27–28.

26. Eric Lott, *Love and Theft: Blackface Minstrelsy and the American Working Class* (New York: Oxford University Press, 1993), 3–4 and passim.

27. Jane Smith, "Everything within Their Vision," unpublished mss., n.d.

28. Ibid.

29. Maurice O. Wallace and Shawn Michelle Smith, *Pictures and Progress: Early Photography and the Making of African American Identity* (Durham, NC: Duke University Press, 2012), 5.

30. The classic account of the New Negro is Alain Locke's essay "Enter the New Negro," which appeared in *Survey Graphic* 52, no. 11 (March 1925). See also Alain Locke, ed., *The New Negro* (New York: Albert and Charles Boni, 1925). The quotations are from "Enter the New Negro," 631.

31. Reprinted in "The New Negro: What He Wants," *Daily Progress,* Feb. 16, 1921.

32. Ibid. Soon afterward the *Daily Progress,* which was owned, edited, and largely read by whites, published an editorial condemning Buckner's "foolishly radical propaganda" and warning that "the circulation of such absurd tirades and impossible proposals . . . only serve[s] to make the problem of the law-abiding and the respected element among the colored people that much harder" ("Misleading the Colored Race," *Daily Progress,* Feb. 18, 1921).

33. For more on the Ferguson family, shown in figure 7, see Susan Svrluga, "D.C. Woman to Get the High School Diploma She Was Denied during Desegregation Battle," *Washington Post,* May 25, 2013, www.washingtonpost.com/local/dc-woman-to-get-the-high-school-diploma-she-was-denied-during-desegregation-battle/2013/05/24/9c92f06c-c3f8-11e2-914f-a7aba60512a7_story.html?utm_term=.577f67854ife.

34. BRC report, 21.

35. Ibid., 4.

36. James Baldwin, "Introduction," in *The Black Photographers Annual, vol. 3,* ed. Joe Crawford (New York: Black Photographers Annual, 1976), n.p.

THE ORIGINAL
FALSE EQUIVALENCY

ELIZABETH R. VARON

"There was a right side and a wrong side in the late war, which no sentiment ought to cause us to forget." So proclaimed the famed abolitionist Frederick Douglass in 1878, fighting back against an ascendant movement among whites for "reconciliation"—a movement premised on the idea that Americans should honor both the Union and Confederate veterans of the Civil War for their martial valor. Douglass knew that such a movement drew a false moral equivalency between the Union cause and the Confederate one—and he knew the danger such a false equivalency represented for him and other African Americans.[1]

In the aftermath of the violent white supremacist riot in Charlottesville in August 2017, Donald Trump fulfilled Frederick Douglass's prophecy. Trump attempted to draw a parallel between neo-Nazi rioters, the Ku Klux Klan, and anti-Semites on the one hand, and counterprotesters on the other. The president's moral relativism was roundly condemned by scholars and by the mainstream and progressive media, but such condemnations failed to set the record straight. In October 2017 White House Chief of Staff John F. Kelly weighed in, describing the Civil War as a conflict in which "men and women of good faith on both sides made their stand." Kelly defended Robert E. Lee, whose statue stood at the heart of the Charlottesville turmoil, as an "honorable man." A few days later the popular historian Jay Winik published an op-ed in the *Wall Street Journal* entitled "What General Kelly Got Right about Robert E. Lee," in which Winik invoked Lee's image as an icon of sectional reconciliation. "Lee went to great pains to heal the bitterness that cleaved the country after Appomattox," Winik insisted. "Lincoln and Grant gave generous terms to the South, paving the way to reconciliation. But they found a willing partner in Lee. Neither a citizen of the Union he once loved nor of the Confederacy that ceased to exist, Lee publicly rejected the idea of a guerrilla struggle. Most important, by April 1865 he no longer spoke of the Confederacy as 'we' or 'our country.' Now he spoke as a U.S. citizen, thereby forging the path to a reunited country."[2]

This view of Lee as an honorable man and "willing partner" to Grant in peacemaking is itself a false equivalency, the product of two converging memory traditions that had their origins in the war's aftermath and that still reverberate today. The Reconciliation tradition, which crystallized in the late nineteenth and early twentieth centuries, emphasized the need for Americans to put aside sectional animosities and focus on achieving national prosperity and international power. Championed by prominent veterans such as Union general Joshua Chamberlain, and embraced by political leaders such as Theodore Roosevelt and Woodrow Wilson, the Reconciliation tradition cast Lee and Grant as "admirable and talented rivals whose strengths reflected well on the societies that produced them," and Appomattox as "the beginning of a healing process that reminded all Americans of their shared history," as the historian Gary W. Gallagher has explained. Reconciliation swept under the rug the painful and tragic history of American race relations and minimized the significance of emancipation and the role of African Americans in Union victory.[3]

From the start, the Reconciliation tradition was "characterized by a measure of Northern capitulation to the white South" and relied on a second powerful memory tradition: that of the Lost Cause. Championed by Confederate veterans such as Jubal Early and by descendants' organizations like the United Daughters of the Confederacy, the Lost Cause tradition emphasized the righteousness and blamelessness of the Confederacy and cast the war as a valiant struggle against overwhelming odds, waged to defend the constitutional principle of states' rights. Lee stood at the center of this memory tradition. As the sponsors of Charlottesville's Lee statue put it when that statue was unveiled in 1924, Lee was the "stainless leader of a stainless cause," the perfect symbol of military heroism and of the Southern elite's entitlement to political power within the restored Union. Many white Northerners, motivated by nationalism, racism, and nostalgia, proved receptive to the message that Lee deserved to be revered as a hero; they found the image of him as a peacemaker at Appomattox particularly palatable. Indeed Northern admirers of Lee's, most notably the elite New Englander Charles Francis Adams Jr., contributed, in the early twentieth century, to crafting Lee's reputation as a nationalist and symbol of reunion. "Nothing embodies the power of the Lost Cause in Civil War memory," the historian Barbara Gannon has written, "more than the unquestioned acceptance of Lee as an American hero for more than a century after his efforts to destroy the Union."[4]

Together the Reconciliation and Lost Cause traditions fostered the idea that Union and Confederacy could share the moral high ground in American memory of the war. These two traditions sought to displace and suppress a pair of rival memory traditions, each with its own long history and champions: a Won Cause tradition, advanced by Union veterans through organizations such as the Grand Army of the Republic, emphasizing the superior righteousness of the cause of Union and the superior valor of the federal army; and an Emancipation tradition, championed by black leaders such as Frederick Douglass, who held up the abolition of slavery as the noble purpose and great achievement of the war. As a rich modern scholarship on Civil War memory has revealed, the Lost Cause and Reconciliation traditions held sway over American culture for much of the twentieth century.[5]

In the modern day, scholars and the general public alike have tended to see Lee, who died in 1870 before the Reconciliation and Lost Cause memory traditions were ascendant, as a symbol enshrined by others as a "marble man," rather than as an agent who actively shaped his own memory.[6] This essay hones in on Lee's comportment in the immediate aftermath of his 1865 surrender, to show how he maneuvered to advance the Lost Cause and to discredit the Won Cause interpretations of the war. Lee served, for defeated Southerners in the postwar era, as a model of measured defiance. That defiance—of Northern political power, of black freedom, of social change—was at the heart of the Lost Cause mythos and found enduring expression in the Southern landscape through statues like the Lee monument in Charlottesville.

Many of the essays in this volume examine the local contexts for the Lee statue controversy: the role of University of Virginia as a bastion of proslavery and white supremacist ideology and Charlottesville's longstanding structural inequalities and cultural erasures. This essay calls attention to the regional and national scope of the Lee cult and Lost Cause propaganda. Many of the essays explore the temporal context of the 1920s, when the statue to Lee was erected in the city: it was an era of Jim Crow segregation, eugenic pseudoscience, a resurgent Klan, and white anxiety over the growing militancy of black Southerners. This essay focuses on the deep roots of the Lost Cause and of white supremacist terrorism, tracing them back to the moment of Confederate defeat. As the historian John Hope Franklin observes in his pioneering book *Reconstruction after the Civil War* (1961), the

Klan's violence and propaganda were not reactions to Radical Reconstruction but instead "a reflection of the general character of Southern life" in the Civil War era. To understand the events of August 2017, we need to go back to April of 1865.[7]

LEE'S LOST CAUSE

General U. S. Grant's Appomattox terms of April 9, 1865, "paroled" the defeated Confederates in Lee's Army of Northern Virginia, setting them free on the promise that they would never again take up arms against the United States, and stipulating that if they obeyed the laws in force where they resided, Confederate veterans would "remain undisturbed." In Grant's eyes, these terms were calculated to effect the Confederates' repentance—Grant believed that he could be merciful because he had rendered Lee utterly powerless and his cause discredited and hopeless.

But Lee viewed the surrender terms in a different light, as a two-sided compact: Confederates agreed to lay down their arms, he believed, on the condition that honorable Southern men would not be treated dishonorably by the victorious Yankees. Snatching victory from defeat, Lee signaled, unmistakably, that white Southerners were willing to "reconcile" with the North only if they could lay claim to their own piece of the moral high ground. The first such signal was Lee's iconic "Farewell Address" (penned by his aide-de-camp Charles Marshall under Lee's oversight) to his defeated army at Appomattox, Virginia, in April of 1865. The address attributed the Union's victory to its "overwhelming numbers and resources." In the context of proslavery ideology, this was a kind of code, conjuring up for white Southerners images of the allegedly heartless efficiency of Northern society. "Numbers" conjured up a Northern army of mercenaries and hirelings who had been seduced or coerced into service and had no real moral stake in the fight. "Resources" conjured up images of Northern factories and cities in which an exploited underclass churned out the material of war at the behest of rapacious capitalists. The Union victory was, in Lee's view, a show of brute force, not of courage and skill: a triumph of might over right. He knew that by denying the legitimacy of the North's military victory, Confederates could deny the North the right to impose its political will on the South.[8]

Two weeks after his surrender, on April 24, 1865, Lee (now back at his home in Richmond) gave a revealing interview with the *New York Herald;* this newspaper was welcoming of Grant's lenient terms and hopeful that the new president, Andrew Johnson, would prove magnanimous to the South. Lee initially adopted the posture of a peacemaker. He deplored the recent assassination of Lincoln as a terrible crime, "beyond execration." Lee claimed, according to his interviewer, Thomas Cook, that the South had long been anxious for peace and had waited only for "some word or expression of compromise or conciliation from the North"; this was standard anti-Republican cant, part and parcel of the charge that Lincoln needlessly prolonged the war in order to effect a social revolution in the South. But even as he offered up professions of good will, Lee also issued a stern warning to Northerners. The peace terms at Appomattox, he argued, were conditional—and Southerners would hold Northerners to the observance of the conditions. Lee put special emphasis on the following point: "Should arbitrary or vindictive or revengeful policies be adopted, the end was not yet." The South still had "sources of strength," which "harsh measures" on the part of the North would "call into action." Lee warned that the "South could protract the struggle for an indefinite period"; if "extermination, confiscation and general annihilation" were the North's policy, Southerners would renew the fight, and "give their lives as dearly as possible."[9]

Nine months later, in February 1866, Lee gave his most extensive testimony on the nature of the peace when he was summoned by the Republican-dominated Joint Committee on Reconstruction, convened to investigate conditions in the South. Much had changed since April 1865: President Andrew Johnson, after initially promising to hold traitors accountable, had instead offered broad amnesty to former Confederates, permitting them to regain control of Southern state governments and to impose, through "black codes" and extralegal violence, a regime of white domination over the freedpeople. Over the course of the winter and spring of 1866, the Joint Committee conducted interviews with 144 witnesses, to expose the flaws of the president's program and justify the need for congressional control over reconstruction. The committee interviewed Lee to gauge the disposition of former Confederates toward the federal government.[10]

When asked about the "state of feeling" among former Confederates in Virginia, Lee responded, "As far as I have heard . . . they are for co-operating with President Johnson in his policy." Lee continued: "Persons with whom I have conversed express great confidence in the wisdom of his policy of restoration." Lee's use of the word "restoration" piqued the committee, and they pressed him: Did Southerners support Johnson out of a desire for "peace and good feeling in the country," Congressman Henry Blow, a Missouri Republican asked Lee, "or from the probability of their regaining political power?" Lee answered, cagily, "So far as I know the desire of the people of the south, it is for the restoration of the civil government, and they look upon the policy of President Johnson as the one which would most clearly and most surely re-establish it." Blow would not let the question go: when his turn next came to interrogate Lee, he asked again— did Southerners want peace, or to regain their lost power? This time Lee answered that he was not inclined to separate the two points. Southern states sought to have their equality with Northern ones restored; the North should be generous because it was the best way of regaining the "good opinion" of the South.[11]

Throughout this interview Lee was defiant. Ideologically, he did not concede an inch. When asked about race relations, he averred that blacks were "not as capable of acquiring knowledge" as whites; they were an "amiable, social race," who liked their "ease and comfort." They were, he insisted, being well treated in the postwar South by their former masters. Lee's testimony went against the grain of that offered by most of the committee's other witnesses. Unionist Southerners and their Northern allies presented the committee with hundreds of pages of testimony describing the hostility of former Confederates to the Union and the suffering and vulnerability of the freedpeople. For example, Thomas Bayne of Norfolk, Virginia, observed, "It is not uncommon to hear threats such as this: we will kill one negro, at least, for every rebel soldier killed by them." Lee, on February 17, 1866, looked his questioners in the eye and denied the reality of antiblack violence in the postwar South. In telling the Joint Committee of the "kind feelings" whites in Virginia had for blacks, Lee revived the prewar Southern fantasy of "paternalism": the idea that masters had been the kindly custodians of their black wards, extending them care in exchange for their submission. Its postwar corollary was the fantasy that only the Southern elite could steward the freedpeople through a transition—not to equality, but to a new form of benign subordination as a class of perpetual serfs.[12]

The Southern press held up Lee's testimony as a political beacon. "The words that fall from the lips of such a man as General LEE must be heard with great respect. He has shown himself a great and good man through a testing ordeal," the *Richmond Examiner* insisted. It praised Lee for having taken a strong stand: Lee demonstrated in his congressional testimony that he had "the proper idea of the colored man's intellect" and that he regarded Johnson's policies as "wise and humane." Lee's testimony before the Joint Committee not only lent his prestige to Johnson's policies—it fortified white Southerners, as Lee's "Farewell Address" had, in the conviction that they were blameless.[13]

In short, ex-Confederates did not see Lee as a symbol of submission and healing. They saw him instead as a symbol of the enduring righteousness of their cause. The North Carolina poet Mary Bayard Clarke put it most succinctly. Urging Southerners to model their behavior on that of Lee, she wrote in the summer of 1866 that he had not "stooped his grandly proud head one hair's breadth since he surrendered to Grant." Confederates would observe their parole terms, but "more than this," she insisted, "an honorable enemy should not desire. It is idle to attempt to force them to say and feel they were wrong. They were right."[14]

MEMORY WARS

From the very start, leaders of the Union such as Abraham Lincoln, Ulysses Grant, and Frederick Douglass rejected Lee's "might over right" interpretation. In their view, the Union victory was the triumph of right over wrong, attributable to the courage, skill, and righteousness of the Union army and the moral and material power of free society. In the eyes of Northern soldiers and their commanders, the Union fought a war of liberation. Liberation initially connoted the deliverance of the white Southern masses from the domination of slaveholding oligarchs. Over the course of the war, most loyal Americans came to see the emancipation of slaves and the enlistment of black troops as essential to Union victory. By the war's end, the Union army reflected America's diversity. More than 25 percent of Union soldiers were immigrants. Two hundred thousand African Americans, the majority of them Southerners, fought for the Union. Many of these Union soldiers hoped that their patriotic sacrifices would earn for them full acceptance and integration into an American society that had oppressed or marginalized them.[15]

No Americans were more hopeful that the surrender augured a new era than were African Americans. Seven United States Colored Troops regiments had participated in the Appomattox campaign. Their views were represented in the Northern free black press, in letters they wrote on the campaign. "We the colored soldiers have fairly won our rights by loyalty and bravery," wrote William McCoslin of the 29th Regiment U.S.C.T., summing up the case that the surrender was a vindication of the cause of freedom and black citizenship.[16]

Loyal Americans did not, in the immediate aftermath of the surrender, view Robert E. Lee as a peacemaker. Instead they viewed him as a dissembling traitor. While Grant embodied the moral virtue of free society, Lee embodied the immorality of the South. An article in the *Christian Recorder,* the organ of the African Methodist Episcopal Church, insisted that it "was no mere game of chance" by which Lee was "so beautifully checkmated" into capitulating at Appomattox. "On the one side was a cool, determined and skillful General, conscious of the final victory, and fighting for his country's honor. On the other a desperate and oath-breaking leader, seeking individual renown, even when mindful of the utter hopelessness of his espoused cause." Northern commentators interpreted Lee's "Farewell Address" as a cynical ploy to manipulate public opinion. For example, an article in the *New York Evening Post,* edited by Radical Republican William Cullen Bryant, excoriated Lee for his references in the address to the Confederates' "devotion to their country" and their satisfaction in "duty faithfully performed." That Lee dared to congratulate the rebels at the moment of defeat was nothing less than a "slap in the face to loyal soldiers." Lee had chosen to "blurt out his treason, and to use his influence over the army which he had surrendered, to rouse them to new rebellion and justify future insurrection." Lee's interview with the *Herald* also elicited criticism bordering on disbelief—how could Lee, the *New York Times* fumed, deny that he was a traitor and seek political immunity and equality with the victors? Lee was, the *Times* insisted, a fearsome villain, not a tragic hero.[17]

Republicans in Congress themselves weighed in, concluding, based on the Joint Committee's interviews with Lee and other defeated rebels, that "the evidence of intense hostility to the federal Union, and an equally intense love of the late Confederacy, nurtured by the war, is decisive," as the majority report of the Joint Committee read. They found Lee to be utterly lacking in repentance and took him to be representative of his fellow Confederates. Johnsonian policies had revived the Southern temper, and the ex-rebels now brazenly sought "to participate in making laws for their conquerors."[18]

As for Grant, he came to fear in the year after the war that Johnson's lenience and Lee's recalcitrance were fueling a process by which the North's victory was slipping away. Grant was radicalized by the resurgence of the Southern elite under Johnson's program, and he came to embrace the congressional program of Reconstruction, of which black voting was the centerpiece. Confronted with what he dubbed the "foolhardiness of the President and the blindness of the Southern people to their own interest,"

Grant adapted: "[I] gradually worked up to the point where, with the majority of the people, I favored immediate enfranchisement" for blacks, as he put it in his memoir. This was the only way to dispel the ex-Confederates' pretension that "they would be able to control the nation . . . and were entitled to do so."[19]

Grant singled out Lee for criticism in an interview he granted, on May 12, 1866, to the editor of Maine's *Lewiston Falls Journal.* Grant revealed that the conviction at the heart of his Appomattox terms remained unchanged: war had been the South's punishment, peace its chance for atonement. But the promised atonement had not come. Southerners, Grant told his interviewer, were "much less disposed now to bring themselves to the proper frame of mind than they were one year since," when the victory was new; "Now they regard themselves as masters of the situation."[20]

Grant then took to task Lee, who was "behaving badly," in his view: "He is conducting himself very differently from what I had reason from what he said at the time of surrender, to suppose he would. No man at the South is capable of exercising a tenth part of the influence for good that he is, but instead of using it he is setting an example of forced acquiescence so grudging and pernicious in its effects as to be hardly realized." Such an assessment strongly suggests that Grant had read Lee's testimony before the Joint Committee and perhaps his *New York Herald* interview, too. But it raises the question: How exactly had Grant hoped Lee would behave? Grant offered a clue when, in this interview, he praised the comportment of Generals Joseph Johnston and Richard Taylor; these men were urging Southerners to "throw aside their old prejudices and conform their course to the changed conditions of things." Neither man, as it turned out, would stand by Grant or the Republican Congress in the long term. But in the coming years, a few prominent rebel leaders—such as Appomattox veteran James Longstreet and the famed "partisan ranger" Colonel John Mosby—would embrace the Republican Party.

Was Lee's standing among Southerners so exalted that he could have, had he so chosen, reconciled them to the "changed condition of things"? The question was moot. Lee chose, in the wake of the surrender, to play a nervy game. Grant had hoped, at Appomattox, that he and Lee together would show the world how soldiers win, and lose, with courage and candor. Instead, Lee had spoken to his followers in code, encouraging them to denigrate the Union victory as a mere show of force; to resist change in the name of restoration; and to obscure Southern violence behind the veil of paternalism.[21]

As Lee encountered Northern hostility to this interpretation of the war's meaning, he dug in his heels and became more entrenched ideologically. He came to firmly believe that "THE ONLY DIFFICULTY IN THE WAY OF AN AMI-CABLE ADJUSTMENT WAS WITH THE REPUBLICAN PARTY," as he stridently put it to Sir John Dahlberg Acton, a pro-Confederate British politician and historian, in December 1866. During 1867 Grant would move to the center stage of American politics as the man designated to unseat Johnson, while Lee would move to the wings, where he disavowed any political ambitions even as he studiously made known his political opinions. Grant won the election of 1868, as the candidate who stood for *"both* sectional harmony *and* the guarantee of the freedpeople's newly gained political and economic freedoms," to quote his biographer Joan Waugh. Lee and two dozen other former Confederate generals and politicians had recently endorsed a treatise, the "White Sulphur Manifesto," which condemned the black suffrage and called anew for "restoration"; he considered Grant's election a tragedy. Lee wrote to his cousin: "I grieve for posterity, for American principle & American liberty. Our boasted self Govt. is fast becoming the jeer & laughing stock of the world."[22]

THE LONG SHADOW OF THE LOST CAUSE

During Grant's presidency former Confederates ratcheted up their propaganda campaign designed to preempt and turn back social change. That campaign disparaged Union soldiers as "mongrels" and "mercenaries"; cast race relations as a zero-sum game in which any advances for blacks would spell the degradation of whites; and conjured the violence the Klan and other white supremacist terrorists used to drive the Unionist coalition out of Southern politics. Former Confederates again and again invoked their interpretation of the Appomattox terms, and particularly the "remain undisturbed" clause, as a shield against social change. Republican efforts to give freedpeople a measure of equality, as well as opportunity and protection, were met by white Southern protests that such a radical agenda was a betrayal of the Appomattox agreement—that the prospect of black citizenship, as one Virginia newspaper put it, "molests and disturbs us."[23]

No one did more to press that argument than John Brown Gordon, former general in the Army of Northern Virginia and one of Lee's right-hand men at Appomattox. In 1871 Gordon, a leader of Georgia's Ku Klux Klan and future U.S. senator and governor, was summoned to testify before a Joint Committee of Congress investigating the "condition of affairs in the

Southern States." In his testimony, Gordon repeatedly invoked the Appomattox terms. "We should not be disturbed, so long as we obeyed the laws": this was the pledge, Gordon said, that Grant had made to the Confederates. Peace would have come swiftly and surely, Gordon continued, if Radical Republicans had not betrayed the spirit of Appomattox by telling Confederates, "Your former slaves are better fitted to administer the laws than you are." Gordon's message was clear: the only way to restore peace was to leave the white South alone to manage its own affairs. Former Confederates systematically sowed chaos and then blamed it on the agents of change, claiming that the violence would end only when the old order was restored. These tactics stoked the fears and prejudices of Northern and Southern whites alike and set the stage for the Reconciliation movement among them that obscured the history of emancipation and black military service, even as it incorporated key elements of the Lost Cause creed. Gordon himself embodied the melding of the Lost Cause and Reconciliation traditions: he crafted a reputation as an icon of reunion by praising white Union veterans for their bravery, even as he "preached the gospel of white supremacy" and insisted that the righteous Lee had been "overpowered" during the war but "never really beaten."[24]

Confederate memorials such as the Lee statue in Charlottesville are, among other things, monuments to a false equivalency—to the idea that Confederates are equally deserving of a place of honor in modern America as Union soldiers. To remove such statues is not to erase history, as so many have claimed. It is vitally important to preserve the artifacts and documents of Confederate history in the places—libraries, museums, national battlefield parks—designed for such purposes. But Lost Cause memorials, looming large in public squares, are themselves erasures of history. They seek to deny the true nature of the Civil War: a triumph of right over wrong, not might over right.

NOTES

1. Frederick Douglass, "There Was a Right Side in the Late War, May 30, 1878," in *Frederick Douglass: Selected Speeches and Writings,* ed. Philip S. Foner (Chicago: Lawrence Hill, 1999), 632.

2. For Civil War historians' reactions to the events of August 11 and 12 and to President Trump's comments on those events, see, for example, David Blight, " 'The Civil War lies on us like a sleeping dragon': America's Deadly Divide—And Why It Has Returned," *Guardian,* Aug. 20, 2017; and Karen L. Cox, "Why Confederate Memorials Must Fall," *New York Times,* Aug. 15, 2017. On Kelly's comments, see

Jay Winik, "What General Kelly Got Right about Robert E. Lee," *Wall Street Journal*, Nov. 3, 2017.

3. Gary W. Gallagher, *Causes Won, Lost & Forgotten: How Hollywood and Popular Art Shape What We Know about the Civil War* (Chapel Hill: University of North Carolina Press, 2008), 35.

4. Gallagher, *Causes Won, Lost & Forgotten*, 33; Brendan Wolfe, "History Writ Aright," http://brendanwolfe.com/lee-monument, accessed Feb. 12, 2018; Barbara A. Gannon, *Americans Remember Their Civil War* (Santa Barbara, CA: Praeger, 2017), 78. On Lee's transformation from a Southern hero into a national one after the war, see Thomas L. Connelly, *The Marble Man: Robert E. Lee and His Image in American Society* (Baton Rouge: Louisiana State University Press, 1977), 116–17, 161; and Gaines M. Foster, *Ghosts of the Confederacy: Defeat, the Lost Cause, and the Emergence of the New South* (New York: Oxford University Press, 1987), 120–21.

5. On the Won Cause (or Union Cause) and Emancipation traditions, see Gallagher, *Causes Won, Lost & Forgotten*, 25–33; Gannon, *Americans Remember Their Civil War*, xvii; David Blight, *Race and Reunion: The Civil War in American Memory* (Cambridge, MA: Harvard University Press, 2001); and Caroline E. Janney, *Remembering the Civil War: Reunion and the Limits of Reconciliation* (Chapel Hill: University of North Carolina Press, 2013).

6. Connelly, *Marble Man*, 212; Foster, *Ghosts of the Confederacy*, 47–51.

7. John Hope Franklin, *Reconstruction after the Civil War* (Chicago: University of Chicago Press, 1961), 153.

8. Elizabeth R. Varon, *Appomattox: Victory, Defeat, and Freedom at the End of the Civil War* (New York: Oxford University Press, 2013), 68–71.

9. *New York Herald*, April 29, 1865; Varon, *Appomattox*, 186–89.

10. Franklin, *Reconstruction after the Civil War*, 58.

11. *Report of the Joint Committee on Reconstruction, at the First Session, Thirty-Ninth Congress* (Washington, DC: Government Printing Office, 1866), part 2, pp. 129–36.

12. Franklin, *Reconstruction after the Civil War*, 58–59; *Report of the Joint Committee*, part 2, pp. 51–59, 129–36. On paternalism, see Lacy Ford, *Deliver Us from Evil: The Slavery Question in the Old South* (New York: Oxford University Press, 2009).

13. *Richmond Examiner*, March 21, 29, and 30, 1866.

14. Varon, *Appomattox*, 235–36; Terrell Armistead Crow and Mary Moulton Barden, eds., *Live Your Own Life: The Family Papers of Mary Bayard Clarke, 1854–1886* (Columbia: University of South Carolina Press, 2003), 212, 228.

15. Varon, *Appomattox*, 80–93; William W. Freehling, *The South vs. the South: How Anti-Confederate Southerners Shaped the Course of the Civil War* (New York: Oxford University Press, 2001).

16. Varon, *Appomattox*, 93–101 (quote on p. 95).

17. *Christian Recorder* (Philadelphia), April 8, 1865; *New York Evening Post*, as quoted in the *Liberator*, May 5, 1865; *New York Times*, June 4, 1865.

18. *Report of the Joint Committee*, xx–xxi.

19. Ulysses S. Grant, *Personal Memoirs* (New York: Penguin, 1999), 615–17, 625, 634, 640.

20. Reprinted in the *New York Times*, May 24, 1865.

21. *New York Times,* May 24, 1865; Eric Foner, *A Short History of Reconstruction, 1863–1877* (New York: Harper & Row, 1990), 145.

22. Letter of General Lee to Lord Acton, Dec. 15, 1866, https://leefamilyarchive.org/9-family-papers/832-robert-e-lee-to-sir-john-acton-1866-december-16, accessed Feb. 12, 2017; Joan Waugh, *U. S. Grant: American Hero, American Myth* (Chapel Hill: University of North Carolina Press, 2009), 109; Varon, *Appomattox,* 246. For a text of the "White Sulphur Manifesto," see *Staunton* (VA) *Spectator,* Sept. 8, 1868.

23. *Valley Virginian* (Augusta County), Feb. 27, 1867; Varon, *Appomattox,* 245.

24. *Report of the Joint Select Committee Appointed to Inquire into the Condition of the Affairs in the Late Insurrectionary States* (Washington, DC: U.S. Congress, 1872), 316–17; Varon, *Appomattox,* 250–51; Janney, *Remembering the Civil War,* 144, 158, 194.

"VAE VICTIS!"

Antisemitism as Self-Victimization (and What Spinoza Knew about It)

ASHER D. BIEMANN

Baruch Spinoza's *Theologico-Political Treatise* of 1670 begins with a memorable observation:

> Men would never be superstitious, if they could govern all their circumstances by set rules, or if they were always favored by fortune: but being frequently driven into straits where rules are useless, and being often kept fluctuating pitiably between hope and fear by the uncertainty of fortune's greedily coveted favors, they are consequently, for the most part, very prone to credulity. The human mind is readily swayed this way or that in times of doubt, especially when hope and fear are struggling for the mastery, though usually it is boastful, over-confident, and in vain.[1]

In the twenty-first century we rarely speak of "superstitions" and rightly hesitate to do so. Religious beliefs and practices have acquired, over the course of modernity and its enduring afterlife, an increasingly private and, at the same time, cultural-anthropological significance, allowing us to suspend the problematic judgment over "true" and "false" beliefs, "right" rituals or "correctness" of worship, as long as these beliefs and practices do not interfere with everyday civility. "Not every prejudice or weakness we seem to detect in our fellowmen is equally harmful," wrote the Jewish enlightener Moses Mendelssohn a century after Spinoza's *Treatise,* and he concludes: "It seems to me that anyone who leads men to virtue in this life cannot be damned in the next."[2] Since religious faith eludes empirical proof, or as Immanuel Kant put it, "assertorial knowledge," and since ritual practice was deemed by the Enlighteners "ceremonial" but not universally required, superstition and prejudice could philosophically (and politically) be tolerated as harmless human error that, at times, might even have inspired virtuous behavior.

Until, of course, this error ceased to be harmless. Spinoza well understood that superstition alone is not merely an error or false belief but the inevitable result of fear and hope struggling for mastery over the human mind. There is, he claims, no ruler more potent than superstition. Since fear and hope spring from human emotion rather than reason and understanding, superstition and prejudice, no matter how harmless they may initially seem, must ultimately be maintained through the very power of emotions that created them: through "hatred, anger, and deceit." Spinoza's Jewish ancestors came from Spain and Portugal, which at the end of the fifteenth century—then under the crown of the Catholic empire—persecuted, forcefully converted, and expelled some 250,000 Jews, as well as deporting its entire Muslim population; he was extremely attentive to the power of emotions, especially the power of fear, which he considered the root of tyranny. And he was attentive to the fact that fear begins not with real-life situations but with "believing the phantoms of imagination"—and, ultimately, with imagining oneself as their victim.

Antisemitism can be regarded as one such "phantom of imagination"; in its modern form, it was not yet known to Spinoza's generation (though some scholars rightly argue that the Spanish inquisition's ideological pedigree of religion and *limpieza de sangre*—"purity blood"—anticipated modern racial fantasies). More specifically, however, it could be regarded as a perpetual exercise in self-victimization, for it is rooted in older forms of Judeophobia, which remained inseparable from common demonophobia. Antisemitism, in this sense, functions like a modern superstition. But this embarrassing genealogy does not render it timid. To the contrary, as all superstition is guided by fear and hope (hope, for Spinoza, being another form of fear), antisemitism, rather than succumbing to its own weakness, becomes "boastful and overly confident," as fearful constructs often tend to be. What begins in fear and in a feeling of powerlessness soon turns into a superstition of superiority, of supremacy, into the idea of a "master-race." This, for Spinoza, was superstition's true peril.

It might have been unthinkable, before August 2017, that this sort of peril would come to haunt the quaint and seemingly peaceful town of Charlottesville, Virginia. But what unfolded during that fateful weekend was neither a fluke in history nor the mere echo of a bygone age. It was a chilling example of modern superstition mobilizing, once again, the crowds; it was an example of fear and phobia becoming boastful, violent, and deadly. To the organizers of the Unite the Right rally, antisemitic symbols merged effortlessly with their white supremacist agenda and the ostensible mission to "save" a monument to Robert E. Lee (and, with it, the entire Confederate legacy). Observers of the rally were shocked by the carnivalesque array of Nazi insignia affixed to banners and crudely fashioned armors, the swastika being only one of them. They were unsettled by chants of "Blood and Soil" and "You [the Jews] will not replace us," and by T-shirts worn to display quotes from Hitler's pen. They were struck by the carefully choreographed Friday night parade across university grounds invoking a notorious scene from Leni Riefenstahl's Nazi propaganda film *Triumph of the Will*, complete with tiki torches, Nazi flags, and Hitler salutes. They were startled by armed demonstrators in fatigues threatening the local synagogue as Shabbat prayers went on inside; and they were aghast when crowds responded to white supremacist leader Richard Spencer mocking Charlottesville's "little Mayor Signer," who happens to be Jewish, by sneering in one voice, "Jew, Jew, Jew."[3]

That antisemitism was not merely incidental to the racist rallying cries of Charlottesville but was, in fact, an integral part of them can hardly be overlooked. This is not to say that antisemitism competed with, much less overshadowed, the profoundly antiblack racism defining the white supremacist agenda. Rather, its unmistakable signs seamlessly attached themselves to the symbols of the Confederacy, both strains complementing each other into a cohesive (though not coherent) state of mind, joining forces in hate, no matter how historically absurd this fusion seemed to be. Indeed, to celebrate the legacy of a Civil War general with Confederate symbols *and* swastikas; to greet fellow Americans, whose grandparents had risked and lost their lives fighting the Nazi tyranny, with the ultimate symbol of loyalty to the *Führer*—the Nazi salute; to express what they consider Southern pride with chants of blood and soil, all this had to appear like an unfathomable perversion of historical time and place. But it was not. It was merely the perilous marriage of timeless and deliberately unhistorical ideologies seeking to write their *own* history, to make sense of their *own* place. In Charlottesville white nationalists and supremacists wanted "their" history to be heard, "their" place to be affirmed. They came to seek "justice." Or as Spencer, who is known also for his earlier episodes of Holocaust denial, told his followers in a livestream: "We have a place in this country. We have a place in this conversation. We have a right to exist."[4]

Encapsulated in this shameless plea for existence is the essential creed of all superstition: that there is a dark, powerful world dominating the innocent—a world so foreign, so other, that it is destined to remain humanly untranslatable, unknowable, and unrelatable. To mingle with this world would mean a metaphysical blemish, to ward off its darkness the only hope for survival. Viewing themselves under siege by what appears to them as a mysterious "nonwhite" majority, white supremacists, like antisemites, and more often *as* antisemites, assume and embrace the role of victims and saviors at once. Their ideology, which is nothing less and nothing more than a reckless eclecticism of hate capitalizing on credulity and fear, teaches, paradoxically, both inferiority and superiority, powerlessness and power. It teaches its followers that they are the last remnant in a vanishing world.

One cannot begin to make sense of the hodgepodge of hate that filled the streets of Charlottesville without considering the fact that hatred stems not merely from spontaneous emotion, that it means no simple loss of control, but that it has a *tradition,* a learned legacy that is often the convergence of multiple traditions. It required little genius for the organizers of Unite the Right to figure out that the affinities of hate can generate a sense of universal kinship, that the "right" is a vast receptacle of the likeminded. Within that kinship, antisemitism has always been a trusted member, sometimes central and at other times auxiliary to the dominant cause. If I briefly reflect now on the history of antisemitism, it is not to diminish the full range of racism white supremacy encompasses, but to illustrate, in one example, how fear and self-victimization have shaped a tradition of their own.

The term "antisemitism" was coined around 1873 by Wilhelm Marr, a German intellectual and disgruntled journalist whose 1879 pamphlet, *The Victory of Judaism over Germandom from a Non-Religious Perspective,* became the essential proof text for most subsequent antisemitic literature. As founder of the Antisemiten-Liga (League of Antisemites), Marr articulated a new form of Jew-hatred, anchored not in religion or in popular tradition but in modern "science" and reason and, most of all, in urgent fear. Germany, and indeed *humanity,* had become, at last, a victim of Judaism. In his pamphlet Marr expressed this fear, as antisemitic texts commonly do, through a rhetoric of hyperbole and satire. Thus he begins:

> It is not a pretentious prophecy, but the deepest inner conviction which I here utter. Your generation will not pass before there will be absolutely no public office, even the highest one, which the Jews will not have usurped. Yes, through the Jewish nation, Germany will become a world power, a western New Palestine. And this will happen, not through violent revolutions but through the compliance of the [German] people. . . .

By now, a sudden reversal of this process is fundamentally impossible, for if it were, the entire social structure, which has been so thoroughly Judaized, would collapse.[5]

A "Judaized" society, which National Socialist ideologues would later call *"verjudet,"* was Marr's greatest worry.[6] The clandestine revolution of Jews "usurping offices" and cunningly transforming Bismarck's Germany into the "New Palestine" of the West seemed, to Marr, a completed fact, irreversible and made possible by the silent complicity of liberal-minded Germans who themselves had enabled these Jews to become "good citizens of the Christian State." Indeed, Marr invoked a historical inevitability that resembled the tragedy of fate: "We should not reproach the Jewish nation. It fought against the western world for 1,800 years, and finally conquered and subjugated it. We were vanquished and it is entirely proper that the victor shouts 'Vae Victis!' "[7]

Woe to the conquered! This would become the battle cry, and call for action, of antisemites then and now. Indeed, the urgency of the moment, in antisemitic imagination, is not that Jews might, one day, conquer Germany, the West, the world, but that they already *had.* If another notorious ideologue of German antisemitism, the British-born Houston Stewart Chamberlain, wrote in his 1899 book *The Foundations of the Nineteenth Century* that "we live today in a 'Jewish Age,' " then it was precisely this perception of a conquered world that seemed to justify and to necessitate forms of antisemitic "resistance." In fact, continues Chamberlain, if the process of Jewish mastery "were to go on for a few centuries, there would be in Europe only one single people of pure race, that of the Jews[;] all the rest would be a herd of pseudo-Hebraic mestizos, a people beyond all doubt degenerate physically, mentally, and morally."[8]

For Chamberlain, then, Jewish "power" culminated in the ultimate desire to "infect the Indo-Europeans with Jewish blood." For Marr, however (while he did not dispute the "historical fact that Israel became the leading social-political superpower in the nineteenth century"), the global Jewish "infection" was an even more elusive matter: "Not individual Jews, but the Jewish spirit and Jewish consciousness have overpowered the world."[9]

Antisemitic literature—which included occasional examples of Jewish self-hatred, such as Otto Weininger or Arthur Trebitsch—routinely invoked such a "spirit" or "consciousness" to depict Judaism as a sinister force beyond empirical grasp, as a paranormal power that could accommodate entirely contradictory qualities and attributes: Jews as communists as well as capitalists, Zionists, and cosmopolitans, as effeminate weaklings and power-hungry beasts, as *Untermenschen* and *Übermenschen;* Jews as a race that, at the same time, was called the "race of racelessness"; Jews unable to assimilate, yet assimilating so well that they had turned into dangerous chameleons.[10] "It is precisely the baptized Jews who infiltrate furthest, unhindered in all sectors of society and political life," wrote the German philosopher and economist Karl Eugen Dühring in 1881.[11] Thanks to this modern *coincidentia oppositorum,* antisemitism ultimately advanced to an ideology inherently immune to falsification and any rational analysis. It became the theory of inescapability par excellence.

More has been written about the "eternal" antisemite than I can possibly here summarize. However, antisemitism represents not only a modern superstition (or as Leo Pinsker put it in his 1882 pamphlet *Auto-Emancipation,* a "hereditary psychosis") but also an intellectual *tradition,* a fact that cannot be emphasized enough.[12] Antisemitic tropes require little reinvention. They exist and are passed down ready-made with or without the presence of Jews. They exist as a distinct literary genre. Antisemitism encompasses a total worldview; it works like a closed system of thought that can be entered at any time by any person from any intellectual persuasion, whether "right" or "left." It is, in this respect, a truly universal tradition and a universally *available* tradition, a commodity of the mind. And like all spiritual traditions striving for permanence and perpetuity, antisemitism remains unperturbed by history and time.

Antisemitism remains strangely impervious also to the ambitions of higher education. Nineteenth-century antisemitism itself was a product of established intellectuals, university professors, and privileged literati, whose first—though by no means last—disciples were students and educated readers; it continues to exist in ever-new and subtle intellectual guises, such as anti-Americanism (especially the anti–East Coast kind), antiglobalism (for Jews are deemed, after all, quintessential cosmopolitans), or anti-Zionism (as an angry ideology rather than thoughtful critique). There lies, in all of these ideologies, a tendency toward self-victimization and not seldom the self-perception of their propagators as prophets outcast. On the other hand, of course, the ubiquity of antisemitism and the practice of spotting an antisemite in every critic or unfavorable neighbor can quickly become a story of self-victimization in itself. Hannah Arendt, in fact, considered the theory of "eternal antisemitism" its own form of superstition.[13]

The trajectory from Marr's "Vae victis!" to Spencer's "The Jews will not replace us!" is thus a logical one; not a rational one, to be sure, but one following the inner logic of an irrational tradition. Wilhelm Marr responded to the chimerical reality of a Jewish world dominion with his own call for resistance and resilience: "Resigned to subjugation to Jewry, I am marshaling my last remaining strength in order to die peacefully, as one who will not surrender and who will not ask forgiveness." Unapologetically, Marr concealed his irrational fears in a language of bravery and courage, modeling the rhetoric of antisemitism for the following century. In 1923 Adolf Hitler wrote the infamous line in *Mein Kampf:* "I had ceased to be a weak-kneed cosmopolitan and become an antisemite. . . . By defending myself against the Jews, I am fighting for the work of the Lord"; in doing so he created the ultimate fusion of victim and divine servant that would enable and necessitate the "Final Solution."[14] It is precisely this lethal fusion that invites us to recall once more Spinoza's reflections on theopolitics: "As though God had turned away from the wise, and written his decrees, not in the mind of man but in the entrails of beasts, or left them to be proclaimed by the inspiration and instinct of fools, madmen, and birds. Such is the unreason to which terror can drive mankind!"[15]

How, we might wonder, can one defeat the terror of superstition? How can one defeat fear, folly, and hate? One thing is abundantly clear if we study the history of antisemitism: its ideas are as unremarkable as are its adherents. Far from being an "extremist" ideology, antisemitism exudes a sense of normalcy, a "normal" hatred, a "normal" fear that attracts the ordinary and poses as self-evident, which makes it all the harder to defeat.

But there is another obstacle to fighting modern Judeophobia: not all fear is suffering. It can also be fun. It is fun to write nonsense and to spread its gospel. It is fun to go to war against an enemy whose supposed power is but chimerical. It is fun, actually, to hate. Countless photographs from the early days of fascism and National Socialism reveal, with unsettling clarity, how much fun these movements really were for their adherents, how much fun it was to burn synagogues, loot Jewish-owned property, and watch their Jewish neighbors, no matter how frail, clean sidewalks on their knees.[16] It is not enough, then, to "understand" the grievances of these enthusiasts, their fears, their superstitions, their fantasies; one must also consider the degree of pleasure and recreational zest such hateful ideologies offer to their followers, old and young, wealthy and poor, men and women. Fascism is fun (and many students agree that studying it, in a perverted way, can be fun too), and marching with tiki torches and self-made insignia of hate has a disturbing share in that tradition of fun. So addressing real grievances alone—as necessary as this first step undoubtedly may be—cannot suffice. Nor will education be able to fully educate away the fear and fun antisemitism has to offer. Traditions, for better or worse, are known to be supremely resistant to new ideas. And when education remains but a gateway to a career, when it is measured in "outcomes" and starting salaries, then intellectual curiosity and the willingness to be unmoored from past assumptions are not necessarily given. Only when learning becomes a value in itself, when it offers time for introspection, will the fabrics of tradition and prejudice sustain the very cracks and lesions needed for change.

Antisemitism may be the oldest tradition of fear, but it certainly is not the *only* one. White supremacist and other racist superstitions, xenophobia, and sometimes even homophobia offer an endless repertoire of similar tropes; they all belong to the same genre of fear whose hideous arguments and penchant for the fake and counterfactual render them not, as one might hope, fragile and short-lived but, to the contrary, steady and perpetual. Reason, as Spinoza already knew, has little power beyond itself. It needs leadership, sovereigns, and politicians to ensure that the mind, because it is powerless, will always remain free.

For Spinoza, freedom—the liberation from fear—was the sole purpose of a polity. To liberate from fear, however, freedom must itself be fearless. Accordingly, only fearless leaders can let freedom flourish and remain unafraid of the power of superstition. There can be no justice, no compassion in a world ruled by fear. In the liberation from fear, reason and politics unite for a common purpose. Where this common purpose retreats, tyranny must follow. Spinoza ultimately understood tyranny as a politics of passion and panic, as a politics of fear having become boastful and overly self-confident to conceal its weakness. Since few of us are able to extricate ourselves from the "self-imposed tutelage" of our fears and prejudices, to paraphrase again Immanuel Kant, the sovereign must tolerate and keep free also our errors and superstitions, as long as his or her actions do not violate what Spinoza, following the tradition of his ancestors, considered the foundation of any society: acts of *zedaka* (justice) and *hesed* (charity), the unity of *din* (judgment) and *rahamim* (compassion, literally from the Hebrew word for "womb"), without which freedom would revert into another kind of bondage. And here the true fearlessness of a leader manifests itself: to protect freedom of thought and freedom of error, to tolerate superstition, but to prevent, at all cost, fear from rising to power and freedom from losing compassion.[17]

Perhaps reading Spinoza will help us direct our responses to the newly manifest acts of racism and antisemitism—*acts* indeed, acts of violence, not merely cognitive errors—away from the crowds having fun and toward the very guardians of freedom in our polity, toward the very leadership plagued by fears and insecurities of its own. One cannot and must not ignore hate. The histories of antisemitism and racism belong to the darkest histories of human civilization. Knowing these histories at once adds a sense of urgency to the events of August 2017 in Charlottesville and removes a sense of surprise and shock from them. Historically speaking, everything looks familiar and unspectacular: the return of an old tradition, the repetition of dehydrated tropes, the stubborn resistance to common sense. There may be a limit to what we can do to restore reason in a world guided by fear and prone to panic. But perhaps we can begin by reaching out to others targeted as "others" by getting to know each other, not by comparing victimhood, nor by indulging in it, but by learning from each other and by developing, if nothing else, strategies of solidarity—another kind of *unity*. It may be true that we learn very little from history except, perhaps, this one thing: that there is a right side and a wrong side and that we must, from time to time, make an effort, even at the risk of oversimplifying the world, to defend the right one.

NOTES

1. Benedict de Spinoza, *A Theologico-Political Treatise,* trans. R. H. M. Elwes (New York: Dover, 1951), 3.
2. Moses Mendelssohn, "Letter to Johann Caspar Lavater," in *Modern Jewish Thought: A Source Reader,* ed. Nahum N. Glatzer (New York: Schocken Books, 1977), 8.
3. Regarding *Triumph of the Will,* see Bonnie Gordon's thoughtful essay in this volume, "On Listening," which offers additional analysis and literature on this obvious parallel. These and other examples of antisemitic rhetoric during the Charlottesville rally have been well documented and commented on in the media, including Israel's *Ha'aretz*. See, for instance, Allison Kaplan Sommer, "From Swastikas to David Duke: Nazism and anti-Semitism Take Center Stage at Charlottesville Rally," *Ha'aretz*, Aug. 13, 2017. Yet there has also been criticism about the lack of response to the distinctly antisemitic tone of the rally: see Jenny Singer, "Why Can't I Find One High-Profile Celebrity Who Acknowledged the anti-Semitism in Charlottesville?," *Forward*, Aug. 14, 2017; Emma Green, "Why the Charlottesville Marchers Were Obsessed with Jews," *Atlantic*, Aug. 15, 2017; Mike Evans, "Hatred of the Jews Returns with a Flourish," *Washington Post*, Aug. 17, 2017; Dahleen Glanton, "Neo-Nazis, anti-Semitism, and the Cycle of Hatred in America," *Chicago Tribune*, Aug. 28, 2017.
4. Doha Madani, "Richard Spencer and Fellow White Nationalists Return to Charlottesville," *Huffington Post*, Oct. 7, 2017.

5. Wilhelm Marr, *Der Sieg des Judenthums über das Germanentum vom nicht confessio-nellen Standpunkt betrachtet* (Bern: R. Costenoble, 1879), 32–33. I follow the translation by Paul Mendes-Flohr and Jehuda Reinharz, printed in *The Jew in the Modern World: A Documentary History*, ed. Mendes-Flohr and Reinharz (Oxford: Oxford University Press, 1995), 331. One might compare this to a recent statement by former Klansman David Duke: "It's ultimately Jewish racism, it's tribalism and supremacy. They're the supremacists. They want to not only have their Zionist ethno-state of Israel, but they want to have supremacy over our media, over what we discuss, over our banking system, and over our political system. They're the most powerful force in campaign financing and campaign organization in America, in the world. . . . If we don't overthrow this Zio-garchy over us then we have no future." Quoted in Anti-Defamation League report, "Anti-Semitism on Full Display in Charlottesville," Aug. 15, 2017, www.adl.org.

6. Hence the repeated calls by white supremacists to "unjew America."

7. Marr, *Der Sieg des Judenthums*, 33.

8. Houston Stewart Chamberlain, *The Foundations of the Nineteenth Century*, trans. John Lees (New York: John Kane Co., 1914), 331.

9. Chamberlain, *Foundations*, 331; Marr, *Der Sieg des Judenthums*, 34.

10. For examples of Jewish self-hatred, see Theodor Lessing, *Jüdischer Selbsthass* (Berlin: Jüdischer Verlag, 1930); and, more recently, Paul Reitter, *On the Origins of Jewish Self-Hatred* (Princeton, NJ: Princeton University Press, 2012).

11. Karl Eugen Dühring, *Die Judenfrage als Racen, Sitten- und Culturfrage* (Karlsruhe: Reuther, 1881), 3–4. This translation is from Mark Gelber, in *The Jew in the Modern World*, ed. Mendes-Flohr and Reinharz, 333.

12. Leo Pinsker, *Auto-Emazipation* (Berlin: Jüdischer Verlag, 1934), 8.

13. Cf. Hannah Arendt, *Antisemitism* (New York: Harcourt Brace Jovanovich, 1968), 7.

14. Adolf Hitler, *Mein Kampf* (1923), trans. Ralph Manheim (Boston: Houghton Mifflin, 1943), 65.

15. Spinoza, *Theologico-Political Treatise*, 4.

16. For startling examples of this culture of fun in Nazi Germany, see Alon Confino, *A World without Jews: The Nazi Imagination from Persecution to Genocide* (New Haven, CT: Yale University Press, 2014).

17. Spinoza champions here, of course, a theory of free speech. On that subject, see the important reflections by Frederick Schauer, "In the Shadow of the First Amendment," in this volume, and Leslie Kendrick, "The Answers and the Questions in First Amendment Law," also herein.

SPEAKING

Political Perspectives

IN THE SHADOW OF THE
FIRST AMENDMENT

FREDERICK SCHAUER

No other country protects controversial speakers with the zeal of American First Amendment doctrine. But whether American free speech exceptionalism is a good thing remains deeply contested, and the Charlottesville events of August 11 and 12 show why.

America's extremely protective approach to free speech, even at the expense of other values, takes many forms. Public officials and public figures, for example, must clear a daunting array of First Amendment hurdles before they can win a libel suit against their critics, even when what is said about them is plainly false. Other countries disagree, and believe the United States sacrifices too much of the value of reputation on the altar of free speech—just as American free speech enthusiasts believe that the approach elsewhere leaves too little breathing room for harsh criticism of those who make and influence public policy.

Similarly, the United States protects free speech and free press against the claims of privacy more vigorously than do other countries, and it is more permissive of publishing unlawfully obtained information (as with the Pentagon Papers in 1971). More relevant to the Unite the Right rally of August 12 and the opposition to it, the United States, as a result of Supreme Court rulings going back to the 1960s, erects an almost insurmountably high bar before it will punish those who advocate or incite illegal action: the advocacy must be explicit, the illegality advocated must be imminent, and the incitement must produce an actual likelihood of that imminent illegality. Short of explicit and immediate encouragement to violence of an angry mob, therefore, the United States—alone among nations—tolerates almost all advocacy, even advocacy of unlawful violence.

Where the United States departs most dramatically from the approaches elsewhere is with what is commonly called "hate speech"—speech that incites or encourages race-based violence or discrimination, or denigrates or insults people because of their race, religion, ethnicity, sexual orientation, or gender. Even though many people in Charlottesville and at UVA believed, correctly, that the Klan, the neo-Nazis, and other white supremacist groups who rallied on July 8, August 11, and August 12 engaged in hate speech, many people also believed, incorrectly, that the offenders had violated the law in doing so. That conclusion would be correct for much of the world, where authorities prohibit incitement to racial hatred, Holocaust denial, racial vilification, racial insult, and other forms of hate speech, but not in the United States. Supreme Court decisions dating, again, to the 1960s have made clear that not only does the Constitution not recognize the category of hate speech, but it also plainly prohibits targeting speakers because their message is racially hateful, hurtful, or outrageous.

Indeed, when in 1977 the National Socialist Party of America, self-described as Nazis, proposed to march in Skokie, Illinois—a community with a majority Jewish population and an especially large number (approximately 5,000 out of a total population in Skokie of 60,000) of Holocaust survivors—federal and state courts rebuffed the city's efforts to prohibit the march, and the Supreme Court refused to hear any of the Skokie cases. While the court's refusal to hear a case is not a decision on the merits, many understood the denial of review, in the context of the dispute's national prominence, as tantamount to a ruling that the law protected the marchers.

America's unique approach to hate speech remains highly controversial, even in America. Our parents admonished us that "sticks and bones may break your bones, but names will never hurt you," but they were wrong. Insults, epithets, and racially abusive language can produce mental anguish, contribute to the marginalization of targeted groups, encourage illegal discrimination, and help create an atmosphere in which racial violence increases. No matter how racist, homophobic, sexist, or otherwise dangerously offensive the speech at issue happens to be, however, American courts have consistently refused to let government restrict speech, parades, marches, demonstrations, or rallies based solely on their content.

Perhaps this aversion to what is called "content regulation" or "content discrimination" reflects a longstanding American distrust of government. Perhaps it embodies a characteristically American libertarianism about regulation of anything. Perhaps it is a reaction to the excess suppression of speech during the Red Scare of 1919 and the McCarthy era in the late 1940s and early 1950s. But whatever the cause, regulation of content crosses an inviolable line in American First Amendment doctrine. Whatever the cause, the effect—refusal to allow regulation of hate speech because of its hatefulness—is by now well entrenched in legal doctrine.

THE PROBLEM OF CONTENT DISCRIMINATION

Much of American free speech law is premised on the principle that government—whether it is the executive branch, the legislature, or the courts—cannot make distinctions based on the *content* of someone's speech, especially if the distinction is based on preferring one point of view over another. And thus, although the views the white supremacists espoused in their August marches were as wrong and false as they were offensive, American free speech law reflects what Supreme Court Justice Lewis Powell observed in a 1974 libel case: "Under the First Amendment there is no such thing as a false idea."

The opening qualification of Justice Powell's pronouncement is important. Justice Powell was no relativist or postmodernist. He believed there were true and false facts, and true and false ideas. But he believed as well, as did his Supreme Court colleagues, that the dangers of allowing officials to determine the truth or falsity of expression outweighed the dangers stemming from the proliferation of false facts and false ideas. And thus, although there is absolutely no moral or political equivalency between the white supremacist protesters in Charlottesville and the counterprotesters who opposed them, treating that which is not morally equivalent as legally and constitutionally equivalent is a century-old keystone of the American First Amendment tradition, even if it is not a keystone, as European and other approaches illustrate, of the very idea of free speech itself.

Here again reasonable minds and reasonable nations have disagreed, but the aversion to content discrimination remains firmly embedded in American constitutional law. However false and harmful white supremacist ideology is, American free speech doctrine worries even more about granting officials the power to determine which ideas are false and which are harmful. If today's officials can suppress coalitions on the right, then tomorrow's will have the power to suppress a united left. Or so it is almost always argued by free speech advocates. Republicans in power would be able to suppress Democrats, capitalists would be able to suppress socialists, and vice versa, depending on how the political pendulum swings or the wheel of the world turns.

And so American law has long held. Other countries are not nearly so worried about the discretion of officials to determine the falsity of white supremacy or the harm of anti-Semitism, but the American approach—encapsulated by the phrase "content discrimination" and the traditional American fear of it—is to the contrary.

THE PUBLIC FORUM

On the day before the August 12 Unite the Right rally, the city tried to relocate the planned demonstration away from Emancipation Park (formerly Robert E. Lee Park) and the confines of downtown to McIntire Park on the north end. Although content neutrality was an issue, as noted below, more than content neutrality came into play to thwart the attempt. The city also had to overcome the strong constitutional protection of a "public forum." Although the city owns Emancipation Park, the Supreme Court has held since the 1930s that municipal authorities cannot close off streets, sidewalks, and parks to parades, picketing, demonstrations, or other forms of speech. When the journalist A. J. Liebling observed a century ago that "freedom of the press is guaranteed only to those who own one," he reminded us that free speech requires not only a speaker but also the resources to make that speech possible. The same holds true for picketing, parading, rallying, or demonstrating, all considered forms of speech. The participants need the physical space to perform their activity, and so the First Amendment requires the authorities to keep public sites open to them.

This mandatory right of access is not absolute. Cities may adopt reasonable "time, place, and manner" regulations, but such regulations must be content neutral. Charlottesville may regulate noise levels, time of day, and size of crowd, for example, but must do so without regard to the views of the speakers. Thus, when U.S. District Judge Glen E. Conrad ruled that the organizers of the Unite the Right rally could not be compelled to move their event to McIntire Park, he based his ruling in part on the fact that only the Unite the Right demonstrators, and not those who were demonstrating against them in other parks, were required to move. For Judge Conrad, the city had drawn a distinction based on the views expressed and thus violated the First Amendment in a way that an order to move all the demonstrations would not have.

The arrival of torch-carrying neo-Nazis to Grounds August 11 presented a more nuanced public-forum issue. As a public institution on state land, the university's open spaces are subject to the First Amendment, but they are also subject to regulation, so long as it is content-neutral regulation. As such, the open areas on Grounds can be considered so-called limited-purpose public forums. The administration may, for example, limit the use of its property to those who have some connection to the university, but it cannot favor certain connections over others based on a group's views or politics. So it was that UVA found itself forced to allow demonstrations by those whose views essentially the entire university community found abhorrent.

Since then, the Board of Visitors has put tighter regulations in place, including reclassifying the Academical Village as a "facility," subject to a permitting process and firearms prohibitions (see "Turning Point," uvamagazine.org/articles/turning_point). In enforcing those rules, the university will need to treat all would-be demonstrators alike, regardless of whether their grievance is anti-Semitic, anti-Trump, antiwar, pro–civil rights, or even anti the serving of meat in UVA cafeterias.

THE PROBLEM OF THE HOSTILE AUDIENCE

The Unite the Right protesters drew counterprotesters or, in the parlance of First Amendment analysis, the speakers drew listeners. The clashes that ensued between them raise the constitutional issue of the "hostile audience." Before the civil rights and antiwar demonstrations of the 1960s, the common solution was to restrict speech likely to spark violence between speakers and audiences. Since the 1960s, however, the courts have rejected that approach as empowering a hostile audience to silence contrary but protected speech, known as the "heckler's veto." Courts and law enforcement alike now accept that their first responsibility is to protect speakers exercising their First Amendment rights, even the if the rights being exercised are racist or otherwise hateful and harmful.

Although the law is now clear about the initial responsibilities of officials and law enforcement, it is less clear about when, how, and on what basis the authorities can step in to restrict the speaker or force an end to a previously constitutionally protected event. When we learn that the University of California, Berkeley, recently spent almost $2 million to protect just three highly controversial right-wing speakers (Ann Coulter, Ben Shapiro, and Milo Yiannopoulos); that the University of Florida incurred expenses of greater than $500,000 to manage a speech by Richard Spencer; and that it cost Charlottesville more than $30,000 to provide law enforcement and related services for the July 2017 Klan rally and another $70,000 for the Unite the Right rally on August 12, even apart from the costs to the university, to the County of Albemarle, and to various state law enforcement agencies, we wonder just how much a city, a state, or a university is required to do. Must they call on the state police before disallowing or closing an event? Must they ask the governor to call out the National Guard? How quickly can they close an event when actual violence seems imminent? There is also an evidentiary issue: Can a speaker's past record of inciting violence be used to restrict the person's upcoming appearances in a way that would otherwise be impermissible?

The recent Charlottesville events bring these difficult questions to the fore, and existing law provides little guidance. The issue is not only with First Amendment doctrine, however. It lies as well with the frequent unwillingness, appropriate or not, of courts, law enforcement, and universities to impose harsh punishments on those who, out of morally admirable motivation, attempt to restrict hateful groups from exercising their First Amendment rights. And as long as that is the case, there is little reason to believe that the problem of the hostile audience will disappear.

Short of an openly hostile audience, there are also the cases where the interference with the speakers is less violent but nonetheless interfering. Counterprotesters can assert a heckler's veto in nonviolent ways, such as using drums or horns to prevent speakers from being heard, or with attempts to block speakers from reaching the location designated for their speech. Should such actions be applauded as part of the civil disobedience tradition? If so, should those who interfere be willing, as so many civil disobedients have been, to accept their punishment? Or should such actions, even if technically legal, be condemned as attempts to interfere with someone's free speech rights? And have we achieved a fair balancing of interests between offensive speakers and offended listeners if we refuse to prevent even the most unacceptable of words and ideas from being heard?

SPEAKING ABOUT SPEECH

The point of the First Amendment is, in part, to encourage dialogue, but, ironically and regrettably, we seem to have little serious public dialogue about the First Amendment. Those who oppose this or that speech restriction parrot standard platitudes, such as "the remedy for bad speech is good speech," without stopping to consider whether this ultimately empirical proposition is actually true. On the other side, those who favor restrictions trot out Oliver Wendell Holmes's 1919 observations that speech can be restricted when there is a "clear and present danger" and that no one has a right falsely to shout "Fire!" in a crowded theater, all the while ignoring almost a century of legal embellishments and qualifications on what were originally little more than offhand remarks. And as the opposing parties hurl hackneyed slogans at each other, we find little serious public thought about the values of freedom of speech and the qualifications that should be imposed on it.

The problem is exacerbated by the all-too-frequent failure to distinguish what the law is from what it should be. It is entirely appropriate to consider what is wrong with the existing constitutional law of the First Amendment, but students, faculty, staff, and administrators at a state university remain subject to the law as it exists, warts and all. We should recognize that officials have the obligation to follow the law, even when they disagree with it. We should also recognize, however, that just because the law is the law doesn't make it immune from criticism or change.

THE ANSWERS AND
THE QUESTIONS IN
FIRST AMENDMENT LAW

LESLIE KENDRICK

So much more matters to what happened in Charlottesville in August 2017 than free speech. After all, the fundamentals of current First Amendment law have been in place for at least forty-five years. During most of that time, Nazis and white supremacists were not regularly converging on American cities for flagrant engagement in bigotry, anti-Semitism, and racial intimidation. Anyone wondering why this happened when it did will not find the answers in free speech law.[1]

Still, once Nazis and white supremacists decided to target Charlottesville, it was the First Amendment that allowed them to be here. In that way, the First Amendment is a cause of everything that happened—only one cause among many, but still a cause. And for that reason, some may conclude that the First Amendment has a lot to answer for.

The First Amendment is a part of Charlottesville, of Boston and Berkeley, of Shelbyville, Tennessee, and of whatever may occur on future occasions. These events take shape around various features of First Amendment law. Some of these features are clear and foundational, others hidden and oblique. These are the answers and the questions in modern First Amendment law: the fundamental precepts that current events implicate and the myriad more hidden, but no less important, problems that they expose. In what happened in Charlottesville, and what may happen elsewhere, both the answers and the questions play an undeniable role. Here I will focus on one key answer—the status of hate speech under the First Amendment—and one key question—who, in a close case, gets the benefit of the doubt.

In America, hate speech is not a legal category. The First Amendment protects most speech on matters of public concern, even if that speech is racist, anti-Semitic, or otherwise counter to our nation's commitment to the fundamental equality of all people. Only if speech meets the demanding criteria of certain narrow categories—incitement, true threats, defamation—can the law regulate it. In short, under American law there is no such category as "hate speech."

This principle mattered a great deal in Charlottesville. It meant that when Jason Kessler applied for a permit to use a public park for the Unite the Right rally for August 12—or indeed, when the Ku Klux Klan applied for a permit for July 8—the City of Charlottesville had no power to reject these groups because their message was hateful or repugnant to American values. Their message was presumptively protected by the First Amendment, unless it could be shown to fit within a narrow, exceptional category, such as incitement or true threats. And because these narrow categories depend on the content of specific utterances and their likely effects in a particular context, it is extremely difficult, if not impossible, to use them to restrict an entire event before it even occurs.[2]

In our robust protection for hate speech, we are virtually alone among Western democracies.[3] Canada and European countries prohibit inciting racial hatred. Many European countries also expressly prohibit Holocaust denial. This is not surprising—we are the world's most speech-protective society, period. We are an outlier in how we protect defamatory statements, campaign contributions, commercial speech, and other forms of speech as well. Indeed, one could read the First Amendment as being designed from its inception to reject some forms of speech regulation historically accepted in other countries, most clearly English print licensing.

So the United States has generally not taken other countries' practice as a guide. But in the area of hate speech, worldwide practice is not the only force that might counsel in favor of more regulation. The United States is a democratic republic, based on the fundamental equality of all persons. Our nation cannot claim to have lived up to that ideal consistently, but it has been there since the Declaration of Independence, it is there in our form of government and our jurisprudence, and we continue to try to perfect our practice in light of our ideals. This being so, speech that denies the basic equality of all persons is, at bottom, antidemocratic and anti-American. It is not simply that it is wrong, in the same way that saying the earth is flat is wrong. It rejects a foundational tenet of our government. Why, then, should it find refuge in the First Amendment? Why should the Constitution protect speech that rejects it?

First Amendment case law offers several reasons to protect speech on matters of public concern. Most of them do not work here.

One argument is that free speech provides a safety valve for harmful thoughts.[4] The theory is that absent free speech, antisocial thoughts or destructive ideologies would fester and possibly explode. This is ultimately an empirical claim that involves counterfactual speculation about what would happen in a society that did not tolerate the speech in question. As such, it is impossible to disprove, but it is impossible to prove as well. Arrayed against it is a wealth of evidence that rather than containing, say, white supremacy, speech can encourage its spread. Also standing against it is the bare fact that the presence of racially and ethnically inflammatory speech or symbols does not tend to be a sign of an otherwise enlightened society. At the least, given the speculative quality of the claim, it seems a meager reed on which to hang the crucial question of a society's treatment of hate speech.

Closely related is the idea that free speech enables surveillance of people who might be inclined to turn from speech to action. This, too, is an empirical claim that depends on weighing how much more violence, discrimination, and antisocial conduct free speech encourages against whatever improvements in prevention and enforcement it enables. This is an interesting question, but its answer seems too uncertain to provide much of a basis for First Amendment jurisprudence.

One of the most famous arguments for free speech is that it is necessary for the search for truth.[5] Although freedom of speech may or may not lead to truth in a given case, free exchange of ideas is more likely to lead to truth than a system of censorship that takes certain possibilities off the table at the outset. John Stuart Mill was so committed to this idea he argued that if an idea becomes so strongly rejected that it has no proponents, someone should be appointed its advocate, just so society can have the benefit of considering it thoroughly and rejecting it.[6]

The search for truth is closely related to the marketplace of ideas, a metaphor that got its start in a famous dissent from Justice Holmes:

Persecution for the expression of opinions seems to me perfectly logical. If you have no doubt of your premises or your power, and want a certain result with all your heart, you naturally express your wishes in law, and sweep away all opposition. To allow opposition by speech seems to indicate that you think the speech impotent, as when a man says that he has squared the circle, or that you do not care wholeheartedly for the result, or that you doubt either your power or your premises. But when men have realized that time has upset many fighting faiths, they may come to believe even more than they believe the very foundations of their own conduct that the ultimate good desired is better reached by free trade in ideas—that the best test of truth is the power of the thought to get itself accepted in the competition of the market, and that truth is the only ground upon which their wishes safely can be carried out. That, at any rate, is the theory of our Constitution. It is an experiment, as all life is an experiment. Every year, if not every day, we have to wager our salvation upon some prophecy based upon imperfect knowledge. While that experiment is part of our system, I think that we should be eternally vigilant against attempts to check the expression of opinions that we loathe and believe to be fraught with death, unless they so imminently threaten immediate interference with the lawful and pressing purposes of the law that an immediate check is required to save the country.[7]

As the passage makes clear, Holmes himself was largely a skeptic about truth. But while he was not sure how much "truth" was attainable, he was sure about how not to attain it—by censoring ideas and prohibiting dangerous opinions. Only when speech posed a "clear and present danger"—another phrase we owe to Holmes—was suppression appropriate.

But the argument for truth is not particularly helpful here. While there are many, many questions that are uncertain, our system takes the fundamental equality of persons as truth. We do not need to subject this question to the so-called marketplace of ideas. We have decided it, and we keep deciding it, in continuing to maintain our system of government.

So why protect hate speech? American jurisprudence offers two reasons. One is that the legitimacy of our system depends upon it. Speech regulation determines what ideas get discussed in our society. Those discussions form the inputs into our democratic decision making. Legitimate democratic outputs depend on uncensored inputs.

This is precisely why censorship is a pervasive feature of repressive regimes. It is much easier to control outputs—whether through illegitimate elections, or no elections at all—when one controls the inputs. Many societies across the globe live out Holmes's observation that censorship is "perfectly logical. If you have no doubt of your premises or your power, and want a certain result with all your heart, you naturally express your wishes in law, and sweep away all opposition." In contrast, democratic legitimacy depends not just on a government's allowing people to vote but on its not interfering with the information they use to vote.

At the end of the day, this view of legitimacy may be driving Mill and Holmes at least as much as an interest in truth seeking. For Mill, the important thing is that society has had an opportunity to consider and reject an unpopular idea—its opportunity to do so makes its rejection of the idea legitimate. For Holmes, skeptic as he was about "truth," the best a society could hope for was a choice, inevitably made with imperfect knowledge, but made freely by the people without interference.

Holmes was writing in a case involving the prosecution of a socialist for publishing socialist leaflets during World War I. There too, the argument could have been made—and was made—that socialism is anti-American, and the Constitution is under no obligation to protect viewpoints that reject its basic tenets. But Holmes, and ultimately American jurisprudence, concluded that a legitimate system depends on inputs from all viewpoints, up to the point of a clear and present danger. This argument for legitimacy requires a reason to treat racist or anti-Semitic speech differently from how we treat other antidemocratic speech. It requires a reason to conclude that our democratic outcomes are sufficiently legitimate despite the suppression of certain viewpoints. This is not to say that such a response is never possible; just that this is what is at stake.

The second argument for protecting hate speech is that we have a terrible track record with regulation. We have a history of censoring abolitionist pamphlets in the South before the Civil War, of punishing socialists (what Holmes called "the surreptitious publishing of a silly leaflet by an unknown man") during World War I, of prosecuting a large-scale witch hunt against Communists during the McCarthy era, and of leveraging the more repressive speech rules of the time to allow Southern states to target the NAACP and block out-of-state newspapers' coverage of the civil rights movement.[8] History suggests that, when it comes to speech, the cure has arguably been worse than the disease.

The alternative to protection for hate speech is not regulation of speech along the lines of any one of our personal preferences. If the First Amendment does not intervene, regulation occurs through regular democratic processes. This primarily means that legislatures, state and federal, would be in charge of speech regulation, with executives, state and federal, participating in the development of a legislative agenda and exercising veto power. It might also mean executive speech regulation through executive orders or administrative agencies.

It is worth considering what this means at this moment. President Trump has expressed interest in reforming the First Amendment, but his suggestions are that defamation laws should be modified to make it easier for public figures to sue newspapers and that the press should be regarded as the enemy of the people.

It is also worth regarding what more regulation means in the long term. Rights are checks on democratic decision making. Historically, the First Amendment has protected the proponents of unpopular ideas against the will of majorities. This is true whether the unpopular belief in question is white supremacy in 2017 Charlottesville or equality in 1964 Birmingham. The alternative to the First Amendment is not hate-speech regulation as devised by a philosopher-king. It is putting some questions back into the hands of majorities.

This is not to say that our current regime has no costs. It has many costs, and they are borne disproportionately by non-Christians and people of color.[9] Our discourse on the First Amendment too often ignores those costs. But when it comes to speech protections, every alternative has costs.

There is a final point to be made about First Amendment protection of hate speech. It is unlikely to change anytime soon. The arguments I have just given are the best justifications for the approach we have now. Whether any one person finds it justified or not, however, the current approach to hate speech enjoys widespread support among the judges who interpret the First Amendment. Charlottesville highlighted the costs of that approach. But it appears not to have changed the commitment to it in any fundamental way.

Where Charlottesville and this moment may make a lasting impact is on a second, more hidden free speech question: Who gets the benefit of the doubt?

Unlike the status of hate speech, this is not a legal question per se. Not because it could not be—the law formally sets an answer to this question in all sorts of contexts, most famously in criminal trials, where the accused gets the benefit until guilt is proven beyond a reasonable doubt. But the First Amendment does not have doctrinal answers to this question in most contexts. Instead, there are a host of areas, big and small, where this question matters, and judges make the decision on their own or guided by past practice rather than articulated precedent.

This much is clear: if the government tries to regulate public discourse in public parks and streets or on private property because of the content of the speech—that is, because of its subject matter, its viewpoint, its message—the presumption is strongly against the government. For its regulation to survive, the government must meet the stringent "strict scrutiny" test by showing that the regulation is narrowly tailored to a compelling governmental interest.

Also clear: if the government tries to regulate such speech for reasons that don't hinge on content—say, for decibel level or maintaining ingress and egress for public parks and sidewalks—it faces a much more deferential level of scrutiny, one that generally does not have a formal name in First Amendment law but is often tantamount to the "rational basis" review that exists in some other areas of constitutional law. So-called time-place-manner regulations fall under this heading: the whole idea of the time-place-manner label is that speech is being regulated for something other than content. The upshot, then, is that such regulation receives a great deal of deference. When regulating for content-neutral reasons, the government gets the benefit of the doubt.

What is not at all clear is who gets the benefit of the doubt as to *whether* the government is regulating for content-based or content-neutral reasons. There is only one clear doctrinal rule on this. If a law, on its face, regulates different content differently—if it bans only "offensive" speech, or "political" speech—and it does this in public streets and parks or against purely private activity, then the law will receive strict scrutiny and likely be struck down.

But if a law or an official decision is not content-based on its face, there is no clear protocol for deciding if government is regulating for a good reason or a bad reason. Sometimes, there is little guidance on what even counts as a good reason or a bad reason. And so courts are left to decide, in so many ways, who gets the benefit of the doubt. Below are a few choices that arose in the context of Charlottesville and will arise again.

Numbers vs. words. Questions of capacity are some of the most clearly content-neutral reasons that a locality can offer for regulating a rally or protest. A park can only hold a certain number of people. The area surrounding a park may not be well designed for holding overflow without interrupting traffic. A permit to use a park does not entitle the holder to appropriate the surrounding area and commandeer the neighborhood to its own purpose.

A city could easily be concerned that an event is likely to be much larger than a permit holder has claimed it will be and much larger than the permit allows for. This would be a neutral reason for delaying, canceling, or moving an event.

At the same time, a permit holder is likely to view this as detrimental action motivated by dislike for its message. Precisely that issue arose in

Charlottesville, and the benefit of the doubt was given to the speaker. The conclusion was that the city's action was driven not by concern about the number of demonstrators but by dislike of their words.

This issue is particularly acute in the case of repugnant speakers whose views any reasonable city or state government would disavow. Government officials can and should state frequently and publicly that they deplore the views of Nazis or white supremacists that seek to use their public spaces. But every such statement becomes evidence to white supremacists that any actions they view as unfavorable were taken *because* of the government's opposition to their views, not for other reasons. On paper, the First Amendment requires the government to tolerate repugnant views but leaves it free to endorse different values of its own. In practice, government officials might worry that by speaking out they will give courts reason to give the Nazis and white supremacists the benefit of the doubt.

Security and the "heckler's veto." Another unresolved question is how much governments can rely on security as a content-neutral reason. Cities have security-based reasons for seeking to regulate when, where, and on what terms inflammatory speakers can utilize public space. Officials may be able to predict that certain dates, days of the week, or times of day are likely to be more dangerous than others. They may be able to predict that certain spaces are more accessible to protesters and counterprotesters or less conducive to maintaining distance between the two groups. They may conclude that certain times or places are simply not compatible with certain types of events, at least not without a serious risk to public safety.

At the same time, the mere fact that an event presents a risk of violence cannot be a reason to shut it down, or even to treat it on terms that are significantly different from other events. Otherwise, officials could always repress or contain the most unpopular speech just by citing security concerns. This would amount to a "heckler's veto": letting the opponents of speech veto it by threatening disruptive or violent opposition. By regulating based on the reaction to speech, the state risks turning regulatory authority over to the hecklers. Doing so undermines the First Amendment's protection for unpopular speech by letting the majority—or a different, well-coordinated minority—decide what gets said. If this does not sound like a problem in the context of white supremacists and Nazis, consider how it sounds in the context of a group that you support that does not enjoy widespread popularity.

The problem is whether every security consideration amounts to a heckler's veto or whether the government sometimes can take into account security judgments that turn in part on the likely reaction to speech. Can the government ever take the likely number of counterprotesters into account in deciding the appropriate time or venue for an event? Is doing so tantamount to giving way to a heckler's veto? Is *not* doing so unrealistic? If the event seeking a permit were a parade, the number of spectators would certainly be taken into account in considering whether to issue the permit. Are the same number of people simply to be ignored when considering the impact of a protest?

As of yet, the doctrine supplies no clear answers. Practice would suggest that the speaker—and the problem of the heckler's veto—gets the benefit of the doubt, but any limit is unknown.

Financial costs and the heckler's veto. The same is true of the heckler's veto and financial costs. In the last year universities and cities have paid multi-million-dollar price tags for the controversial speech of a handful of speakers. Berkeley, university and city, spent over $2 million on three individual speaking events, while the University of Florida and nearby jurisdictions spent an estimated $500,000 on a one-day appearance by Richard Spencer. The vast bulk of these funds is spent attempting to provide security in an environment in which officials can predict large numbers of protesters and counterprotesters and some likelihood of physical violence. (In Florida a supporter of Richard Spencer fired a gun at counterprotesters, and he and two associates were charged with attempted murder.)

Absent concerns about the heckler's veto, a local government might look at some of these price tags and say to a group, "We're sorry, we just don't have the money to host you." But the result could be that only popular groups are able to use public spaces. The result could also be to galvanize the opposition to certain groups to make clear that the response to them will be so costly that states and localities should deny them space in the first place. This is the definition of a heckler's veto. It also underscores that the enormous cost of security comes from a (reasonable) prediction that protesters and counterprotesters will not remain peaceful, will not respect each other's right to speak while voicing their own opposition, and will engage in or at least threaten violence. To recognize these tendencies is in some ways counter to the view of humanity present in First Amendment jurisprudence, where rational people engage in reasoned argument. To take away the speaking rights of every individual within a group, because either their opponents or some few among their number cannot be trusted not to engage in violence, is in some tension with the First Amendment's overarching ideals.

At the same time, no limit at all seems untenable. It seems absurd that cities, First Amendment ideals notwithstanding, can predict the risk of violence with statistical certainty yet have no recourse but to spend hundreds of thousands of dollars. It seems absurd that a fringe group should be entitled to what amounts to a public subsidy of their speech, with absolutely no limiting principle. It is countermajoritarian in the extreme to conclude that a single speaker can blow a hole in a locality's budget, no matter the consequences to public schools, public safety, and the many other interests that public funds support. Also, if the funding principle has no limit, speakers essentially enjoy the power to bankrupt a public entity that they do not like. This is the mirror image of the heckler's veto: if the speaker's opponents should not have an incentive to shut him down through costly opposition, should the speaker enjoy a power to shut down localities through extreme financial cost?

Neither extreme here seems inviting. And perhaps this is one of those areas where some vagueness is salutary. If courts tried to set a limit—say, by holding that localities only have to pay a certain amount for security and no more—that might just create clearer incentives for gaming on one side or another. For now, the bulk of the case law puts the benefit of the doubt on the side of the speaker and against the government and the heckler's veto. But, practically speaking, recent events suggest there must be some limit to that. For better or worse, we do not know what it is.

Guns and speech. Another issue about who gets the benefit of the doubt involves what gets characterized as "speech" and what gets called "conduct." Prior to August 11 and 12, few people were focused on the fact that many white supremacists who showed up for the Unite the Right rally were likely to be heavily armed. They characterized themselves as speakers, and the law did as well. In agreeing to represent Jason Kessler in a lawsuit challenging the City of Charlottesville's attempt to relocate the rally to another park, the ACLU of Virginia suggested that the role of guns in the protest was irrelevant to speech protections.

The images from August 12, however, suggest something different. The salient aspect of many images is the paramilitary weaponry and outfitting of many protesters. Having a quiet conversation, let alone a vociferous protest and counterprotest, is quite different when one side is heavily armed. Words and symbols of racial intimidation are quite different when one side is heavily armed. Perhaps at one point in our history, First Amendment doctrine was silently built on an awareness of the potential for gun violence in speech confrontations, but it does not seem to be so any more.

In the aftermath of August 12, the ACLU announced that it would not represent demonstrators who insist on carrying loaded firearms.[10] There is an ongoing nationwide conversation about how guns relate to speech, and how the Second Amendment relates to the First.[11] Prior to August 12, a speaker carrying a firearm was given the benefit of the doubt as a speaker. Whether that will continue remains to be seen.

In these and other ways, Charlottesville laid bare the hidden yet important, minor yet monumental decision points concealed within First Amendment law. All of them involve who gets the benefit of the doubt. None of them involves comprehensive written rules of the First Amendment, but it is fair to say that in practice, on most fronts, the benefit of the doubt goes to the speaker. It is worth considering whether this practice, while likely to be unpopular when the speaker in question is a white supremacist, holds up fairly well over the mine run of cases. But it is also worth considering where the limiting principles are. Charlottesville cast light on several issues for which limits seem vital and undefined.

As a Jewish free speech lawyer living in Charlottesville, I think about August 11 and 12 every day. I think about it personally, professionally, legally, morally. It casts light on the limits of the First Amendment, on the answers that are clear but sometimes painful, and on the questions that have no answers. It casts light on the fact that there is no perfect answer to any of these questions and every decision comes with its costs. It ultimately shows that, though a repressive speech law can probably damn a society, no speech law alone can save it. We alone can do that, in the values we affirm day after day. Given the choice, in this perilous experiment, it is up to us to choose rightly.

NOTES

1. But several pieces in this volume offer a good place to start.
2. See *Brandenburg v. Ohio*, 395 U.S. 444 (1969) (overturning a Klansman's conviction because his speech at a rally was not shown to have been "directed to inciting or producing imminent lawless action and [] likely to incite or produce such action"); *Virginia v. Black*, 538 U.S. 343 (2003) (rejecting a conviction under Virginia's cross-burning statute because it was not shown that the defendant burned the cross with an intent to intimidate).
3. See Frederick Schauer, "In the Shadow of the First Amendment," in this volume.
4. See, e.g., Thomas Emerson, *The System of Freedom of Expression* (New York: Vintage Books, 1970), 7.
5. See, e.g., John Milton, *Areopagitica* (1644).

6. John Stuart Mill, *On Liberty* (1859) (Cambridge: Cambridge University Press 1989), 24.

7. *Abrams v. United States,* 250 U.S. 616, 630 (1919) (Holmes, J., dissenting).

8. Id. at 628.

9. See Leslie Kendrick, "How to Defend the Constitution When the KKK Comes to Town," CNN.com, July 12, 2017, www.cnn.com/2017/07/12/opinions/free -speech-isnt-free-kendrick-opinion/index.html.

10. Joshua Barajas, "Charlottesville Violence Prompts ACLU to Change Policy on Hate Groups Protesting with Guns," PBS.org, Aug. 17, 2017, www.pbs.org/news hour/nation/charlottesville-violence-prompts-aclu-change-policy-hate-groups -protesting-guns.

11. For examples, see Risa Goluboff, "Where Do We Go From Here?," in this volume; Dahlia Lithwick and Mark Joseph Stern, "The Guns Won," Slate, Aug. 14, 2017, www.slate.com/articles/news_and_politics/jurisprudence/2017/08/ the_first_and_second_amendments_clashed_in_charlottesville_the_guns_won .html; and Leslie Kendrick, "Guns v. Speech," Backstory, Aug. 23, 2017, www .backstoryradio.org/shows/guns-v-speech.

WHERE DO WE GO FROM HERE?

RISA GOLUBOFF

The title of this essay comes from Martin Luther King Jr. and a book he published in 1967. He wrote it while holed up in Jamaica, seeking perspective about a civil rights movement unsure of where it was headed given its enormous accomplishments to date. The question is a good one. It implies that we have already moved from one place to another, but that movement has now generated a new set of choices ahead.

When white supremacists gathered in Charlottesville and at the University of Virginia on August 11 and 12, 2017, it became clear that we are, as a nation, a town, and a university, in just such a moment. As the variety of contributions to this volume alone suggests, any number of people would identify the critical issues of this moment in different ways. For me, a civil rights historian, constitutional law scholar and teacher, and law school dean, the most obvious and pressing questions about where we have been and where we are headed are legal ones. The law played a crucial role in what happened in August 2017 and beyond—in setting baselines, mediating expectations, justifying behaviors, providing a language of rights and obligations, and rationalizing the use of force.

As we reflect on what happened and how it will affect what happens next, three questions about the law's role require special consideration. One concerns the long problematic relationship between speech and violence generally and the newly problematic relationship between speech and guns in particular. A second stems from the fact that speech itself can be and do violence, and it addresses the intersection of white supremacist speech and racial equality. The third concerns constitutional protection for racial equality itself.

FREEDOM OF SPEECH AND THE RIGHT TO BEAR ARMS

For many, even discussing the First Amendment in the context of August 11 and 12 seems misplaced. In one sense, the speech itself seemed to be and do violence, a point I will take up in the following section. In a more prosaic sense, so much of what occurred in Charlottesville was not constitutionally protected expression at all. It was physical violence in the form of assault, battery, and even homicide. The fact that white supremacists presented themselves as free speakers, wanted to be thought of as free speakers, and indeed engaged in some protected speech did not immunize the violence and intimidation in which they also engaged. In other words, saying that one is engaged in protected speech does not necessarily make it so. Even as we must continue to protect speech and uphold the First Amendment, we must remain attentive to the possibility that protections appropriately in place at one moment may no longer be warranted at another.

It has become clear in retrospect that the general identification of the white supremacist protesters as free speakers led law enforcement officers and other officials to witness events through that lens, which left a more aggressive response to lag behind as events overtook them. Of course, the stage was set before the protests even began, when a judge denied the City of Charlottesville's attempt to move the planned protests on the ground that it was an unconstitutional violation of free speech. Although neither that decision nor the white supremacists' self-presentation as protected free speakers conferred upon them a special status that would adhere regardless of any unprotected actions the speakers might take, the anticipation of protected speech did serve as something of a framing device for the entire episode. One might say that one of the key lessons of "Charlottesville"—and one reason for its resonance nationally and internationally—was a shared sense of outraged surprise at how quickly what might have been speech turned into violence.

Indeed, as Leslie Kendrick points out in her essay in this volume, if the white supremacists described themselves as free speakers, from the start their physical presence augured something else as well. The many heavily armed and militarized men present projected intimidation and impending violence. Indeed, post-event analysis has concluded that the hesitant response of law enforcement on August 12 resulted not only from the overhang that their role was to protect free speech but also from the fear of being out-armed in the event of conflict between the police and the white supremacists.

That there is a tension between speech and conduct—especially perceived or actually dangerous conduct—goes back to the beginning of American free speech doctrines. Our constitutional free speech doctrine has been fairly stable for almost a century. After World War I, and in the aftermath of severe repression of antiwar speakers and leftist radicals in the Red Scare, the Supreme Court began to recognize judicially enforceable constitutional protection of free speech. Over the last hundred years, the courts have elaborated First Amendment protections as new groups of free speech contenders tried to make their voices heard: labor union organizers and left-wing activists in the 1930s, communists in the 1950s, civil rights protesters and antiwar demonstrators in the 1960s and 1970s, activists on both sides of the abortion debates in the 1980s, political conservatives more recently. At every moment, the courts have attempted to differentiate speech from nonspeech action, what is protected as expression and what is prohibitable as disorder or danger: the protection of speech as distinct from the reality of revolution or espionage or terrorism.

Questions remain about many aspects of First Amendment doctrine, as about most every aspect of constitutional interpretation. But as Fred Schauer describes in this volume, we know the basic contours of free speech rights in public. We know that in open public spaces—which the courts refer to as public forums—free speech must be allowed. We know that cities and other governmental units can limit when, where, and how such speech can take place, through what are commonly referred to as "time, place, and manner regulations." Those regulations must, however, be content neutral. Under Supreme Court doctrine, there cannot be one set of rules for speakers the government likes and another for speakers with whom officials disagree. Courts have elaborated these rules for decades, and despite remaining lacunae, they are fairly well settled.

What is new now, as the events of August 11 and 12 highlight, is constitutional protection for the individual right to bear arms for self-defense. Barely a decade old, this doctrine is a mere baby in jurisprudential terms. In 2008 the Supreme Court decided *Heller v. District of Columbia,* which held that the Second Amendment restricts the federal government's ability to regulate such arms. In 2010, in *McDonald v. City of Chicago,* the court extended that holding to states and local governments.

Those two cases initiated a new jurisprudence that has not yet answered questions about the precise contours of Second Amendment rights or about the circumstances under which governments might be justified in restricting them. Both *Heller* and *McDonald* struck down laws that prohibited the possession of handguns in the home. They did not answer questions about other types of weapons or the possession of handguns or other weapons in other private or public spaces. Despite broader state-level legislative protections—including in Virginia—and rhetoric by gun-rights advocates that implies wholesale protection of such rights, the Supreme Court has actually decided very little. For example, can a government premise all park permits—for a barbecue or a baseball game as much as a rally—on leaving one's weapons at home? Courts might determine that anywhere that large crowds of people gather, the dangers of widely held weapons can be considered and prevented by governments. Hundreds of people carrying weapons, for any reason, in a public park is a far cry from the right to own and possess a handgun in one's home. The court has not yet decided whether such distinctions, and which ones, matter.

More generally, the justices have not identified what standard of review they will use to answer such questions. Would a government hoping to restrict such weapons have to show that they have merely a rational interest, an important one, or a compelling one? How much evidence would they have to amass? In Kendrick's formulation, who would get the benefit of the doubt?

In particular, the courts have not yet asked whether situations like that in Charlottesville on August 11 and 12 might justify greater governmental regulation of weapons. Now that "Charlottesville" has occurred, now that we have witnessed the violence and fatalities that resulted from hundreds of armed and vituperative haters, can those events serve as evidence that a prohibition in a similar circumstance in the future is warranted? Does the right to bear arms mean that time, place, and manner regulations cannot prohibit weapons at gatherings of large numbers of people for free speech purposes?

This first set of questions asks whether the Second Amendment places limits on government time, place, and manner regulations that the First Amendment would ordinarily allow. Another set of questions asks about the claim that the carrying of arms is part of protected expression itself. If the Second Amendment right to bear arms does not in itself authorize the carrying of arms by protesters like those on August 11 and 12, might the First Amendment do so? One can imagine that members of Unite the Right understood not only the carrying of but also the aggressive, visible, militant carrying of arms to be part of their message. Their message, after all, is about the aggressive and militaristic defense of their racialist, aggressive, and militaristic vision of the nation. They are self-described warriors fighting for the survival of their nation, and their weaponry identifies them as such. Under this view, one might see guns as part of the expression of their message, in much the same way that carrying a peace sign or doves would underscore an antiwar message.

The problem, of course, is the vast difference between doves and guns. Even if weapons are part of expression, expression is still subject to reasonable, neutral limitations. First Amendment rights are not absolute. Returning to the earlier tension, governments can take steps to protect the public from danger even as they cannot infringe protected speech. Do the dangers attendant on the widespread open carrying of weapons transform what might be expression into prohibitable behavior? If even law enforcement officers charged with maintaining safety and order feared the armed white supremacists, how can one interpret their arms as mere expression, rather than an outright threat of imminent violence? The line between protectable speech and prohibitable behavior has always been tricky. The recent protection for Second Amendment rights represents the most recent incarnation of this longstanding and troubling tension.

FREEDOM OF SPEECH AND FREEDOM FROM HARM

Condemnation of the white supremacists who marched on August 11 and 12 has taken many forms. While some condemn that the pretense of speech masked the intent to do violence, others condemn the weapons and militarization that made such threats tangible and immediate. For others, however, even if the white supremacists had followed the playbook of the Ku Klux Klan on July 8, 2017—the playbook the police had expected—and marched without weapons or torches in an orderly and physically unthreatening fashion, their message alone should have justified governmental restrictions on their speech. Such claims raise questions not about mistakenly protecting violence that presents itself in guise of free speech but rather about the violence that speech does.

If our first set of questions grew out of the relationship between freedom of speech and the right to bear arms, this next question takes the form of what can best be described as an oft-invoked dichotomy between freedom of speech and freedom from harm. In my view, that dichotomy is false. On one side lies a caricature of vigorous defense of silenced free speakers. The insistence that free speech must be protected at all costs imagines this free speaker, more often than not, as the white supremacist or far-right conservative beleaguered and shut down by intolerant liberals. There is considerable irony to this reversal, given the historical origins of free speech in protests by so many left and liberal groups: communists, anarchists, labor union members, civil rights activists.

Pitted against this caricature of silenced conservatives are the liberals who are silencing them. On this side of the dichotomy is a caricature of liberals—often young, college-age liberals—unwilling to hear anything with which they disagree. Because they share the same image of the free speaker as conservative (and racist), they scoff at the idea of a neutrally protective free speech paradigm. They are scolded for forgetting that the First Amendment once protected those they would call predecessors or allies, for their short-sightedness in not seeing that they too need freedom of speech. They are condemned for their heightened sensitivities and the frequency with which they take offense.

The caricatures on both sides suppress what is a real and enduring tension within our law: an old conflict between liberty and equality. We have seen it before. Sit-in demonstrators in the early 1960s made a claim of equality: you must serve us on the same terms as others. Restaurant owners made a claim of liberty: you cannot force me to serve anyone on my property I do not want to serve. As a society, our balance between the liberty claim and the equality claim is not static. For much of American history, the liberty claim prevailed in our example—the restaurant owner was free not to serve African Americans. After the sit-ins, and especially with the passage of the Civil Rights Act of 1964, the equality claim took priority— the owner's liberty ended where racial discrimination began.

Events like August 11 and 12, as well as less explosive but more frequent racially offensive speech (as well as speech offensive for other reasons, like sex, sexual orientation and gender identity, ability, citizenship status, and religion), have presented new forms of this always dynamic and evolving tension. The freedom from harm is a form of equality claim, pressed against a liberty claim of the freedom of speech. The liberty claim is that I can speak, period. The equality claim is that not everyone is equally situated vis-à-vis certain speech. The impacts of certain kinds of speech fall far more heavily on some than on others. Whether African American students should or should not take offense at and find harmful, say, another student's racial slur, one cannot deny that such speech affects them differently than it affects non–African Americans. It makes no sense to deny that there is what constitutional doctrine would call a disparate impact—a differential impact on different people because of their race. Rather, the question should be whether and how best to take racial difference into account. To ignore the harm, to say "buck up," is akin to what has been said about racial harms in the past that are now recognized as legally or constitutionally cognizable.

In other words, once we take seriously the concerns on both sides, we can see the real issue. To the extent that the First Amendment results in recognizable injury along racial lines, how should we think about that harm?

The discussion in the university setting currently takes two forms. First, as Schauer and Kendrick note, some deny the tension by either failing to understand or refusing to acknowledge that "hate speech" is constitutionally protected at all. Surveys show that many Americans believe that "hate speech" is not protected by the Constitution and therefore prohibitable. That is not the law. Though "hate crimes," where violent or destructive conduct is involved, are prohibitable, hateful and discriminatory speech itself is protected. Public universities and other government institutions flout clear constitutional dictates if they ban what is protected—on peril of lawsuits and certain legal liability. As Schauer suggests, a conversation about the law as it really is and whether and how it might be changed would be far more productive than denying the current state of the law and insisting that those in authority do the same. By the same token, officials who simply ignore those who would wish away the current state, rather than educating them about the law and how it changes over time, squander an opportunity for productive dialogue.

The second conversation addresses an increasingly apparent conflict between two legal regimes: Title VI of the Civil Rights Act of 1964 and the First Amendment. On the one hand, Title VI requires universities to ensure that their campuses are free from hostile racial environments. On the other hand, the First Amendment to the U.S. Constitution requires government actors—which include public universities—not to restrict free speech. Another way to put this is that even if hate speech is protected by the First Amendment, can its unchecked expression lead to sanctions under Title VI? This leads to what some have called a double bind for universities (not only as it concerns race and Title VI but also sexual harassment and Title IX). If universities protect hate speech to comply with the First Amendment, they might run afoul of Title VI. But if they curtail hate speech to comply with Title VI, they might run afoul of the First Amendment.

One way through, or perhaps around, this dilemma might actually be beyond the law. Entitlement to free speech is legally crucial, but it cannot answer every question. Indeed, the insistence that these questions can be answered by the law might be part of the problem. Having a right to do something does not tell us when we might prudently decide not to exercise it to its fullest, or when nonlegal values might shape how we exercise that right. One might think of this as the difference between free speech law and free speech ethics or norms.

There is an extensive literature on the relationship between law and norms—ranging from how ranchers resolve disputes when their livestock wander to how husbands and wives bargain outside of the strict confines of the law of divorce. We live under the law, but just as often we live under social norms that operate in relation to the law. In other words, what the law allows and what a community expects from its members are often different things.

Take, for example, a child bringing a toy he or she owns to the sandbox at the park. The child has complete dominion over that toy. She is free to hoard it, not to share it, to flaunt it in front of other children. Legally, it is hers and she can do with it utterly as she likes, short of physically harming another person with it.

Still, what do parents routinely tell their children as they enter the sandbox with a favorite toy? Share it. The law may give the child dominion, but social norms require some amount of sharing or at least consideration of the other children in the sandbox.

There is obviously a world of difference between parental expectations for children playing in a sandbox and public clashes between white supremacists and antiracists. It is probably too idealistic to apply this lesson to any speech, let alone white supremacist speech, on a national scale or even in a small city like Charlottesville.

Let us begin instead with a university. The modern American university is generally committed to both the personal and intellectual growth of its members and the free exchange of ideas. At our core, we are committed to diversity, humanity, equality, and mutual respect. We invest in the belonging and thriving of every member of our community and support honest and empathetic exchange across our many differences. We challenge our students to be critical thinkers within a community of trust.

Law schools are not only committed to these values; they also have additional professional commitments that should enable such free speech norms. The law as a profession is dedicated to testing ideas through dialogue and persuasion rather than violence and intimidation. Lawyers are trained both to make arguments on all sides of an issue and to listen to ideas and arguments with which they may not agree. Even if those arguments might not be comfortable or attractive in their own right, at the very least they are necessary to hear and engage with in order to strengthen one's own arguments.

In communities with these values and commitments, members do not tend to say hateful things to one another. That does not mean we always agree. That does not mean that we cannot or will not hear things that make us uncomfortable. It does mean that we always and routinely tailor our speech for the context in which we offer it, on the most mundane issues. We routinely offer up our opinions with prefaces like, "I'm not sure you'll agree," or "I don't know if I believe this argument myself, but . . ." When speech goes to the core of our identities, our personhood, our deepest values, we must again, as both speakers and listeners, think about how we speak and listen within a community of mutual respect. We can and should be a model of dialogue across difference, a model of how we simultaneously exercise free speech and embrace empathy and civility.

Given that universities are currently being tested—and often failing—along precisely these lines, perhaps this hope is unrealistic. Indeed, even sandbox sharing often ends in tears. But we try, and in trying we model a solution for what most see only as an intractable problem. The caricatures are just that. Most members of university communities would prefer to find a way through the false dichotomy. As false dichotomies do, this presents itself as unsolvable. Perhaps it is legally: I get to speak, and you cannot stop me. But as a matter of social norms, which universities do so well, it is far more tractable. I continue to hope that law schools and universities will not be the only communities in which such dialogue is possible. If both sides are indeed overdrawn, then to insist on free speech does not have to mean trampling humanity. To insist on mutual respect does not have to mean stifling dialogue. It may in fact advance it.

RACIAL EQUALITY AND THE FUTURE
OF EQUAL PROTECTION

This discussion of the dynamic tension between liberty and equality makes apparent that as a nation and a society we have already come some distance toward racial equality. The events of August 11 and 12 raise legal questions of where we go from here in that context as well: What does August 2017 tell us about the way the courts have interpreted the Fourteenth Amendment's admonition that "no State shall . . . deny to any person . . . the equal protection of the laws"?

When the court decided *Brown v. Board of Education* in 1954, the brief opinion in that case did not clearly articulate the nature of the racial harm prohibited by the equal protection clause. There were indications that the harm might be legally segregating and discriminating against people on the basis of race. If that were the case, then the Constitution would prohibit government decisions based on race. On the other hand, *Brown* and related cases indicated that the harm was not based solely in the government's actions. The harm instead inhered in the reality of racial inequality in our society as a whole. If that were the case, then the Constitution should allow the government to take steps to end such inequality. It might even *require* the government to take such steps. Among legal scholars, the first interpretation has become known as the "antidiscrimination" or "anticlassification" approach to equal protection, in contrast to the second, "antisubordination," approach.

The essence of the problem in an antidiscrimination approach is that the government distinguishes on the basis of race, regardless of who benefits. This is the foundation of constitutional arguments against affirmative action: regardless of whether a government employer or university thinks it is helping racial minorities, it is prohibited from making any decisions on the basis of race. Identifying the essential problem as the existence of racial inequality or subordination, the antisubordination approach assumes that governments are part of the solution as well as the problem and can take steps, like affirmative action, to effectuate racial equality in the world.

Over the past several decades, the first, antidiscrimination, interpretation has increasingly dominated. This legal interpretation is based on, and in turn supports, a particular historical narrative: that we have triumphed over Jim Crow and the oppression for which it once stood. In this story, the civil rights movement ended overt white supremacy. All Americans are now on an equal playing field. (Barak Obama often serves as Exhibit A for this "postracial" world.) It is therefore now historically appropriate to invoke legal doctrines that assume that the greatest constitutional harm is one in which government treats people of different races differently for any reason. The Constitution is "colorblind."

To say that this antidiscrimination approach has become dominant is not to say that everyone embraces it. Activists reveal the immense injustices that persist in the face of constitutional limitations. Legal scholars continue to debate its dominance. Historians continue to articulate alternative historical narratives that challenge the triumphalist story on which it is based. For some time now, however, these arguments have been pushing against the grain within the public sphere, the courts, and the academe.

Moreover, even these more antisubordination-oriented arguments have often presumed that the kind of overt racism that characterized the Jim Crow era is no longer the main justification for legal action. Rather, they claim that because overt racism is far less prevalent, the law must take notice of covert or unconscious bias, enduring institutional racism (the historically embedded remnants of that older overt form of racism), and the continuing disparate impacts of racial inequalities.

What the white supremacist actions of August 11 and 12 make far clearer today, and to many more people, is that the era of overt racism is not past. It is apparent that the legal and social changes we have seen over the last seventy-five years—which have been transformative in many ways—have not been as thoroughgoing as many surmised. Perhaps we should not be surprised. Even as some forms of racial inequality have abated, the antidiscrimination cast to our constitutional and legal framework—and the attendant triumphalist historical narrative—has limited the nature and scope of that change. The United States has always been in a hurry to grow up, move on, declare the past dead and the present and future bright with possibility. But it was naïve to think that a system of racial subordination and white supremacy ingrained for three centuries could be undone in a generation or two.

Moreover, some of the rhetoric of this newly visible white supremacist movement highlights unanticipated consequences of the antidiscrimination approach to equal protection. That approach treats all racial discrimination as constitutionally equivalent. It refuses to differentiate between segregation and affirmative action or, as Justice Stevens once put it, between "a 'No Trespassing' sign and a welcome mat." By making all racial categories equally unacceptable, rather than acknowledging the existence of historical racial inequality against particular groups, the antidiscrimination norm unwittingly set the stage for a new rhetoric of "white discrimination." Whereas many of those who marched on August 11 and 12 identified as "white supremacists," Jason Kessler, one of the organizers, called himself a "white advocate" instead. In shifting from "supremacist" to "advocate," Kessler was taking a page from the antidiscrimination playbook. Minorities are entitled to advocates who articulate the harms they have suffered and the racial concerns they share. So why not whites as well? Such a strategy would fail under an antisubordination approach, which recognizes the historical oppression whites have exercised over people of color. But under an antidiscrimination approach, all races are entitled to call foul, even those who have been, and continue to be, agents of oppression, violence, and dehumanization.

We must accordingly ask what role the law has played in bringing us to this moment and what role it can and must play in moving us forward once again. If one lesson of these events is that racism is more deeply embedded than previously believed and we are not now past its overt phase, then we might revisit the conclusion that, in the words of one Supreme Court opinion, "the way to stop discriminating on the basis of race is to stop discriminating on the basis of race." That approach has served to sweep conversations about race under the rug, rather than allow them to be discussed openly. It has underestimated the entrenchment of racial inequality across all aspects of American society. And it has refused to countenance the force and authority of government to act to oppose it.

CONCLUSION: TAKING THE LONG VIEW

At a law school panel where faculty from across Grounds put the August events into a variety of perspectives, some scholars referred to the white supremacists and neo-Nazis as "unpopular minorities." That phrase is a familiar one within the context of the First Amendment, which has long protected the speech of unpopular minorities as against the majorities who would silence them.

It struck me, however, as a jarring application of the term. In my own work, which focuses on the 1950s and 1960s, the civil rights activists were the unpopular minorities and the white supremacists were the majority. The radical disjuncture between that moment and this elicited in me two distinct reactions. The first is gratification: fifty years after the beginning of the active, classic phase of the civil rights struggle, the unpopular minorities have flipped. Where in the 1950s many white Americans would have identified more with white supremacists than African American protesters, today it is the opposite. Today, even a politically fractured Congress can unanimously denounce white supremacy.

My second response, however, is concern. Because I recall when civil rights activists were the unpopular minority, I know that massive change can happen. My own scholarship details how unpopular minorities make that change happen, and it is apparent that Kessler and his colleagues have been careful students of histories that they view as a roadmap. Moreover, I know that change does not always happen for the better. To prevent backsliding, we must model alternatives. We must articulate a compelling alternative vision of a diverse, inclusive, equal, and humane nation if we are to keep these "unpopular minorities" so confined.

I hope, if I don't quite predict, that when the story of the long march of civil rights is told, the white supremacist violence and intimidation in Charlottesville will be seen as a late and ultimately futile reaction to the successes of the freedom struggles of the last fifty years. The events of August 11 and 12 were violent and disturbing reminders that our narrative of a civil rights movement triumphant was premature, that progress is all too often accompanied by reaction. No less a figure than Thurgood Marshall, the architect of the NAACP Legal Defense Fund's campaign against segregation and the first African American Supreme Court justice, warned as much: "I wish I could say that racism and prejudice were only distant memories. We must dissent from the indifference. We must dissent from the apathy. We must dissent from the fear, the hatred and the mistrust. . . . We must dissent because America can do better, because America has no choice but to do better."

It is up to us to decide how to do better and where to go from here. It is up to us to transform "Charlottesville" from a lament into a call to arms.

LISTENING

Critical Engagements

"THIS CLASS OF PERSONS"

When UVA's White Supremacist
Past Meets Its Future

LISA WOOLFORK

What we view as racial progress is not a solution, but rather a
regeneration of the problem in a particularly perverse form.
—DERRICK BELL

The past and the future merge to meet us here / what luck /
what a fucking curse.
—WARSAN SHIRE, "INTUITION"

Charlottesville faced a two-pronged assault from white supremacists who
rallied in the city on August 11 and 12, 2017. Their strategy of attack was to
strike at the heart of Charlottesville by breaching the Rotunda, the University of Virginia's symbolic center, and by violating the center of the city
itself with incursions in parks, parking garages, and downtown streets.
That weekend, an allied group of Nazis, neo-Confederates, fascists, white
supremacists, and unaffiliated racists converged on Charlottesville to ostensibly protest the removal of a Confederate monument from the city center.
The August 2017 rallies were the culmination of what some local antiracist
activists called the "Summer of Hate." Beginning in May 2017 Charlottesville faced monthly white supremacist rallies with varying degrees of
spectacle and severity. Leading white supremacist and UVA alum Richard
Spencer held what has now become known as a "torch rally" in May. Several
dozen white supremacists holding lit torches and chanting "white heritage"
slogans surrounded the Robert E. Lee statue. In June 2017 a small group of
neo-Confederates convened at the Lee statue only to be met by clergy and
local residents who joined hands for songs, chants, and prayers. In July 2017
a Ku Klux Klan group from North Carolina rallied in Justice Park to protest
its recent renaming. (The park was formerly called Jackson Park in honor
of the Confederate general Stonewall Jackson, whose statue is installed

there.) These events and their mobilization around the removal of Confederate monuments that enshrine white supremacy laid the foundation for the more prolonged action scheduled for August 11 and 12, called Unite the Right. The Unite the Right participants, orchestrated by UVA alum Jason Kessler, assembled in Charlottesville for a weekend of sustained pro-white activism. It all culminated on Saturday, August 12, when pro-white protesters prompted skirmishes with antiracist activists and black community members, resulting in injuries to dozens of people and the death of one counterprotester, who was killed when a white supremacist drove through a crowd of counterprotesters in a deliberate act of terror.

The most significant precursor to the lethal attack of August 12, however, was the violent white supremacist spectacle at the UVA's Central Grounds on the evening of August 11. The white supremacists' fire-fueled march though Grounds and the university's official responses to it are the focal points of this essay. Specifically, I ask: Why has the university arrested more people for protesting white supremacy than for promoting white supremacy? And what might this discrepancy reveal about the weight that white supremacy continues to bear on university life? Why were three UVA students arrested for trespassing—two black and one white—during the university's bicentennial celebration, when three hundred white supremacists (not currently enrolled students) brandishing lit torches could march unimpeded to seize the symbolic heart of the university?[1] The university's official statement explains that because the students disrupted a "ticketed event," they were subject to ejection and legal consequences: "The UVA Bicentennial Launch yesterday on the Lawn was a ticketed event. Any person who interrupts an invited speaker or event shall be requested to leave and removed if they refuse to leave or persist in interrupting any speaker or event."[2] This seemingly neutral preference for order and civility attempts to conceal an important issue that students were trying to address. At the time of their arrest, the students held a large, carefully crafted banner. Styled in a graphic theme similar to the official university bicentennial promotional materials, the banner proclaimed "200 years of white supremacy." When three currently enrolled students are arrested for trespassing but approximately three hundred white supremacists are allowed to march unimpeded through Central Grounds—bearing lit torches and ultimately attacking students and staff in full view of law enforcement—it raises the provocative suggestion that the students' banner had the right of it after all.

My essay turns to documents to better understand the persistence of white supremacy at the university. Some of the texts I consider emerge from the historical record, while others are recently written responses to pro– and anti–white supremacist rallies on Grounds. My purpose here is to use the literary studies skills of textual analysis and close reading to better understand how these texts create a discursive landscape that remains complicated by, if not indebted to, the white supremacy from which the university was stamped at its beginning.[3] In addition, careful study of these documents, statements, and counterstatements produced by, within, and against the university is part of a moral inventory prompted by the challenges of the white supremacist violence that occurred on our campus and in our city. An examination of select archival and contemporary documents allows us to evaluate the meaning of white supremacists marching on campus. Is this act best described as an anomaly, an invasion, or a homecoming?

It is useful to start at the beginning. On August 1, 1818, the commissioners for the University of Virginia met at a tavern in Rockfish Gap on the Blue Ridge. The assembled men had been charged to write a proposal that would be titled the *Report of the Board of Commissioners for the University of Virginia to the Virginia General Assembly*, also known as the *Rockfish Gap Report*. This document would articulate the university's unique and robust educational mission, which included "to develope the reasoning faculties of our youth, enlarge their minds cultivate their morals, & instil into them the precepts of virtue & order."[4] The collective also articulated a vision of education that specifically affirmed racial and racist hierarchy for its students and the commonwealth. Relying on a horticultural metaphor of a "wild & uncultivated tree" that is ameliorated by merging the "savage stock" with a "new tree," the report declares that "education, in like manner engrafts a new man on the native stock, & improves what in his nature was vicious & perverse, into qualities of virtue and social worth." The horticultural symbolism quickly gives way to the racist and eugenic dimensions of education. The commissioners promote the value of higher education by comparing its benefits to those who lack it: "What, but education, has advanced us beyond the condition of our indigenous neighbours? and what chains them to their present state of barbarism & wretchedness, but a besotted veneration for the supposed supe[r]lative wisdom of their fathers and the preposterous idea that they are to look backward for better things and not forward, longing, as it should seem, to return to the days of eating acorns and roots rather than indulge in the degeneracies of civilization." The rhetorical nature of this question—"What, but education, has advanced us?"—leaves little room for the possibility that structural, ideological, and economic factors "advanced" these scions of the white, wealthy, master class who composed this document. A careful inspection of this report suggests that white supremacy, in theory and in deed, was a requisite foundation for the educational benefits essential to progress.

White supremacy was not only useful for helping to promote the value of the *educational* mission of the university. This belief system also played a crucial role in locating the physical space that the university would occupy. As the *Rockfish Gap Report* suggests, in addition to the educational project of the university, the commissioners were required to structure other formal protocols, such as the living arrangements represented by the Pavilions, Hotels, and the Lawn.

Though they considered the power that resided in constructing a radical educational vision previously unknown during their time, the commissioners were also committed to finding the ideal geographical location for this undertaking. Three choices were identified as the most propitious venues: Lexington in Rockbridge County, Staunton in Augusta County, and Central College (Charlottesville) in Albemarle County. Ultimately, however, Central College was deemed the best site on which to build. As the report claims, Staunton and Lexington were also suitable since "each of these was unexceptionable as to healthiness & fertility." The deciding factor that led the commissioners to choose Albemarle County as the site for the university was exclusively its proximity to white people. The commissioners observed, "It was the degree of centrality to the white population of the state which *alone* then constituted the important point of comparison between these places: and the board, after full enquiry & impartial & mature consideration, are of opinion that the central point of the white population of the state is nearer to the central college, than to either Lexington or Staunton by great & important differences, and all" (emphasis mine). The *Rockfish Gap Report* lays the literal and figurative groundwork for the university's interests in and promotion of white supremacy.

The report reveals the practical ways in which white supremacy was the single most important attribute that explains the university's current location in Charlottesville. The commissioners made the determination, based on research that was "impartial" and "mature," to privilege Albemarle County over Lexington or Staunton. Simply put, the University of Virginia was located in Charlottesville because Charlottesville was the site most easily accessed by most of the state's white people. These white supremacist foundations constitute a fundamental element of the university's history that curiously anchors expressions of white supremacy on its grounds today.

Scholars at UVA have increasingly documented the impacts of slavery on the university and the degree to which the peculiar institution's prevalence structured campus life during the antebellum period. Digital projects like The Illusion of Progress, by the Citizen Justice Initiative of the Carter G. Woodson Institute for African American and African Studies, offer rich context and archival documentation of Charlottesville's and the university's investments in white supremacy. Similarly, Jefferson's University Early Life (JUEL) database is a thoroughly constructed archive of digitized primary documents, three-dimensional renderings of buildings and other sites, and essays (including nineteenth-century faculty minutes and student commentary). The President's Commission on Slavery and the University, convened in 2013, was tasked to "provide advice and recommendations on the commemoration of the University of Virginia's historical relationship with slavery and enslaved people."[5] This essay acknowledges this important work and seeks to amplify the role white supremacy played in these historic formations.

My objective is to understand how vestiges of the original determining factor for the university's location in Charlottesville—white supremacy as seen in Charlottesville's "centrality to the white population"—resonate across generations, making contemporary Charlottesville less an idyllic "progressive" town and more a place where its white supremacist roots await activation. One trace element of white supremacy, attributable to the antebellum days, shaped an interpretation of the ways that the neo-Confederates, Nazis, and other white supremacists organized on university Grounds. For the first fifty years of its existence, the university relied on enslaved labor in a variety of positions. In addition, enslaved workers were tasked to serve students personally—cleaning rooms, lighting fires, cooking, running errands, and more. Jefferson believed that allowing students to bring their personal slaves to college would be a corrosive influence, which fit within his paradoxical philosophy in general. Faculty members, however, and the university itself owned or leased enslaved people. This strategy of restricting students' personal ownership of the enslaved while allowing them access to and reliance on enslaved labor had an even more corrosive effect of magnifying the notions of mastery already firmly held among the student population. No enslaved person was the personal property of any student, yet all enslaved persons were meant to obey every student.

Heinous violations of the enslaved are recorded in the archives of the JUEL database, including the first documented rape case that resulted in student expulsion. Though students were punished in this case, there is substantial evidence to support the notion that extreme acts of violence against the enslaved could be accepted as part of the institutional culture of the university. For instance, in 1856 a student who beat a ten-year-old slave girl until she lost consciousness defended himself—and successfully appealed his punishment—by claiming "whenever a servant is insolent I will take upon myself the right of punishing him without the consent of his master."[6] This enslaved child was not this student's property, yet as a slave she was subject to his whims and authority. Appealing his punishment, the student claimed this right. This dispersed form of mastery practiced at the university permitted students access to and control over any slave on Grounds. In this way, the student's beating of a slave who was not his personal property, according to the student, was "not only tolerated by society, but with proper qualifications may be defended on the ground of the necessity of maintaining due subordination in *this class of persons*" (italics mine). This student's beating of an enslaved child conformed to the beliefs and practices already underway at the university. The student's successful appeal of his punishment did more than demonstrate the need to maintain black subjection in "this class of persons." This act of violence and its subsequent endorsement by the faculty—which reversed its original decision to punish the student—had the added benefit of validating widespread white mastery among students. The beating and its exoneration served more than one purpose: it reminded the enslaved child and the enslaved community more broadly that they were meant to obey all students; it also reinforced the idea that mastery at the university could be exerted by physical violence and defended by sophistry. It also reinforced the university's position as a site well suited to promote the rules of the antebellum regime, as UVA historian Kirt von Daacke observes: "The early University of Virginia [was] an incubator for pro-slavery and white supremacist thought."[7]

These foundational moments from 1818 and 1856 sustain an important relationship between white supremacy and the university. This generalized mastery so widely practiced on Grounds in the nineteenth century, bolstered as it was by an equally widespread belief in white supremacy as a theory and practice, shaped the ways in which concepts like power, prestige, and heritage (especially "Southern heritage") would work within and beyond the university. Mastery and white supremacy helped define who the university was while also controlling the boundaries that kept access to the university limited or provisional.

Generalized mastery—the notion that any student could discipline any enslaved person—was a documented practice at the university from its earliest days to the time of the Civil War. Post-Reconstruction, this mastery transformed significantly from legal control over the enslaved to a more nebulous but no less effective form of white social control. This promotion of white supremacy can be traced from the antebellum period all the way through to the university's leading role in eugenics, its contributions to the state's "racial integrity" laws, and its endorsement of massive resistance to desegregation. Just as historians have argued that slavery was less abolished than transformed, so too were the practices of generalized mastery changed at the university. Rather than having enslaved workers vulnerable to the physical violence of white authority, white mastery was exercised in new ways.

At the turn of the twentieth century, both formal and informal means of maintaining the social practice of white supremacy found purchase at the university. In 1900 Chairman of the Faculty Dr. Paul Barringer delivered an address on the "influence of heredity on the negro" to the Tri-State Medical Association.[8] The speech, titled "The American Negro: His Past and Future," railed against the abolition of slavery, declaring that emancipation was a menace to the South because it compromised the devices—legally mandated white supremacy—that curtailed black liberty.

Black freedom was particularly threatening, according to Professor Barringer, since his study of heredity revealed that "fifty centuries of savagery in the blood cannot be held down by two centuries of forced good behavior if the controlling influences which held down his savagery are withdrawn as they have been in this case."[9] These alarmist predictions of unchecked black "savagery" would be borne out in such fiction as Thomas Dixon's *The Clansmen: A Historical Romance of the Ku Klux Klan* (1902) and in the nation's first blockbuster film, *The Birth of a Nation* (1915). Professor Barringer's lecture on the "biological" inferiority of black people was received with the highest acclaim. The association published his remarks, by unanimous vote, and disseminated the document "to all the medical societies in the South."[10] In addition to arguing that slavery benefitted black people by ameliorating their natural "savagery," Barringer claimed that slavery also served as a laboratory for how heredity could be altered: "Two hundred and fifty years of close association, as slave and master, produced changes in the race, the like of which has never been seen before or since." Interracial proximity on the condition of white supremacist authority was, in Barringer's estimation, a cause for optimism: "Fortunately for us, experience (history) has shown that these savage traits can be held down, and we have seen that if held down long enough, they will be bred out. In this one fact lies the hope of the South."[11]

These words would have a curricular effect on the university. In subsequent years, white supremacy at UVA, which had taken the form of white mastery in the nineteenth century, became legitimized in the twentieth century as a scientifically objective and academically viable course of study. UVA was a national leader in the field of eugenics: a discipline based in biology that promoted white supremacy (and the defense of the "American race" and "civilization") by advocating for sexual reproduction of only the best white people while curtailing the growth of black, Jewish, and immigrant populations. Based in large part on the faculty's work in eugenics, the highest levels of university administration cultivated the institution's reputation as modernized yet committed to a Southern way of life. Faculty trained disciples in the study of eugenics and sent graduates into Virginia legislatures, classrooms, and hospitals throughout the South. Ultimately, the eugenic curriculum set the stage for the university's contributions to white supremacist medical practices, social policy, and political action.

From the 1920s until the late 1950s, UVA was a veritable powerhouse of white supremacist ideology, scientific racism, and massive resistance to desegregation. In 1921 a Virginia chapter of the Ku Klux Klan recognized the university's commitments to white supremacy by pledging $1,000 for the construction of Memorial Gymnasium. As part of a larger centennial endowment drive, the Klan's contribution was offered "with the deepest devotion for the University as an institution which inculcates virtue and fosters pure American patriotism."[12] President Alderman acknowledged the donation by "heartily" thanking the KKK for "its generosity and good will."[13] The bonds of kinship between the early twentieth-century university and the Klan are further strengthened by the appearance of the university's own KKK chapter—"the University of Virginia Klan Number Five"—in 1922.[14] President Alderman would usher in a new age of racist scientific discovery by forming a close relationship with the faculty's leading eugenicist, Dr. Ivey Foreman Lewis, Miller Professor of Biology and Dean of the University of Virginia. Following the advice of Lewis, who taught at the university from 1915 to 1953, President Alderman would shape the university into a pioneer of modern white supremacist ideology.[15] As Gregory Michael Dorr suggests in his study of Lewis, "Alderman wanted to move the University of Virginia into the top tier of American universities, but he was not willing to compromise the university's southern heritage. With the hiring of Ivey Lewis, Alderman gained an ally in his quest."[16] Eugenics confirmed the university's reputation as a progressive institution that centered on its Southern heritage. In this way UVA could boldly march into the scientific future (eugenics) while remaining firmly ensconced in its white supremacist past.

The university's aggressive eugenics program, which promoted "the purity of the white race," shaped the thinking of generations of elite Virginians.[17] These men then created social policies and medical programs that aligned with the white supremacist vision of eugenics in which they had been trained. For instance, in 1920 President Woodrow Wilson appointed Hugh Smith Cumming, UVA alum and eugenics advocate, as the surgeon general of the United States. In 1932 Cumming would work with two other UVA eugenics-trained graduates to craft and implement the infamous Tuskegee Study of Untreated Syphilis in the Male Negro, which is now recognized as one of the greatest violations of medical ethics and human rights to impact African Americans since slavery.[18] University of Virginia alumni of the eugenics curriculum were responsible for two additional catastrophic social and medical programs in the state: the Racial Integrity Act of 1924 (SB 219) and the Eugenical Sterilization Act (SB 281). The Virginia General Assembly, which was composed of a substantial number of UVA alumni, enacted these measures to control marriage and sexual reproduction as a hedge against the deterioration of the white race. The Racial Integrity Act stated in part that it was "unlawful for any white person [in Virginia] to marry any [person] save a white person." If the integrity act was a social strategy for the preservation of the white race, the sterilization act took a medical approach by authorizing "capable physicians or surgeon[s]" to sterilize patients "with hereditary forms of insanity that are recurrent, idiocy, imbecility, feeble-mindedness or epilepsy" (SB 281).[19] The UVA eugenics curriculum provided a double-barreled solution to maintain white supremacy in the face of black liberation and rising immigration: keep marriage white and births "pure." This notion of pure births and the anxiety about impure reproduction, as seen in the lectures, letters, and other papers of Professor Lewis, had far-reaching consequences. As Gregory Dorr observes, "In the final estimate, perhaps the most chilling legacy of Lewis and many other eugenicists was their effect on health care. Many of the students who took courses in eugenics went on to become physicians. While it is impossible to know the precise number of University of Virginia trained physicians who performed these operations, it is certain that Virginia alumni performed many of Virginia's compulsory sterilizations between 1927 and 1973."[20] More than eight thousand Virginians would be sterilized under this law; countless more throughout the South would undergo the procedure as the principles of UVA eugenics curriculum gained traction in other states.

The legislative covering of the social institution of marriage and the medical practices to ensure pure birth aligned with the need for racial separation in all aspects of private and public life. The University of Virginia was heavily involved in civic organizations to promote this cause. President Alderman was connected to the Aristogenic Association, which considered that "[white] Race survival and advance depend much on leadership. . . . The study and understanding of the biological characteristics of leaders is therefore of importance."[21] UVA alum John Powell, UVA alum Dr. Walter Peckler, and Methodist minister Earnest Cox founded the Anglo-Saxon Clubs of America in 1921. The goal of these organizations and similar groups was to promote white supremacy and racial integrity though leadership, education, and other forms of civic participation. These groups were the driving force behind Virginia's ardent rejection of school desegregation. Once again, UVA faculty were major contributors to this effort to maintain white supremacy: filing briefs in favor of segregation in the *Brown v. Board of Education* landmark case and, when that failed, using their platform as UVA professors to amplify calls for massive resistance. A particularly useful example of this is Ed Ogelsby, mathematics professor and presiding officer of the group Defenders of State Sovereignty and Individual Liberties. In 1956 Ogelsby, whose group had organized a meeting of about twelve hundred Charlottesville residents to mobilize against integration, told a reporter from the *Nation* that "we've got enough money here in this country to operate private schools for the whites. What the niggers are gonna do, I don't know. If we have to close the schools, of course, the nigger'll have to suffer from it—everybody knows that. . . . Then, if the federal government says we have to operate the schools, and operate integrated schools, we'll be ready to get out the bayonets."[22] Generalized mastery, aggressive eugenics curriculum, and blood-thirsty defense of segregation are but three components of the University of Virginia's practices of white supremacy. On Grounds, in its classrooms, and throughout the entire South, the University of Virginia was an institution that centered whiteness and white supremacy as the basis for civilization and its Southern heritage.[23]

I argue that this history animates an interpretation of the white supremacist action on campus in August 2017, providing a rich context to help frame, if not fully explain, why three hundred white men carrying lit torches were not seen as an actionable menace. To begin an assessment of threat, it is important to consider the ways university officials perceived white supremacy as (merely) a deplorable opinion or objectionable political ideology. In this way, white supremacy as a belief structure or social practice is not inherently violent or threatening. This passive view of white supremacy undergirds President Teresa Sullivan's pre-rally email to the university community. In this message she reiterates the institution's belief "that diversity is an essential element of excellence, and that intolerance and exclusion inhibit progress."[24] This is the position of the modern university, a "diversity champion" that "set the standard for thousands of other campus communities striving for diversity and inclusion."[25] The university that issued this pre-rally statement is one that has travelled far, one might imagine, from the days when students were at liberty to beat black children with impunity if the student presented a well-reasoned justification for that violence.

A powerful yet deleterious slippage, which could indicate an inadvertent return to antebellum thinking, occurs when white supremacist ideology is accepted on the grounds of free speech and expression. Sullivan's remarks execute this neutralization when she states, "We also support the First Amendment rights to free speech and assembly. These rights belong to the 'Unite the Right' activists who will express their beliefs, and to the many others who disagree with them."[26] This perception of white supremacy as a First Amendment issue supports the ways in which the torch-lit rally itself might have been seen as neither disorderly nor dangerous. It creates a false equivalency between white supremacists and antiracist activists as if to see these groups as two factions of a single idea that lacks literal meaning and consequence. An example of the adverse consequence of such an equivalency emerged in President Trump's remarks on the events in Charlottesville, which seemed to take the same neutral approach. After acknowledging "very fine people on both sides," Trump singled out the white supremacists as especially protected by the First Amendment: "You had a lot of people in that group that were there to innocently protest and very legally protest."[27] Trump's insistence on the harmless and legitimate nature of the alt-right torch rally led the New York Times to declare, "Trump Gives White Supremacists an Unequivocal Boost." To frame the alt-right as champions of free expression is a category error, one that seeks to diminish the violence inherent in their ultimate aim to establish a white ethnostate. As law professor Risa Goluboff argues in "Where Do We Go from Here?" (in this collection), a new interpretation of free speech is required in the face of acts of terror: "So much of what occurred in Charlottesville was not constitutionally protected expression at all. It was physical violence in the form of assault, battery, and even homicide. The fact that white supremacists presented themselves as free speakers . . . and indeed engaged in some protected speech did not immunize the violence and intimidation in which they also engaged. . . . Saying that one is engaged in protected speech does not necessarily make it so." Given that white supremacy was once standard operating procedure at the university, it seems vital that this institution consider ways to vigorously resist white supremacy rather than deploy the First Amendment as a paper shield to conceal its violence. As Nicole Hemmer notes, "Clarity cannot come quickly enough to institutions of higher education and the boards and politicians who govern them."[28]

The sequence of events on August 11 suggests that the university did not contest the white supremacists that marched with torches on campus. In September 2017 university police, in conjunction with the Office of University Counsel, published a timeline of the day and evening.[29] This document reveals that university police and officials knew that a march was planned as early as 3 p.m. The hours between the first alert and the actual march were spent liaising with white supremacists' "security" detail and sharing information with city police. By 9:10 p.m. university officers were stationed along the initial march route, though the white supremacists would deviate from it. Though the torch-lit march wending its way through Central Grounds toward the Jefferson statue in front of the Rotunda sparked alarm in some students, staff, and community members, the university made no attempt to impede or halt its progress. This inaction is a consequence of viewing white supremacy as only an idea rather than a social practice rooted in violence. These men marching through campus shouting Nazi slogans like "Blood and Soil," "You will not replace us," or "Jews will not replace us" were treated by the university as if they were merely exercising free speech in a public place, a neutral constitutional right guaranteed all Americans.[30] In this light, and to return briefly to the historical record to better see the university's status as an "incubator for white supremacist thought," this spectacle is a highly charged display of white supremacy that is part of the institution's distant heritage. Protecting the right of men armed with torches (and other weapons), the university police signaled that the distance between the university's white supremacist past and this current eruption was much closer than two hundred years of elapsed time would suggest. For instance, the timeline notes that at 9:52 p.m., the UPD "expresses concern that changed route means that torches will be near buildings and trees on Grounds." It is useful to note that the potential harm for which university police "expresses concern" was the danger the open flames presented to the historic buildings and trees. Three hundred men marching with torches toward the Jefferson statue is not described as a risk that must be repelled or mitigated. Even when the white supremacists swarmed the small group of students, staff, and residents at the base of the Jefferson statue, the timeline does not suggest that this was a cause for "concern" in the same way that potential damage to property might have been. The timeline reads:

— 10:07 pm Group begins to go up Rotunda stairs.
— UTR (Unite the Right) group surrounds counter-protesters at Jefferson statue on north side of the Rotunda.
— University Official and faculty member approach statue to offer assistance to counter-protesters.
— 10:16 pm Disorder is called.[31]

This timeline is a bare-bones accounting of the white supremacists' march through Grounds. Other assessments—from a wide variety of sources, including faculty member Willis Jenkins's powerful essay "Moral Trauma," about the crisis of nonintervention—provide a rich context to understand the stakes and consequences of that evening.[32]

Tyler Magill, a UVA alum and university library employee, provides a vital contribution in detailing his transformation from *observing* the white supremacists to attempting to defend students from them. In a public letter addressed to President Sullivan, Magill explains how he became "rather more involved with the racist riot on August 11th than even [he] intended to be."[33] Magill stationed himself to watch the white supremacists arrive and assemble earlier in the day. When students would stumble on the growing crowd, perhaps looking to park for the library, Magill would dissuade them. In the process of his efforts to de-escalate and deflect potential dangers, Magill encountered a young black man who appeared anxious: "What's happening? he asked. I told him. His face was heartbreaking. I'm a student here, he said. How am I supposed to feel safe here? All I could say was, I'm sorry."[34] Magill's brief yet sympathetic response to a fearful student is the difference between supporting white supremacists and supporting those harmed by them. It also provides a glimpse into why Magill would rush to the aid of those students when they were surrounded by torch-bearing white nationalists. He had considered the ways in which law enforcement's hands-off approach might have emboldened the white supremacists. After police pulled over a vehicle for a traffic violation, Magill notes, "One wonders what the crowd was thinking, and one wonders about the relief they must have felt when the police car drove on, the happiness they felt knowing that they could do whatever they wanted without fear of reprisal."[35]

Magill's description of standing with the students is harrowing for the degree to which law enforcement observed but did not prevent white supremacist violence. Magill recalls, "I stood next to a young person in a wheelchair. And some point I looked down and saw liquid splashing on them, and then the fascists started throwing lit torches at us, in full view of the UVA Police, and behind them, the Charlottesville police. No one stopped them. This was all done in full view of the police." That these incidents could unfold as Magill describes illustrates that the veil of history that separates the past from the present is permeable. I would argue that this unchecked white supremacist attack on students, staff, and residents assembled at the Jefferson statue is an echo from the days when white supremacist violence was permitted free reign. Indeed, racist violence did not disrupt the social order: it was the social order.

In this essay I have explored the ways in which the university's white supremacist past shaped or framed white supremacist action on campus in the present. I would like to turn briefly to a consideration of how the depth and rigor of that white supremacist history is easily, if unintentionally, amplified today. When official responses appear to protect the First Amendment rights of white supremacists to a greater degree than the First Amendment rights of those who advocate for equity and justice, some may conclude that white supremacy trumps antiracism at the University of Virginia. This disparity was most recently observed in a university community message from President Sullivan in response to an antiracist protest at the Rotunda on September 12, 2017. This student-led action supported by faculty, clergy, and other community members began at the president's home and culminated at base of the Jefferson statue, where students draped the statue in black cloth.[36] The president's response was bifurcated in the form of two letters: one letter went to current students and staff ("Members of the University Community"), another was sent to "alumni and friends of the University."[37] (The texts of both emails are reproduced at the end of this essay.) Religious studies professor Karl Shuve found in Sullivan's dual responses an instructive example of "source criticism," a mode of comparative biblical analysis that aims to understand why two similar stories diverge.[38] His chart (see "A Comparative Analysis of President Sullivan's Responses to September 12, 2017 Protest" below) traces the similarities between the two letters. For instance, both of Sullivan's letters mention the protest (though the alumni letter says it was "about forty students" and the current-community letter says "several members of the University and Charlottesville communities"). Both letters discuss Thomas Jefferson: the alumni heard how Jefferson received "abusive treatment" in the media, while students were reminded that Jefferson was a paradox—a lover of liberty who owned slaves.

The most compelling element revealed by comparing the two texts, however, is Sullivan's use of religious language for only one audience. In her letter to alumni, she explained that students "shrouded the Jefferson statue, desecrating ground that many of us consider sacred."[39] The idea that the Jefferson statue and the Rotunda are "sacred" spaces that were tainted by peaceful protest was disturbing. Janet Spittler, a religious studies professor, identified precisely why Sullivan's declaration was problematic when she told Virginia Public Radio, "We've seen that ground desecrated by fascists with torches. The students Tuesday evening were not desecrating anything."[40] President Sullivan described the shrouding of Jefferson's statute as an act of sacrilege. This belief is embedded in the perception that Jefferson and "his" university are holy. How then are we to understand the active role that white supremacy played in Jefferson's framing of the university? How should we understand the ways that white supremacy and white mastery were freely wielded during the university's early years, or grasp the notion that the university formally defended and, in some cases, promoted white supremacy throughout its history up until the 1960s? Are these also sacred ideals that we must revere? Why is it that three hundred torch-wielding white supremacists who attacked students and staff were not described as desecrators but antiracist activists were?

White supremacy is part of the university's deepest and oldest historical archives and played a significant role in its early institutional structures. The university's history of white supremacy—its status as beacon for white supremacist thought and deed in the nineteenth and early twentieth centuries—can illuminate an approach to understanding the events of August 11. I contend that the same white supremacy that anchored the university in Charlottesville in 1818 because of the region's proximity to the "white population," the same white supremacy that linked education to white racial progress, that fueled a widespread model of white racial mastery on campus, that promoted pro-white policies (racial integrity laws) and practices (eugenics as "science" or "medicine") is the same white supremacy that the neo-Confederates, Nazis, and other racists marched on Grounds to support. It is incumbent upon all of us to consider why Charlottesville is now both "epicenter and pilgrimage site," as music professor

Bonnie Gordon says in her essay in this volume.[41] To move forward, we can follow the direction of antilynching activist Ida B. Wells, author of *Southern Horrors: Lynch Law in All its Phases* (1892). As Deborah McDowell, director of the Carter G. Woodson Institute, advised in a message following the events of August 11 and 12, Wells "makes two instructive points, which may serve to guide us in the days ahead: 1) 'the people must know before they can act' and 2) 'the way to right wrongs is to turn the light of truth upon them.' "

PRESIDENT SULLIVAN RESPONDS TO TUESDAY NIGHT PROTEST

Dear alumni and friends of the University,

Last night about forty students held a demonstration on the north side of the Rotunda and as part of this demonstration, they shrouded the Jefferson statue, desecrating ground that many of us consider sacred. I strongly disagree with the protestors' decision to cover the Jefferson statue. University personnel removed the shroud. One person was arrested for public intoxication. These are the facts of the situation, regardless of what you may read in media accounts of those who have their own agenda.

Coming just one month after the August 11 torchlight march by 300 racist and anti-Semitic protesters, a march that became violent, this event has reminded us that there are critical and sometimes divisive issues related to the exercise of free expression in an inclusive community.

I would like to frame this issue somewhat differently. Thomas Jefferson was an ardent believer in freedom of expression, and he experienced plenty of abusive treatment from the newspapers of his day. He would likely not be surprised to find that when there are critical disagreements in the polity, those disagreements will find expression at his University. UVA's importance as a university is underscored by the fact that arguments about free expression, hate speech, and similar issues occur here. Sometimes these arguments are noisy.

In your own college days, many of you experienced protests and activism at UVA. The war in Vietnam, Watergate, 9/11, and many other issues have been discussed, debated, and protested at UVA. We are at another such point. I prefer the process of discussion and debate, and the debate is happening here at UVA with a wide variety of guest speakers, panels, and other opportunities to look at underlying issues. That there is also activism should not be a surprise to any of us.

With my best wishes,
Teresa A. Sullivan
President

PRESIDENT SULLIVAN RESPONDS TO
TUESDAY NIGHT PROTEST

Members of the University Community:

Last night, several members of the University and Charlottesville communities held a protest at the Thomas Jefferson statue located north of the Rotunda, and several protestors covered the Jefferson statue in a black shroud. We have since removed the cover. One person was arrested for public intoxication.

I strongly disagree with the protestors' decision to cover the Jefferson statue. I also recognize the rights of those present at the protest to express their emotions and opinions regarding the recent horrific events that occurred on our Grounds and in Charlottesville. Our community continues to heal, and we must remain respectful of one another if substantive progress can be made on addressing the many challenges and opportunities that we all face.

The University's founder, Thomas Jefferson, made many contributions to the progress of the early American Republic: he served as the third President of the United States, championed religious freedom, and authored the Declaration of Independence.

In apparent contradiction to his persuasive arguments for liberty and human rights, however, he was also a slave owner. In its early days the University of Virginia was dependent upon the institution of slavery. Enslaved people not only built its buildings, but also served in a wide variety of capacities for UVA's first fifty years of existence. After gaining freedom, African Americans continued to work for the University, but they were not allowed to enroll as students until the mid-twentieth century.

The University has acknowledged its controversial history and we continue to learn from it through open dialogue and civil discourse. In 2013, I formed the President's Commission on Slavery and the University to explore UVA's relationship to slavery and enslaved people and to make recommendations for steps UVA can take in response to this history. The Memorial to Enslaved Laborers that the Board of Visitors approved this past June is another example of how the University is reconciling its past with its aspirations for a more inclusive, diverse environment. Recent gains in enrolling students from underrepresented groups and recruiting a more diverse faculty are also testament to our commitment to be a more diverse University.

Today, the University will formally dedicate Pinn Hall in honor of Vivian W. Pinn, M.D., one of the earliest African-American women to graduate from the School of Medicine and a former director of the National Institutes of Health's Office of Research on Women's Health. Later this week, the Board of Visitors will also discuss honoring W. W. Yen, the first student from China to graduate from the University of Virginia, and the first international student to receive a Bachelor of Arts degree from UVA, with a building name.

There is more work to be done, and I look forward to members of our community coming together and recommitting to our foundational values of honor, integrity, trust and respect.

Teresa A. Sullivan
President

A COMPARATIVE ANALYSIS OF PRESIDENT SULLIVAN'S RESPONSES TO SEPTEMBER 12, 2017 PROTEST

ALUMNI LETTER	UNIVERSITY LETTER
"Last night about forty students held a demonstration"	"Last night, several members of the University and Charlottesville communities held a protest"
"desecrating ground that many of us consider sacred."	[No parallel]
"One person was arrested for public intoxication."	"One person was arrested for public intoxication."
"These are the facts of the situation, regardless of what you may read in media accounts of those who have their own agenda."	[No parallel]
[No parallel]	"I also recognize the rights of those present at the protest to express their emotions and opinions regarding the recent horrific events that occurred on our Grounds and in Charlottesville."
"Thomas Jefferson was an ardent believer in freedom of expression, and he experienced plenty of abusive treatment from the newspapers of his day."	"The University's founder, Thomas Jefferson, made many contributions to the progress of the early American Republic."
[No parallel]	"In apparent contradiction to his persuasive arguments for liberty and human rights, however, he was also a slave owner. In its early days the University of Virginia was dependent upon the institution of slavery. Enslaved people not only built its buildings, but also served in a wide variety of capacities for UVA's first fifty years of existence."
[No parallel]	"The University has acknowledged its controversial history and we continue to learn from it through open dialogue and civil discourse."
"In your own college days, many of you experienced protests and activism at UVA."	[No parallel]

Courtesy of Karl Shuve

NOTES

I would like to thank Liza Ayres, UVA class of 2019 majoring in political and social thought, for her invaluable research assistance. I am also grateful to Benjamin Doherty, research librarian at the UVA School of Law and member of Showing Up for Racial Justice (SURJ)—Charlottesville.

1. According to a witness, the white student had to insist on being arrested since police seemed initially unwilling to detain her. The students were later convicted for trespassing and fined.

2. "Three UVA Students Arrested during Bicentennial Celebration," NBC29.com, Oct. 21, 2017, www.nbc29.com/story/36544802/3-uva-students-arrested-during -bicentennial-celebration.

3. This phrase is an allusion to Ibram X. Kendi's National Book Award–winning monograph *Stamped from the Beginning: A Definitive History of Racist Ideas in America* (New York: Nation Books, 2016).

4. *Report of the Board of Commissioners for the University of Virginia to the Virginia General Assembly*, Au General Assembly, [Aug. 4] 1818.

5. "U.VA. President Appoints Commission on Slavery and the University," *UVA Today*, Sept. 12, 2013, https://news.virginia.edu/content/uva-president-appoints -commission-slavery-and-university.

6. Kirt von Daacke, "A History of Pro-Slavery Thought and Education at UVA," Sept. 24, 2017, www.facebook.com/notes/kirt-von-daacke/a-history-of-pro -slavery-thought-education-at-uva/10150120482157228.

7. Ibid.

8. Speech excerpted from Paul B. Barringer, *The American Negro: His Past and Future* (Raleigh: Edwards and Broughton, 1900), reproduced and annotated by Stephen Railton, Twain Library, University of Virginia, 2007, http://twain.lib.virginia .edu/wilson/barrnger.html, accessed Feb. 18, 2018.

9. Ibid.

10. Ibid.

11. Ibid.

12. By "calculating the S&P 500 average and compound investment over 96 years," Jalane Schmidt estimates that this $1,000 donation would be currently valued at $16,000,000. See Schmidt, "Excuse Me, America, Your House Is on Fire: Lessons from Charlottesville on the KKK and 'Alt-Right.'" Resist Here, Medium.com, June 27, 2017, https://medium.com/resist-here/excuse-me-america-your-house -is-on-fire-lessons-from-charlottesville-on-the-kkk-and-alt-right-84aafddca685; "Ku Klux Klan Gives a Thousand Dollars to Gymnasium Fund," *College Topics* 32, no. 36 (March 25, 1921), *the Movement in the Archive*, http://civilrights.woodson .virginia.edu/items/show/1251.

13. "Klan Gives a Thousand Dollars."

14. "U. of VA. Klan No. 5," *Daily Progress*, Nov. 6, 1922, http://search.lib.virginia.edu/ catalog/uva-lib:2123262/view#openLayer/uva-lib:2123263/4009.3765377788/ 2088/1/1/1.

15. For a rich and highly detailed study of the influence of Lewis on the university,

including its hiring decisions, Jewish student enrollment, curricular reform, and the legions of students Lewis taught in his long career at UVA, see Gregory Michael Dorr, "Assuring America's Place in the Sun: Ivey Foreman Lewis and the Teaching of Eugenics at the University of Virginia, 1915–1953," *Journal of Southern History* 66, no. 2 (May 2000): 257–96, www.jstor.org/stable/2587659.

16. Ibid., 265.

17. Ibid., 272.

18. Ibid.

19. Citizen Justice Initiative, "The Progressive Era and the Enforcement of Racial Difference," chapter 3 in The Illusion of Progress: Charlottesville's Roots in White Supremacy, Carter G. Woodson Institute for African American and African Studies, University of Virginia, 2017, http://illusion.woodson.as.virginia.edu/index.html, accessed Jan. 31, 2018.

20. Dorr, "Assuring America's Place," 291–92.

21. Ibid., 264–65.

22. Dan Wakefield, "Charlottesville Battle: Symbol of the Divided South," *Nation,* Sept. 15, 1956, p. 212.

23. In the interest of space, I have ended my review of UVA's white supremacist heritage in the mid-twentieth century. To better understand the university climate and students' organizing efforts to change it following the civil rights movement, see Claudrena N. Harold's essay in this volume, "No Ordinary Sacrifice."

24. An Important Message from President Teresa A. Sullivan Regarding August 12, personal email communication, Friday, Aug. 4, 2017, 12:00 p.m.

25. According to Insight into Diversity, the organization that bestowed this award on the university in 2017, "Diversity Champions exemplify an unyielding commitment to diversity and inclusion throughout their campus communities, across academic programs, and at the highest administrative levels," www.insightinto diversity.com/diversity-champions, accessed Feb. 18, 2017.

26. Important Message from President Sullivan.

27. Glenn Thrush and Maggie Haberman, "Trump Gives White Supremacists an Unequivocal Boost," *New York Times,* Aug. 15, 2017, www.nytimes.com/2017/08/15/us/politics/trump-charlottesville-white-nationalists.html.

28. Nicole Hemmer, "Weaponizing Free Speech," *US News and World Report,* Oct. 24, 2017, www.usnews.com/opinion/thomas-jefferson-street/articles/2017-10-24/william-fears-and-the-alt-right-weaponize-free-speech-on-college-campuses.

29. UNIVERSITY POLICE DEPARTMENT (UPD), TIMELINE: AUGUST 11, 2017, posted Sept. 11, 2017, https://response.virginia.edu/system/files/public/upd-timeline.pdf.

30. Hawes Spencer and Sheryl Gay Stolberg, "White Nationalists March on University of Virginia," *New York Times,* Aug. 11, 2017, www.nytimes.com/2017/08/11/us/white-nationalists-rally-charlottesvillevirginia.html?action=click&content Collection=U.S.&module=RelatedCoverage&region=EndOfArticle&pgtype=article.

31. UPD TIMELINE.

32. Willis Jenkins, "Moral Trauma," Medium.com, Aug. 28, 2017, https://medium
    .com/@willisjenkins/moral-trauma-f4c17866ad8c.

33. A letter from Tyler Magill to Teresa Sullivan, president of UVA. Magill was an
    eyewitness to the torch-lit march on UVA's campus on the evening of August
    11, a prelude to the Saturday march in downtown Charlottesville. D. R. Tyler
    Magill, "'The white nationalists were allowed to take the university': A letter
    to U-Va's president," *Washington Post*, Oct. 4, 2017, www.washingtonpost.com/
    news/grade-point/wp/2017/10/04/the-white-nationalists-were-allowed-to
    -take-the-university-a-counterprotester-writes-to-u-va-s-president/?utm_term=
    .de5ad657c950.

34. Ibid.

35. Ibid.

36. It is important to note that this was not the first time that Jefferson's statue had
    been draped by students. In 1928 members of the all-white, all-male student
    body did it as an act of mourning as the state switched from voting Democrat
    to voting Republican for the first time since Reconstruction. *Daily Progress*, Nov.
    7, 1928, www.dailyprogress.com/125yearsofprogress/in-charlottesville-no-fights
    -and-little-booze-on-election-day/article_1a0491be-c3cb-11e7-ad3e-1fc578645c0b
    .html.

37. President Sullivan Responds to Tuesday Night Protest, personal email communi-
    cation, Wednesday, Sept. 13, 2017, 11:30 a.m.

38. Karl Shuve, comparison of Sullivan letters, personal communication with the
    author, Sept. 14, 2017.

39. The entirety of the letter to alumni can be found in the document Counter-
    Statement to President Sullivan's Emails, https://gdoc.pub/doc/e/2PACX-1v
    T7QvSCeIZoFzlHo8g1mkRD9DUujVRjoO1FM709g-6tKevmvV34PpxTylyeqr
    UpkZFnLiw5jZWJZsZv, accessed Feb. 18, 2018.

40. Sandy Hausman, "UVA President Catches Heat over Latest Protest," Radio
    WVTF, Sept. 14, 2017, http://wvtf.org/post/uva-president-catches-heat-over
    -latest-protest.

41. Bonnie Gordon, "On Listening," in this volume.

EUGENICS AT THE UNIVERSITY OF VIRGINIA AND ITS LEGACY IN HEALTH DISPARITIES

P. PRESTON REYNOLDS

Racism was part of the fabric of American medicine in all regions of the country well into the latter half of the twentieth century. Discrimination in access to health-care services was legal; it also became the defining feature of hospital care in the North and South. Jim Crow and its denial of health care and educational and professional opportunities for black persons led to the creation of separate hospitals and health-professions training schools for blacks and whites. Discrimination also facilitated the rise of eugenics as a field of scientific inquiry and justified perpetuation of structural racism in all of America's institutions. Eugenics served as the science of segregation; it also fueled white supremacy and its rhetoric of white superiority. The University of Virginia fed the eugenics movement, populating it with citizen leaders, academic spokespersons, scientists, scholars, and teachers, as well as supplying the grounds that kept this racist movement fertile for decades. Tragically, eugenics ideas persisted within Jefferson's academic village long after this pseudoscience had been debunked nationally and internationally.

Eugenics has a long history at UVA, beginning with faculty in the nineteenth century and lasting well into the 1950s. In the late eighteenth century Thomas Jefferson, founder of the university, argued that archetypal Americans were the white settlers who left England and came to Jamestown, Virginia, and Plymouth, Massachusetts. Their courage, along with a unique set of physical, intellectual, and psychological qualities, enabled them to survive the harsh conditions and colonize the New World. Jefferson, akin to eugenicists centuries later, believed descendants of these persons were of a superior genetic stock. Furthermore, blacks in America, because most were enslaved or descendants of the enslaved, were of a much lower genetic stock and were even savage by nature.[1]

Since blacks were biologically inferior, Jefferson contended they could not be educated into citizenship. He pioneered what later became "race science," or the study of differences between black and white persons. In *Notes on Virginia* Jefferson wrote that the slaves he observed on his plantation lacked beauty, emitted strong and disagreeable odors, were "in reason" inferior, were dull and tasteless in imagination, participated more in sensation than reflection, never conversed in thought above plain narrative, and were never seen participating in even an elementary act of painting or sculpture.[2]

Jefferson, one of the most widely read persons in the eighteenth and nineteenth centuries, believed that "any attempt to assimilate [blacks] with the American polity is a greater threat to the integrity of the republic than naturalizing immigrants."[3] As an eighteenth-century scientist using observation as the primary method of scientific inquiry, Jefferson proposed that "the opinion that [blacks] are inferior in faculties of reason and imagination, must be hazarded with great diffidence. To justify a general conclusion requires many observations, even where the subject may be submitted to the Anatomical knife, to Optical glasses, to analysis by fire, or by solvents."[4]

The University of Virginia became home to faculty who tested Jefferson's hypothesis. With the emancipation of slaves in 1865, the South faced what became defined as the "Negro problem." Edwin Alderman, UVA's first president from 1904–31 (before that time the university was governed by its Board of Visitors), promoted the institution as the place where young citizen leaders could be educated in skills necessary in solving the "Negro problem," as well as in strategies to advance the Commonwealth of Virginia. Among the foundational ideas taught throughout departments and schools at UVA was the discipline of eugenics.[5]

Historically, eugenics was the study of how certain physical, intellectual, and emotional qualities were inherited; the goal of using such knowledge was to speed up evolution by creating "superior" persons through selective procreation. Francis Galton, a cousin of Charles Darwin, first used the term "eugenics" in 1883. From his work, two dominant eugenics policies emerged: positive and negative. Positive eugenics, more common in England, promoted the use of incentives to encourage successful individuals to marry and have children with individuals of superior intellect or talents or of a high socioeconomic class. Negative eugenics, dominant in America, gave rise to policies that restricted the rights of people determined to be "less fit." Over time, "less fit" and "unfit" became defined as racial and ethnic minorities, persons of low socioeconomic status, persons with mental

health and intellectual disabilities, and often persons living in geographi-
cally remote areas of the country, such as Appalachia.[6]

The eugenics metaphor (so called because eugenicists believed their
science represented a monistic philosophy that brought together all disciplines into a unified whole) united political, social, religious, health, and
educational initiatives that were meant to advance society through the production of future generations of people free from disabilities and socially
unacceptable behaviors. Similarly, the eugenics metaphor gave birth to laws
that increasingly restricted the lives of many Americans and denied potential immigrants access to America and its opportunities and freedoms (as
well as its Jim Crow racism).

At UVA expertise in eugenics became a criterion for recruitment of
faculty into various departments, including biology, education, sociology,
psychology, and the school of medicine. These faculty invited nationally
acclaimed eugenics scientists to give university lectures. They joined eugenics organizations and participated in national and international eugenics
conferences. They took their ideas throughout Virginia as part of summer
education circuits. At home they used these ideas to shape campus-wide
policies related to the admission of women and blacks into the university
and its graduate schools, including the law school and medical school. Since
both women and blacks were considered biologically inferior to white men,
their admission into UVA was delayed when compared to other institutions
of higher learning in the state and across the nation. In sum, these leaders created a culture of white supremacy justified by the science of eugenics, which argued all persons other than white men were inferior. Since the
leadership of UVA was white and male, these ideas perpetuated the status
quo. Work in the field of eugenics contributed to the promotion and tenure of individuals who shared such ideologies, thus solidifying a culture of
prejudice and racism.

WHO WERE SOME OF THESE FACULTY LEADERS?

James Lawrence Cabel graduated from UVA in 1833 with the highest degree
obtainable in America, a master of arts. With aspirations to become a physician, he matriculated into the University of Maryland and upon graduation traveled to France to obtain additional clinical training. He joined
the UVA faculty in 1837 as the third professor of medicine. Cabel served
UVA for fifty-two years, primarily as a professor of medicine; however, he
held other leadership roles. In 1846 he became chair of the faculty; today

this title would be equivalent to the university's president. A leader in the field of public health, Cabel advocated for innovations in medicine and surgery; locally, he commanded Charlottesville's Civil War hospital, among other responsibilities.[7]

Cabel and his family were large slaveholders. Cabel himself was a towering figure intellectually, and as such he set out to discover a scientific basis that might justify the enslavement of black persons. He believed the truths in science complimented truths in the Bible. In his book *The Testimony of Modern Science in the Unity of Mankind* (1859), Cabel set forth the idea that although all humans could be saved by God's redeeming grace, not all persons were equal in the physical world. While God had created Adam and Eve, he wrote, subsequent generations of descendants, through environmental pressures, developed a variety of traits, such as skin color, intellect, and emotional temperament, that over time became permanent. These permanent characteristics were then passed down from generation to generation and could be used to distinguish one race from another. Cabel argued that white persons were permanently superior to other races in intellectual, moral, and physical traits, and that black persons were permanently handicapped by intellectual, emotional, and physical limitations.[8] According to Cabel, "Contact with whites under the benign institution of slavery may have been intended by the merciful and wise providence of God as the only means of extricating [blacks] from their otherwise inevitable destiny."[9] Without slavery, blacks were destined to revert back to their savage nature.

Paul Brandon Barringer studied under Cabel as an undergraduate and medical student. After graduating from UVA medical school in 1877, Barringer, like his mentor, traveled to Europe. There he came under the influence of Louis Pasteur, one of the leading scientists in the world, who pioneered discoveries in the areas of bacteriology, including work in the causes of and treatment of syphilis.

Barringer joined the UVA faculty in 1883, the same year Francis Galton coined the term "eugenics" to describe an area of scientific inquiry. Like Cabel, Barringer supported innovations in public health and medicine, bringing the science he learned from Pasteur back to the South. He positioned UVA at the forefront of transformation of medical education when he oversaw construction of its first hospital, which opened in 1901. As chair of the faculty from 1897–1903, Barringer pushed for reform of the medical school curriculum, including the adoption of national curricular standards that required four years of instruction and basic science and clinical teaching. He also had an indelible influence on UVA's students through his promotion of the theories and practices of eugenics.[10] Blacks were denied access to medical services at UVA, and they would be subjected to racist scientific investigations.

Barringer also grew up in a slaveholding family, one distinguished by military service to the South. As a young boy he remembered Emancipation as a traumatic time. Years later he would recount feeling shocked when the family's slaves walked off the plantation, realizing the only thing that held them was a whip. Like Jefferson and Cabel, Barringer held firm to the belief that blacks were biologically inferior to whites. He used his position as a physician, educator, and leader to reinforce these ideas within the UVA and Albemarle communities and throughout the Commonwealth of Virginia.

In a series of papers delivered around the turn of the twentieth century, Barringer argued that blacks, because of their biological inferiority, were unable to fight off disease. Consequently, he argued, significantly higher rates of morbidity and mortality among blacks in cities throughout America, including Charlottesville, were unrelated to their housing, neighborhoods, or work environments (which usually were horrific) but could be attributed instead to their genetic susceptibility to disease, especially syphilis and other contagious illnesses. Extinction of the black race loomed. The "Negro problem" was more than a political problem. Blacks, simply by living in proximity to whites, created a massive public health threat for white persons.

Barringer's solutions to the "Negro problem" were to segregate blacks (moving them into neighborhoods further away from whites), to restrict interaction between the two races through Jim Crow laws and regulations, and to transfer education at all levels from black teachers to white teachers. Barringer believed that blacks should not be educated beyond their roles as laborers and artisans. Furthermore, he contended that "every doctor, lawyer, teacher or other 'leader' in excess of the immediate needs of his own people is an antisocial product, a social menace."[11]

The counterargument that addressed the strikingly greater morbidity and mortality rates of blacks in cities throughout the United States, an argument that was gaining power within the black medical profession and public health movement, was the need to expand sanitation services to black neighborhoods, ensure safe drinking water and food services, and improve housing, jobs, and access to health-care services. The environment (which was broadly defined, but especially focused around military bases and rural and lowland areas) needed to be improved so as not to serve as breeding grounds for vectors of infection, such as mosquitoes, flies, and vermin. Regional and national programs, especially under President Franklin D. Roosevelt's administration, extended the reach of federal funds into smaller communities, which resulted in improved health for many black persons in America. Unfortunately, Virginia (and especially Charlottesville) seemed immune to these innovative theories and remained beyond the reach of these regional and national programs.[12]

As a eugenicist Barringer's overall goal was to use the power of government—which was locally, regionally, and nationally under white authority—to address the "Negro problem." Consequently, he used his influence to promote passage of eugenics laws and to recruit eugenics faculty to the University of Virginia. Although he left UVA to serve as president of Virginia Polytechnic Institute from 1907–14, he retired back to Charlottesville, where he lived until his death in 1941. Back in his home city, he continued to mentor students as future citizen-leaders who would take his ideas about eugenics into the far reaches of the commonwealth and the country.[13]

Barringer left the medical school in able hands with the recruitment of Harvey Ernest Jordan, who joined the faculty in 1907. With a PhD from Princeton, Jordan came to UVA with a background in biology, bacteriology, organic chemistry, and histology. Jordan rose to become one of the most highly respected educators and prolific scientists in the medical school; he published more than 177 articles and three books. His required medical school courses, embryology and histology, ensured students learned his brand of eugenics. His role as dean of admissions, and then as dean of the medical school from 1939–49, gave him greater leverage to shape the faculty and medical school curriculum.[14]

Like other nationally recognized eugenics researchers, Jordan promoted the use of family pedigrees, including those of families living in remote parts of Virginia, to further scientists' understanding of the inheritance of favorable and unfavorable traits. Collaborations with eugenicists at UVA and eugenics scientists around the country ensured the propagation of his ideas among physicians and scientists of his generation, as well as the engagement of medical students and graduate students at his home institution.

As would become more common among eugenicists of his era, Jordan supported sterilization laws to prevent procreation among the "unfit" and marriage restrictions to prevent blacks and whites from marrying, thereby reducing the possibility of weakening the gene pool of the white race by introducing into it black genes. To advance his cause further, he argued for compulsory registration of everyone sick with contagious illnesses, segregation of the sick from the healthy, and sterilization of the ill to prevent the sick from bearing children. Rather than advocate for increased access to health services for sick black persons, as many black physicians and public health experts argued was necessary, Jordan fell in line with other UVA eugenicists who believed in the biologic inferiority of black persons, thus rationalizing the lack of benefit of providing essential and necessary medical care to them.

In another part of the university, the UVA biology department was soon under the leadership of Ivey Foreman Lewis, who like Cabel and Jordan cast a long shadow over the university with service from 1915–53, first as chair, then assistant dean, dean of men, and finally dean of the College of Arts and Sciences. As had other eugenics faculty, Lewis came with a distinguished academic record and connections to leading eugenics researchers around the country. He deepened his collaborations with his eugenics colleagues with regular participation in the summer program at Woods Hole Marine Biological Laboratory.[15]

Like Cabel, Lewis believed science existed as an extension of God's goodwill toward humanity. Hereditary determinism, a natural law created by God and discovered by scientists, could be controlled by man through eugenic science. Furthermore, according to Lewis,

> a society of eugenically "fitter" individuals would operate more intelligently and efficiently, easing the strain of survival. An efficient society left more time and resources for cultivating morality through religion and education, making science more humane. A eugenically improved population would be better equipped to receive moral instruction, for there would be no moral delinquents. Humanity could then refine the "higher things in life" such as courage, honor, a descent [sic] reserve, gentleness, magnanimity, pride in ideals.[16]

As chair of biology Lewis recruited faculty, determined which courses were required for graduation, and shaped the intellectual climate of his department as one that supported eugenic science. As a highly esteemed teacher and mentor of graduate students, he advanced eugenics research within the university. Like Jordan, Lewis believed he had a responsibility to extend the reach of UVA and participated with other UVA faculty on the summer teaching circuit, taking eugenics and its scientific foundation to high school and college teachers throughout Virginia.

In 1917 Robert Bennett Bean joined UVA as chair of anatomy in the school of medicine. Bean, whose family could be traced back to Thomas Jefferson, was ideal for a faculty increasingly seeped in eugenics. He set out to prove that whites had a different brain structure than blacks, thus establishing white intellectual and moral superiority. Using the scientific method of comparative anatomy, he studied the brains of 152 individuals—half from white persons, half from black persons. Bean claimed to have demonstrated that brain size correlated with race and that whites had larger brains than blacks; thus, he said, his anthropometric investigations proved black inferiority. However, Franklin Mall, Bean's teacher at Johns Hopkins University and a nationally renowned scientist, could not replicate Bean's results. Nevertheless, once Bean's conclusions appeared in the scientific literature, they were widely disseminated in the public press.[17]

Bean and others used his data to further support eugenics policies. Bean agreed with Jefferson, Barringer, and Lewis when he wrote: "The object to be attained in training the true [N]egro is to cultivate his natural endowments and to fit him for positions that he can fill. The training should be in manual labor of various kinds, useful in the industrial development of the South, and in intellectual pursuits for the production of men of affairs among their own people, under white male teachers of the highest moral caliber."[18] Bean and other eugenics faculty in the medical school also advocated for different levels of medical care to be provided to persons of different races, since the races were biologically different and blacks were less able to fight off disease. Ideas such as these fueled what later became known as health disparities—differences in disease incidence and outcomes—that were rooted, in part, in denial of access to medical care to blacks, even when such care was essential to good health and survival.

Eugenics faculty were also recruited into other UVA departments and schools. William Henry Heck joined the faculty of the education department in 1905. One of the most visible educational reformers during his tenure at UVA, Heck pushed for and implemented teacher refresher courses. He introduced eugenics formally into the undergraduate curriculum in 1912, later taking these ideas throughout the state in his outreach activities. George Oscar Ferguson was recruited to fill Heck's position after his unexpected death in 1919. Skilled in the use of intelligence testing, Ferguson conducted research on the IQs of blacks, mulattos or mixed-race persons, and whites. Echoing Bean's research on brain size, Ferguson claimed that student IQs correlated with the perceived amount of white blood: "pure" whites had higher IQ scores than mulattos, who scored higher than black persons. Ferguson contended that these results paved the way for truly scientific industrial management: whites again on top and blacks, as before, at the bottom of any job or employment ladder.[19]

Eugenic science served as intellectual justification for Jim Crow laws, for underfunded and segregated health care, and for diminished public education for blacks, as well as for reduced funding for social services to ethnic and racial minorities and other vulnerable populations. Eugenics laws concerning marriage restriction and sterilization of the "unfit" affected citizens of Virginia, and passage of similar legislation in other states deepened the impact of eugenics nationwide. The reach of UVA's eugenics faculty expanded as its alumni, now citizen-leaders, took these ideas into prominent positions in institutions such as the U.S. Public Health Service.[20]

WHAT WERE SOME OF THE CONSEQUENCES OF THE EUGENICS MOVEMENT LOCALLY, REGIONALLY, AND NATIONALLY?

Health care in America, before passage of Medicare in 1965, was characterized by prejudice and structural racism. White physicians, as well as the hospitals that cared for the seriously ill, routinely refused services to blacks, Native Americans, and immigrants.[21] With reforms in medical education at the turn of the twentieth century, all but two of the medical schools where most black persons received training closed, and the predominantly white medical schools that remained open refused to admit black students. Consequently, the number of black health professionals, including physicians and nurses, failed to increase to meet the needs of expanding black and immigrant populations.[22]

UVA's University Hospital segregated black patients into two basement wards, a practice common in hospitals that did admit blacks for medical care. Charlottesville's Martha Jefferson Hospital refused admission to blacks under any condition, a practice also common in hospitals throughout the South. At University Hospital, all black patients, including patients with mental health illnesses, were housed in the same quarters, as there were no private or semiprivate rooms for blacks until the hospital expanded into new buildings in 1960. The lack of separate beds devoted to black patients with mental illnesses, and policies that refused admission of blacks to the specially designated mental health ward for whites, made the care of black patients in all disease categories even more difficult. Children were placed in a segregated pediatric ward and newborns in a separate nursery.

As with adults, the facilities for children were not equal. In addition to diminished clinical care, hospitalized black pediatric patients had less access to recreation and entertainment compared to the programs offered to white children.[23]

Today, elderly black persons who grew up in Charlottesville and surrounding counties remember the dark, crowded, poorly ventilated University Hospital basement unit where they or their family members received care—a painful reminder of the era of Jim Crow. These memories remind us that eugenics, with its rabid racism, gave license to degrading, disrespectful, and substandard care. Some would describe it as inhumane. As a scholar noted in 1949, "Because of the present facilities for [black] children at the University Hospital, it has been said that many [black] parents are reluctant to use this facility . . . and adult patients on the [black] wards have been known to insist that they be allowed to return to their homes to die rather than suffer the inconvenience, discomfort, and exposure they often undergo during the course of their hospitalization."[24] At the height of the eugenics movement in the 1930s and 1940s, physicians at University Hospital did not provide any medical care to black adults in their outpatient clinics. Nor did they provide surgical treatment for tuberculosis. Yet the black population in Charlottesville was ravaged by TB and other chronic diseases. In the period between 1935–48, the rate of TB among blacks in the city was more than four times higher than it was for whites in every year but three. In 1937 alone it was seventeen times higher. Nor did blacks have access to institutional medical treatment for TB in or near Charlottesville. The only sanatorium in the state that admitted blacks was in Burkeville.[25]

The lack of access to preventive or curative medical treatment contributed to higher rates of illness from all contagious diseases, including syphilis, and higher rates of death among blacks. In 1936 the death rate from syphilis among blacks in Charlottesville was 72.6 percent, compared to 7.2 for whites; in 1941 the rate for blacks was 48.1 percent, for whites, 6.5. Death rates for blacks exceeded those for whites in all disease categories: cancer, heart disease, pneumonia, kidney disease, and infections. Their longevity, or life expectancy, was a decade less than whites.[26]

Some blacks living in Charlottesville were spared these horrific health disparities. They were the upper- and middle-class persons of color living in good neighborhoods. As James Barksdale argues in his study of Charlottesville after World War II, the great majority of blacks faced additional barriers to good health that included poor housing characterized by filth and vermin, overcrowding, and lack of indoor plumbing to provide sanitation and clean water. Most blacks in the area also lacked access to well-paying jobs. In nearly all job categories that Barksdale examined, blacks were hired into positions classified for "Negroes" that paid less and had little opportunity for advancement. In no area did blacks supervise whites.[27]

In the late 1940s six ministers, three dentists, two doctors, two nurses, and thirty-three teachers comprised Charlottesville's black middle and upper classes. There were a few small businesses owned by black persons, such as barbershops, grocery stores, and funeral homes. The remainder of black adults worked in domestic and food services, labor, maintenance, and bottom-level industrial positions. UVA was one of the largest employers in Charlottesville of black persons in these low-paying job categories.[28] Educated black residents of Charlottesviile sent their children to college; at graduation these young adults found more lucrative and professional opportunities in larger cities in the North and South.

The reach of eugenics ideas was felt throughout the country, especially after the Supreme Court ruled in 1927 in support of Virginia's sterilization laws, a lawsuit born, in part, out of a tragedy that occurred in Charlottesville. Other states followed the lead of Virginia, Indiana, and California by passing similar eugenics laws that opened the door to sterilization of the "unfit": those persons classified as feeble-minded, those who were burdensome wards of the state, or those considered socially deviant and beyond reform. Nationally, more than sixty thousand people were sterilized; in Virginia over seven thousand persons succumbed to this injustice.[29]

In Virginia marriage restriction was practiced as another way to preserve the purity of the white race. Passage of the Marriage Integrity Act in 1924 enabled the director of the Virginia Department of Public Health to require all individuals planning to marry to first provide proof of their racial integrity. Whites were considered pure if there were no black ancestors (at all) and no Native American ancestors four generations back (one-sixteenth). In 1967 the U.S. Supreme Court overturned this antimiscegenation law in *Loving v. the State of Virginia,* when it ruled in support of Mildred Loving, a black woman, and Richard Loving, a white man, who married and faced a year in prison for their decision.[30] For over forty years the fundamental human rights of people throughout the state had been violated with this one piece of legislation. That same year sixteen states had similar eugenics laws on their books.

One of the most egregious examples of eugenic science was the Tuskegee Study of Untreated Syphilis in the Male Negro. Three individuals in leadership roles in the Tuskegee syphilis study were graduates of UVA medical school, and all were proponents of eugenics. They included Dr. Hugh Smith Cumming, the surgeon general of the U.S. Public Health Service; and two assistant surgeons general, Drs. Taliaferro Clark and Raymond Vonderlehr. Historians have argued that, viewed through the lens of eugenics, the Tuskegee syphilis study was a way for its architects to test their theory that blacks were biologically different from whites and thus would manifest clinical symptoms of syphilis differently from whites. They believed these differences should be measured and added to the body of knowledge about syphilis in the black race.[31]

The study leaders recruited almost four hundred black men in the 1930s thought to have syphilis, which at the time had no cure. These men were never told they had syphilis, only "bad blood," but they were followed clinically for nearly forty years, and manifestations of the disease were documented. Periodically, leaders of the study presented their findings at national meetings and published them in the scientific literature. One of the tragedies of the study is that when penicillin was discovered in the 1940s and determined to be a cure for syphilis, these men were not offered treatment by the physicians of the U.S. Public Health Service overseeing the study or by the local physicians and nurses helping to administer it. The Tuskegee syphilis study is not only an example of violations of fundamental ethics and human rights; it is also a denial of human decency and respect for the lives of persons of color and of these black men and their families.[32]

SUMMARY AND AFTERMATH

Eugenics persisted at UVA after World War II, at a time when the rest of America had ended its affair with the eugenics metaphor. In 1951 Professor Ivey Foreman Lewis, in his role as president of the biology section and vice president of the American Association for the Advancement of Science (AAAS), gave his parting address to association members. In his talk, titled "Biological Principles and National Policy," Lewis once again lauded the power of eugenics to make America the greatest nation in the world. Outraged, the AAAS council broke precedent and refused to publish Lewis's address in its prestigious journal, *Science*.

Lewis's terms as chair of biology and dean of Arts and Sciences ended in 1953; however, he was replaced as chair by Professor Ladley Husted, one of Lewis's former students, who carried forward his mentor's adherence to eugenics ideas. Other eugenics faculty, such as Orland E. White, who retired in 1957, were also succeeded by faculty who remained committed to the idea of eugenics as a strategy for gradual improvement of humanity. Hired as a visiting professor in 1957, Henry Garrett, former chair of psychology at Columbia, led a resurgence of hereditarian and racial psychometrics within the psychology department.[33] The medical school was slow to admit black students and even slower to hire black physicians and nurses onto the faculty and staff, and the textbooks medical students used for classes, some written by UVA medical school "eugenics" professors, prevented these emerging health professionals from understanding the common biology of all persons. The hospital remained segregated in effect, as black persons received preventive and chronic care in clinics far from where white persons were seated in private waiting rooms and doctors' offices.

In conclusion, UVA's leaders and some of its most prominent and influential faculty members were seeped in "race science" and its later iteration, eugenics, for more than a century. Edwin Alderman, UVA president for over twenty-five years, set out to strengthen the university by investing in its research foundation; he did so through the science of eugenics. Eugenics framed the dialogue in classrooms, laboratories, fieldwork, medical care, and university outreach activities. The fact that eugenics was a pseudoscience with no real substance eluded these UVA leaders and faculty, in part because they were determined to maintain a social hierarchy that placed white men above all other social groups and to reinforce the idea that blacks were biologically inferior. They clung to the notion that this—supposedly inherited and immutable—moral, physical, intellectual, and social weakness of blacks, as a distinct group, made them incapable of achieving what white persons, both men and women, did.

These UVA leaders and faculty believed so much in their flawed ideas that they set out to protect the public from harm through eugenics laws and policies that in fact helped create the outcomes they erroneously believed were biologically determined. The legacy of eugenics in medicine, in general—and the crimes of the Tuskegee syphilis study, specifically—resulted in health disparities and fostered the lack of trust many people of color have toward physicians, especially those who are white, as well as toward hospitals and medical care in general. Explicit racism is no longer ethically tolerated in medicine; however, implicit bias and other forms of discrimination, such as structural racism, still impact access to health care and overall health outcomes of minority persons and limit career opportunities of racial and ethnic minority health professionals and women.[34] The racism of eugenics fueled not only Jim Crow but also white supremacy and all of the prejudices these ideologies bear today.

NOTES

1. Gregory M. Dorr, *Segregation's Science: Eugenics and Society in Virginia* (Charlottesville: University of Virginia Press, 2008), 14, 28.
2. Ibid., 27–30.
3. Ibid., 30
4. Ibid., 27.
5. Ibid., 48–52, 70–72.
6. Dorr, *Segregation's Science*, 9–10; Edward J. Larson, *Sex, Race, and Science: Eugenics in the Deep South* (Baltimore: Johns Hopkins University Press, 1995); Paul A. Lombardo, *Three Generations, No Imbeciles: Eugenics, the Supreme Court, and Buck v. Bell* (Baltimore: Johns Hopkins University Press, 2008); Paul A. Lombardo, ed., *A Century of Eugenics in America: From the Indiana Experiment to the Human Genome Era* (Bloomington: Indiana University Press, 2011); Kenneth M. Ludmerer, *Genetics and American Society: A Historical Appraisal* (Baltimore: Johns Hopkins University Press, 1972).
7. Dorr, *Segregation's Science*, 25–26, 34.
8. Ibid., 34–37.
9. Ibid., 37.
10. Dorr, *Segregation's Science*, 22–25, 33, 38–47.
11. Ibid., 45.
12. Edward H. Beardsley, *A History of Neglect: Health Care for Blacks and Mill Workers in the Twentieth-Century South* (Knoxville: University of Tennessee Press, 1987), 77–185, especially "Black Physicians and the Health of Their People," "Civic Crusaders and Corporate Reformers, 1900–1940," "Blacks and the Southern Public Health Establishment, 1900–1932," and "The Federal Rescue of Southern Health Programs." See also Gertrude Jacinta Fraser, *African American Midwifery in the South: Dialogues of Birth, Race, and Memory* (Cambridge, MA: Harvard University Press, 1998), 59–104, especially "Race and Regulation" and "Race and Mortality."
13. Dorr, *Segregation's Science*, 42–47.
14. Ibid., 47, 53–65.
15. Ibid., 72–77; Gregory M. Dorr, "Assuring America's Place in the Sun: Ivey Foreman Lewis and the Teaching of Eugenics at the University of Virginia, 1915–1953," *Journal of Southern History* 66, no. 2 (2000): 257–96.
16. Dorr, *Segregation's Science*, 75.
17. Ibid., 77–82.
18. Ibid., 80.
19. Ibid., 66–69, 83–86.
20. Dorr, *Segregation's Science*; Larson, *Sex, Race, and Science*; Lombardo, *Three Generations, No Imbeciles*; Lombardo, *Century of Eugenics*; Ludmerer, *Genetics and American Society*; Paul A. Lombardo and Gregory M. Dorr, "Eugenics, Medical Education, and the Public Health Service: Another Perspective on the Tuskegee Syphilis Experiment," *Bulletin of the History of Medicine* 80 (2006): 291–316.
21. Beardsley, *History of Neglect*; David Barton Smith, *Health Care Divided: Race and the Healing of a Nation* (Ann Arbor: University of Michigan Press, 1999); Thomas

J. Ward Jr., *Black Physicians in the Jim Crow South* (Fayetteville: University of Arkansas Press, 2003); P. Preston Reynolds, "The Federal Government's Use of Title VI and Medicare to Racially Integrate Hospitals in the United States, 1963–67," *American Journal of Public Health* 87 (1997):1850–58; P. Preston Reynolds, "Professional and Hospital Discrimination and the US Court of Appeals Fourth Circuit," *American Journal of Public Health* 94 (2004): 710–20.

22. W. Montague Cobb, *Medical Care and Plight of the Negro* (New York: NAACP, 1947); W. Montague Cobb, *Progress or Portents for the Negro in Medicine* (New York: NAACP, 1948); Dietrich C. Reitzes, *Negroes and Medicine* (Cambridge, MA: Harvard University Press, 1958); Ward, *Black Physicians;* Todd Savitt, "Abraham Flexner and the Black Medical School," in *Beyond Flexner: Medical Education in the Twentieth Century,* ed. Barbara Barzansky and Norman Gevitz, 65–81 (New York: Greenwood Press, 1992).

23. James Worsham Barksdale, "A Comparative Study of Contemporary White and Negro Standards in Health, Education, and Welfare in Charlottesville, Virginia," Phelps-Stokes Fellowship Papers, no. 20 (1949): 27–30.

24. Ibid., 30.

25. Ibid., 34–38.

26. Barksdale, "A Comparative Study."

27. Ibid., 39, 73–82.

28. Ibid., 73–77.

29. Dorr, *Segregation's Science;* Larson, *Sex, Race, and Science;* Lombardo, *Three Generations, No Imbeciles;* Lombardo, *Century of Eugenics;* Ludmerer, *Genetics and American Society.*

30. Dorr, *Segregation's Science,* 9, 144–66, 207–10.

31. Lombardo and Dorr, "Eugenics, Medical Education."

32. Allan M. Brandt, "Racism and Research: The Case of the Tuskegee Syphilis Study," *Hastings Report* 8, no. 6 (1978): 21–28; James H. Jones, *Bad Blood: The Tuskegee Syphilis Experiment* (New York: Free Press, 1981); Susan M. Reverby, ed., *Tuskegee's Truths: Rethinking the Tuskegee Syphilis Study* (Chapel Hill: University of North Carolina Press, 2000); Susan M. Reverby, *Examining Tuskegee: The Infamous Syphilis Study and Its Legacy* (Chapel Hill: University of North Carolina Press, 2009).

33. Dorr, *Segregation's Science,* 217–19.

34. Institute of Medicine, *Unequal Treatment: Confronting Ethics and Racial Disparities in Health Care* (Washington, DC: National Academy Press, 2002); J. F. Dovidio et al., "Disparities and Distrust: The Implications of Psychological Processes for Understanding Racial Disparities in Health and Health Care," *Social Science and Medicine* 67 (2008): 478–86; Z. D. Bailey et al., "Structural Racism and Health Inequities in the USA: Evidence and Intervention," *Lancet* 389 (2017): 1453–63; J. Feagin and Z. Bennefield, "Systemic Racism and U.S. Health Care," *Social Science and Medicine* 103 (2014): 7–14; D. Lewis and E. Paulsen, eds., *Proceedings of the Diversity and Inclusion Innovation Forum: Unconscious Bias in Academic Medicine* (Washington, DC: Association of American Medical Colleges, 2017).

NO ORDINARY SACRIFICE

The Struggle for Racial Justice at the University of Virginia in the Post–Civil Rights Era

CLAUDRENA N. HAROLD

On the night of May 4, 1970, fifteen hundred students at the University of Virginia assembled on the historic Lawn in a moving display of political solidarity and self-determination. Earlier that day, campus activists at Kent State had launched their fourth round of demonstrations against President Richard Nixon's deployment of U.S. troops to Cambodia. The Kent State protest turned deadly when the Ohio National Guard fired into the large crowd of demonstrators, wounding ten students and killing four others. Anger engulfed the nation as more than four hundred colleges and universities witnessed massive demonstrations over the Kent State murders. Over the next ten days, students at UVA boycotted classes, occupied buildings, and pushed the university's president, Edgar Shannon, into a heated showdown with state legislators in Richmond. Not content with simply challenging the war in Southeast Asia, student activists addressed larger issues facing the university, including its role in the militarization of U.S. society, its integration of African Americans and women into the student body and key administrative positions, and its commitment to improving the economic conditions of low-wage workers on Grounds.

At the center of much of the student organizing was James Roebuck, a graduate student from Philadelphia and an alumnus of Virginia Union University who several weeks before the Kent State massacre had been elected as the first African American president of UVA's student council. A gifted leader working toward his doctorate in history, Roebuck had the task of mediating the brewing conflict between his peers, the university's president, and a seemingly trigger-happy state all too ready to rely on force to quell dissent. On the second day of their protest, Roebuck and other leaders composed a list of demands that ranged from ending ROTC to removing all law enforcement officials from Grounds to UVA publicly committing itself "to accepting 20% as a goal for the enrollment of black students throughout the University."[1] Two days after submitting the students' demands to administrators, Roebuck faced his greatest challenge when local police and the National Guard harassed and arrested dozens of students, invaded several fraternity houses on Rugby Road, and all but turned the university's storied Academical Village into a war zone. To restore order, as well as regain the confidence of his students, President Shannon fiercely condemned the state for its excessive use of force. The former Navy veteran also reiterated his frustration with "the continued alienation of our young men and women owing largely to our nation's military involvement in Southeast Asia." Ever the diplomat, Shannon arranged meetings between student activists and key Virginia lawmakers to discuss the critical issues facing the nation: "It is my firm conviction," Shannon explained in a letter to Senators William Spong and Harry Byrd, "that student views and questions on this matter need to be heard by those in a position to influence and shape national policy."[2]

Far from an isolated event, the May upheaval at UVA was part of a larger wave of protests that engulfed American colleges and universities throughout the 1960s. That black student activist James Roebuck would find allies among a growing community of young white progressives should not surprise us. "By the late sixties," historian William L. Van Deburg writes, "university communities had become accustomed to student protests. In an important sense, the black students' expression of rage at 'the system' reflected their membership in a vital, militant youth culture that sought self-definition and power for all college-aged Americans."[3] This militant youth culture, as Jeffrey Turner reminds us in his seminal book *Sitting In and Speaking Out,* was not confined to the centers of higher learning in the Northeast and on the West Coast.[4] Several institutions below the Mason-Dixon Line, including UVA, were the sites of important student rebellions over administrators' commitment to desegregation and compliance with Title VI of the Civil Rights Act of 1964, the creation and funding of Black Studies units, the integration of athletic departments, and the treatment of low-wage workers, among other issues. During these transformative years, progressive students and faculty at UVA set in motion a series of events that would transform the social, cultural, demographic, and intellectual landscape of the college. In many ways, these students established a legacy of political protest and civic engagement that has continued well into the twenty-first century.

This legacy of student protest at UVA weighed heavily on my mind as former students, colleagues, and family members inundated me with questions after white supremacists staked their claims on the university and Charlottesville. Were the white supremacist marches and rallies of August 11 and 12 isolated incidents or simply another manifestation of the entrenched racism within and beyond the campus of UVA? How would new and returning African American students function in such a hostile environment? And if white supremacists followed through on their promise to return to Grounds, could black students depend on or even reasonably expect protection from law enforcement officials? How could parents of current and prospective black students trust a university willing to cede public and moral space to unapologetic white supremacists? And finally, were black students adequately prepared to deal with the many challenges and pressures of the upcoming semester? To the latter question, my response frequently centered on the long tradition of protest at the university, a tradition that has become increasingly familiar to me in my multiple roles as professor of African American Studies and History, faculty advisor to the Black Student Alliance (BSA), and codirector (with my UVA colleague Kevin Jerome Everson) of six short films on the African American student experience at UVA. Of course, this tradition was well known to many UVA graduates who contacted me in the days after August 12. Frequently they interpreted events through their own experiences at the university. Take as a case in point their discussion of law enforcement officials' response to the white supremacist rallies. On more than one occasion, both young and older black alumni mentioned the long history of strained relations between African American students and local law enforcement officials. The anger engulfing many of these graduates (as well as the larger Charlottesville community) emerged not just from the events associated with the "Summer of Hate" but also from years of frustration surrounding African Americans' position in the local political economy, the hyperpolicing of black youth and their high rates of exposure to the criminal justice system, and the devastating effect of urban renewal, gentrification, and the city's progrowth policies on black Charlottesville.

Much has been made in recent months about the need for the university to confront its legacy of slavery and Jim Crow segregation/exclusion. Such work is necessary, but our critical engagement with the university must also attend to the more recent past. Turning our attention to the ongoing struggle for racial justice at UVA enables us to put recent political initiatives and demands in a broader historical context. It also helps us understand why some white supremacists and nationalists feel the need to reclaim the university many of them regard as a stronghold of the political and cultural left. Toward these goals, this essay traces the history of political protest at the University of Virginia during the post–civil rights era, focusing in particular on the political demands and intellectual concerns of African American students. It revisits themes and issues that have long been a part of the political conversation at UVA, including but not limited to the university's social responsibilities and moral obligations to the City of Charlottesville. If nothing else, the more recent history of student activism and race relations at UVA proves that the passage of the Civil Rights Act of 1964 did not mark the culmination of the black freedom struggle, but instead inaugurated a new phase in African Americans' ongoing quest for racial justice. To prove this point, we begin with the politically tumultuous year of 1968.

On Tuesday, November 12, 1968, student council members Bud Ogle and James Roebuck presented a series of resolutions to their colleagues. These resolutions called for the university to establish an African American Studies program; appoint an African American administrator in the Office of Admission; ban the use of "Dixie, rebel flags, and other prejudicial symbols" at school activities; raise the students activities fee by five dollars in order to adequately fund the newly created Martin Luther King Scholarship Fund; actively recruit students from Howard, Virginia State, and Virginia Union for its graduate programs; and immediately integrate its athletic department. Consistent with national trends, the students prioritized the establishment of an African American Studies program and viewed the diversification of the school's curriculum as central to the university's desegregation agenda and intellectual transformation. "At present most students here are culturally deprived insofar as they are confined to a white upper-middle class ghetto," Ogle and Roebuck complained. "Needless to say, if we are going to receive an adequate education for our contemporary world such circumstances must change." Ogle and Roebuck were equally passionate about addressing the university's role as Charlottesville's largest employer. The university, they argued, had failed to "adequately deal with Charlottesville's social and economic problems." Such negligence was unacceptable given the school's centrality to the local economy: "The University, as the city's largest employer, source of income and influence, has a special responsibility to the larger community."[5]

The resolutions put forth by Bud Ogle and James Roebuck set the tone for the spring semester of 1969, which witnessed an upsurge in student protest and organizing. In mid-February progressive students initiated a three-day campaign designed to draw attention to the university's "racist atmosphere." On the last day of the protest, student leaders put forth numerous demands, including the integration of African Americans into all areas of campus life, the elimination of application fees for low-income students, administrative support and endorsement of workers' right to collectively bargain, and the hiring of an African American as associate dean of admissions. Several weeks after the protest, the Black Students for Freedom (BSF) submitted a seventeen-page proposal outlining its curriculum and vision for the Afro-American Studies (AAS) program. As their proposal made clear, BSF leaders envisioned a comprehensive program that would fundamentally transform academic life at the university. They demanded that the AAS program be intellectually rigorous, politically relevant, and adequately financed by the university's administration.

Their demands did not fall on deaf ears. Envisioning the creation of an AAS major as an important component of the university's push to improve black student enrollment (the number of African Americans stood at an embarrassing 1.9 percent in 1969), the College Faculty–Committee on Academic Legislation approved the interdisciplinary major in African American Studies on March 25, 1970. Four months later, the State Council of Higher Education, along with UVA's Board of Visitors, stamped their approval on the major. The fledgling program added two new hires: literary scholar Houston Baker and theologian Joseph Washington. Recounting his time at the university, Charles Conyers attributed a great deal of his intellectual maturity to his relationship with Professors Washington and Baker. "They did not play. They believed in rigor, they believed in accountability." Noting how black students "had few to no role models," Conyers readily admitted modeling his style and demeanor after Washington, who served as chair of the AAS program. "I thought he was one of the deepest brothers I ever met."[6]

The establishment of an AAS program was not the only promising development at UVA. Over the period between 1968 and 1976, African American students laid the foundation for the institutional infrastructure of "Black UVA." No organization contributed more to the vibrancy of black student life than BSA, which developed out of the BSF and adopted its current name in 1971. Another important organization was Black Voices, a gospel choir founded in 1972. The first half of the 1970s also witnessed the arrival of various black Greek-letter organizations. These organizations significantly enriched African Americans' social life. Their probates, step shows, and block parties provided temporary respite from the rigors of academic life and a conduit to a richer cultural tradition.

Even as African Americans expanded their numbers and constructed a vibrant social and cultural life on Grounds, many black students still questioned the institution's commitment to racial justice. Especially vocal in this regard was the first group of African Americans who integrated the university's athletic department. The last school in the Atlantic Coast Conference to integrate its sports teams, UVA moved at a glacial pace in its response to campus activists' demand for more African American student athletes and coaches. On December 15, 1969, the university finally signed its first black candidate for a football grant-in-aid: Stanley Land, a six foot three, 210-pound defensive back from Waverly High in Rockbridge, Virginia. A few months later, the football team added three other African Americans to its recruiting class: Kent Merritt, John Rainey, and Harrison Davis. No signee garnered more attention than Merritt, a Charlottesville native who was an all-American in both track and football. Football and track were not the only sports breaking the color line. In April 1970 Al Drummond became the first black basketball player to sign a grant-in-aid to UVA.

Reflecting on his time at the university in an interview with Daniel Artin, Harrison Davis recalled his tenure as UVA's first African American quarterback as one of great struggle. Coupled with the typical pressures associated with playing the most scrutinized position in sports, Davis endured a great deal of racism from within and outside the university community. His encounters with racial prejudice and intimidation ranged from facing derogatory comments from fans to receiving hate mail from the Ku Klux Klan threatening him and his family.[7] "It wasn't easy," Kent Merritt remembered as he reflected on the challenges facing the first group of black scholarship athletes. "There was not much for us to do on the Grounds, as well as in Charlottesville. I think some other students might have seen us being here as accommodations as a result of the various civil rights laws that were on the books at the time. So I can't really say the student body was accepting, I think they were just tolerant."[8] Another black athlete, Mike Dove, was more blunt: "I don't think they want us here. I hope things get better but I don't think they want us here."[9]

Such feelings intensified for other African American students in 1974, when the *Cavalier Daily* published a series of explosive articles on the large number of UVA administrators, including President Frank Hereford, who held memberships in the all-white Farmington Country Club, which still barred African Americans and other people of color. "Our worst suspicions, our most grievous concerns have been confirmed," the paper bemoaned as it revealed the list of high-ranking officials at UVA who belonged to Farmington. This list included President Hereford, seventeen department chairs, seven deans, and eight Board of Visitors members.

Debate over Farmington continued well into 1975 as Hereford maintained his membership in the exclusive club. The conflict between Hereford and his critics hit a breaking point on the night of October 7 when approximately three hundred students stormed Carr's Hill (the president's campus residence) to confront him about his conspicuous absence at the student council's open forum on minority affairs. Student council president Paul Freeman had informed the restless crowd that UVA's president wanted to hear the students' concerns, but a previously scheduled luncheon in Washington, D.C., prevented his attendance. The crowd's frustration quickly turned to outrage when Eston E. Melton, the editor in chief of the *Cavalier Daily,* revealed that Hereford had just been seen at Culbreth Theatre. Disgruntled students then marched to Carr's Hill to "demand an explanation for Hereford's failure to attend the forum."[10]

This protest, along with the upheaval of the past year, laid the foundation for the creation of the Office of Afro-American Affairs (OAAA), which opened on March 4, 1977, and would become an anchoring institution for many black students. Another important milestone occurred in 1977: the number of African American undergraduates on Grounds reached five hundred for the first time. Notwithstanding the steady increase in the black student population, the struggle to desegregate higher education in Virginia was far from over. In 1977 the U.S. District Court, District of Columbia ruled in *Adams v. Califano* that the desegregation plans accepted by the Department of Health, Education, and Welfare (HEW) in 1974 failed to meet the requirements earlier specified. A year later HEW accepted the plans of Arkansas, Florida, and Oklahoma but rejected those from Georgia, North Carolina, and Virginia. Finally, in 1982 the CRO declared the state of Virginia in compliance with the Civil Rights Act.

Of course, African American students as a whole had never equated the attainment of desegregation benchmarks as evidence of full integration or equality. To be sure, UVA had made steady progress in increasing the black presence on Grounds, but student activists were far from satisfied. On April 28, 1983, one hundred students demonstrated outside Luther P. Jackson House in an effort to communicate their frustration at the state of affairs at UVA. The cultural arm of OAAA, Jackson House administered various cultural and enrichment programs specifically designed for African American students. Counted among the group of demonstrators at the rally was the university's most famous undergraduate, Ralph Sampson, who joined BSA chairperson Louis Anderson in presenting a list of grievances to Student Affairs Vice President Ernest Ern. Their grievances included the shortage of African American faculty and administrators, the high percentage of black students tried and convicted in honor trials, the absence of an African American Studies department, the ineffectiveness of Jackson House, the customary allocation of funds and office space for black student organizations, and the decline in financial aid.

Many (but not all) of these students' concerns were amplified in 1986, when UVA commenced preparations for its decennial reaccreditation for the Southern Association of Colleges and Schools. University president Robert O'Neil appointed the Steering Committee for the Self-Study, which had as one of its tasks the evaluation of the university's recruitment of African American students and faculty. The committee eventually suggested the formation of a separate task force that would focus solely on investigating the state of race relations on Grounds and defining "an appropriate policy aimed at achieving full and genuine integration at the University."[11] O'Neil impaneled a committee of sixteen faculty members, students, and administrators to conduct such a report. The extent to which the university had transformed its culture would be the subject of *An Audacious Faith: A Report of the Task Force on Afro-American Affairs,* a sprawling document that offered a rare look into the university's past, present, and future. While conceding that there had been some progress in race relations, the task force concluded that the "self-transformation of the University of Virginia into a genuinely integrated institution equally receptive to people of all races is far from complete." It continued:

> The mere elimination of flagrant and overt racial barriers, the admission under legal pressure of black students (who now constitute but 6.5 percent of the student body in a state where blacks compose 18 percent of the citizenry), the recruitment of a relatively small number of black faculty members and lower level administrators (many of whom have not chosen to remain here), the initiation and tenuous maintenance for the past decade of a student-demanded unclearly defined Office of Afro-American Affairs, and the less than enthusiastic offering over the years of a handful of transitory, under-funded academic programs for students with special needs do not taken together constitute achievement of genuine integration at the University of Virginia.[12]

Though written in 1987, the *Audacious Faith* report illuminated the paradoxical nature of race at UVA not just during the 1980s but well into the 1990s. It was a period many former students remember as the best of times and the worst of times. Let's start with the milestones and accomplishments: The black undergraduate population reached an all-time high of 1,366 in 1991 and the African American retention and graduation rates ranked among the highest in the nation. Established organizations like Black Voices reached their peak in membership, while informal spaces like the Black Bus Stop were culturally vibrant hangouts for African Americans. At the same time, the *Cavalier Daily* routinely ran stories in which black students cited incidents of racial harassment on "The Corner," a popular dining and tourist spot adjacent to Grounds, and black students spoke of unfair treatment at the hands of local police. And then there was the university's honor system, which many claimed unfairly targeted African Americans. A key component of student self-governance, the honor system enforced a single-sanction policy in which a student found guilty of an honor offense was expelled from the university. On September 11, 1996, the Honor Committee's Diversity Task Force released a report that documented honor violations, accusations, and trials. African American students accounted for 35 percent of honor investigations and 23 percent of students dismissed. Asian Americans constituted 12.9 percent of students charged with honor violations and 23 percent of those expelled. The parent of one expelled African American student filed a complaint with the Office of Civil Rights (OCR), which decided to investigate not just that case but the entire honor system for evidence of any violation of the Civil Rights Act of 1964. Two members of the OCR listened to trial tapes, reviewed case files, and interviewed members of the Honor Committee. On July 8, 1997, the office delivered its verdict: the honor system did not violate Title VI of the Civil Rights Act. Notwithstanding the OCR's ruling, many African American students continued to look at the honor system with great suspicion.

A similar disposition characterized some black students' relationship with university police, which had never been great. "The most racism I've felt here at the University has been at the hands of the police," one student told the *Cavalier Daily* in 1997. In a decade in which African American culture and politics turned greater attention to the problem of police harassment and brutality, UVA students refused to see one of their generation's biggest issues as something that only mattered in New York or Los Angeles. "We need to understand the patterns of police brutality which have surfaced year after year in our community," student leader Porsha Burke insisted.

"We need to be able to discuss these issues of longstanding ill will between black students and police with appropriate powers and see actions taken. We only can hope that the necessary dialogue will reach the ears of all who need to hear it, and that it can impact the change so desperately required."[13]

Another topic of great discussion on Grounds as well as in the larger Charlottesville community was the troubling findings in the Office of Equal Opportunity Programs (EOP), which released *An Examination of the University's Minority Classified Staff (Muddy Floor Report)* in 1996.[14] The report discovered "glaring disparities" in employment opportunities, performance evaluations, and disciplinary sanctions between white and black employees. As had long been the case at UVA, African Americans were overrepresented in unskilled positions and virtually nonexistent in high-salaried, managerial positions. Though constituting only 17.6 percent of the entire classified workforce, they made up 54.8 percent of the service/maintenance workers. Perhaps even more disturbing were the sharp racial disparities in job performance evaluations and disciplinary actions. The EOP's analysis of job-performance evaluations for the years 1993–95 reveals that whites were much more likely to receive "exceptional" ratings than their African American counterparts. In 1994, a year the university awarded merit raises based on job-performance ratings, African Americans received an exceptional rating only 8.8 percent of the time, while whites received an exceptional mark 23.5 percent of the time. To further compound matters, African Americans were much more likely to experience disciplinary action. Though blacks constituted 17.9 percent of the total classified workforce, they received 48 percent of the written notices. They also suffered from a disproportionate rate of termination.[15]

The *Muddy Floor Report,* the ongoing conversations about the discriminatory politics of the honor system, and the heated debates over affirmative action, among other issues, fueled the activism of the BSA and motivated newly formed organizations like the Black Empowerment Association (BEA). Created by Shaheed Minder in 1995, BEA drew inspiration from the Black Power movement of the 1960s and 1970s, as well as the resurgence of black cultural nationalism during the 1990s. BEA galvanized students frustrated with the growing problem of mass incarceration, the public policies of the New Right, and President Bill Clinton's welfare-reform agenda. Looking back at the 1990s, UVA alum Minder viewed the period as a politically intense time in which students thought deeply about the ways in which racism and economic exploitation adversely affected the life chances and experiences of African Americans. The country was in the throes of great political, economic, and cultural change, and the university provided an ideal site for young women and men seeking to make sense of those changes: "It was a bunch of intellectuals in the black community there at the same time, and that was pretty extraordinary."[16]

The political fervor of the 1990s continued in the early years of the twenty-first century as students battled rising tuition costs, shifts in black enrollment trends, the continued problem of police brutality, and the disproportionate impact of the 2001 and 2008 recessions on African Americans. Then there was the spate of isolated attacks on African American students that marred race relations in the early 2000s and led to the formation of the Center for the Study of Race and Law and the Office of Diversity and Equity.

Students also remained attentive to the problems facing an important though often neglected constituency of UVA's black community: low-income workers. On February 21, 2006, the Living Wage Campaign released *Keeping Our Promises: Toward a Living Wage at the University*. The report called for the administration to adopt a living wage ($10.72 per hour) for classified staff and contract employees. "The University's stated commitment to diversity," the report noted, "must confront the fact that people of color, particularly women, form a disproportionate number of those receiving less than a living wage."[17] The report had the support of public officials, faculty members, state and national political groups (ACORN, the Virginia Organizing Project, and the Virginia AFL-CIO), and various student organizations (the Black Leadership Institute, BSA, and the University Democrats).

The Living Wage Campaign intensified its struggle on April 12, when seventeen students staged a sit-in at Madison Hall. For the next three days, the Living Wage Campaign captured the attention of students, administrators, faculty members, community leaders, and the media. School administrators instructed the students to either end their sit-in or face arrest for trespassing. Theirs was no idle threat. On Saturday evening, April 15, at around seven p.m., local police arrested the students occupying Madison Hall and hauled them off to the Charlottesville Regional Jail.

The plight of low-wage workers is but one of many issues of importance to student activists. As evident by the list of demands issued by the BSA in response to the events of August 11 and 12, many African American students still view the university as a site of racial and economic injustice. Not just in their demands but in their public statements, they express grave concerns about the university's commitment to racial justice, the fate of African Americans on Grounds, the disturbingly low percentage of blacks on faculty, the values communicated through the school's historical landscape and symbols, and administrators' willingness to acknowledge, confront, and rectify UVA's racist legacy through substantive policy initiatives geared toward improving the material conditions (income and housing) of Charlottesville's low-income citizens. They call for more remedies than symbolic gestures that fail to address larger structural inequities. And yet, despite these challenges, many black students and their allies still envision themselves as agents of change, heirs of a great legacy of political protest and engagement. They have drawn on their own political and cultural resources, but they have also built on the lessons of those who came before them.

Watching my students incorporate those lessons over the past few months has buoyed my spirits and strengthened my faith in the possibility of change and radical transformation. To be certain, it is easy to turn to cynicism and despair in these trying times, but we must heed the call of the late historian Vincent Harding, who challenged us to "cultivate not only indignation and anger but also vision and hope."[18]

NOTES

1. Robert Buford, Peter Shea, and Andrew Stickney, *May Days: Crisis in Confrontation* (Charlottesville, VA: n.p., 1970).
2. *Daily Progress,* May 10, 1970.
3. William L. Van Deburg, *New Day in Babylon: The Black Power Movement and American Culture, 1965–1975* (Chicago: University of Chicago Press, 1992), 66.
4. Jeffrey Turner, *Sitting In and Speaking Out: Student Movements in the American South, 1960–1970* (Athens: University of Georgia Press, 2010).
5. *Cavalier Daily,* Nov. 14, 1968.
6. Black Fire at UVA, May 20, 2014, https://blackfireuva.com/2014/03/20/one-of -the-deepest-brothers-i-know-reflections-on-joseph-washington.
7. Ibid., https://blackfireuva.com/2015/01/12/in-conversation-with-harrison-davis -the-first-african-american-quarterback-at-uva.
8. Ibid., https://blackfireuva.com/alumni-interviews-2.
9. *Cavalier Daily,* Nov. 2, 1973.
10. *Cavalier Daily,* Oct. 8, 1975.
11. *An Audacious Faith: A Report of the Task Force on Afro-American Affairs,* University of Virginia, June 1987, p. 14, https://blackfireuva.files.wordpress.com/2012/05/ an-audacious-faith.pdf.
12. Ibid.
13. *Cavalier Daily,* April 14, 1997.
14. Classified staff refers to employees employed directly by the university rather than those who are outsourced through a third party (i.e., Aramark).

15. *An Examination of the University's Minority Classified Staff (The Muddy Floor Report)*, https://blackfireuva.files.wordpress.com/2012/02/an-examination-of-the-universitys-minority-classified-staff-the-muddy-floor-report.pdf.

16. Shaheed Minder, interview with the author, April 2015.

17. Workers and Students United for a Living Wage, *Keeping Our Promises: Toward a Living Wage at the University of Virginia in 2012*, http://livingwageatuva.wixsite.com/lwc-uva/keeping-our-promises, Feb. 21, 2006.

18. Vincent Harding, "Is America Possible?," On Being, https://onbeing.org/blog/is-america-possible, accessed Feb. 22, 2018.

ON LISTENING

BONNIE GORDON

On Friday, August 11, 2017, my family and I went from a small Shabbat service at Charlottesville's one synagogue, Congregation Beth Israel, to an interfaith service at St. Paul's Memorial Church, located about two hundred yards from UVA's central campus, known as the Lawn. The large prayer meeting, led by interfaith leaders from around the city and the nation, including Traci Blackmon and Cornel West, deliberately echoed the spirit of the civil rights movement. Churches were spaces for political and spiritual strength, and singing performed spiritual cleansing before fighting hate. Despite the incessant buzz of helicopters and the sight of white men with large guns trickling into town, the mood felt hopeful. But as the service ended, cell phones vibrated. I received a text from a local friend and UVA alumna with whom I went to synagogue as a child: "Holy shit are you at the Lawn? You have to get out of there, huge marches, torches as far as you can see, chanting 'Jews will not replace us,' 'Fuck off commies this is our town now,' and 'Blood and Soil.'" She sent pictures from her Facebook feed and called to help us figure out if there was a way we could get to our car without running into screaming Nazis. By the time we figured out what to do, the church was on lockdown. The pastor said, "We're going to need y'all to sit and prepare to duck and take cover." My ten-year-old son held my hand tightly and said, "I knew it was a bad idea to go to church on Shabbat." He whispered, "Has anyone thought to call the police?" Thanks to various external reviews we know now that there was no law enforcement plan to protect the seven hundred people inside the church and that by the evening local police forces, university administrators, and city officials knew about the torch rally.[1]

Richard Spencer, a white supremacist who advocates for peaceful ethnic cleansing, directed the August 11 and 12 production. He graduated from UVA in 2001 with majors in English and music and went on to write a master's thesis at the University of Chicago on Wagner, Adorno, opera, and anti-Semitism. As an undergraduate he made stage sets for Shakespeare on the Lawn, a student-run theater group, and after graduate school he worked on opera productions in Germany. So he knew exactly what he was deploying when he used the chant "Blood and Soil." Although he and his followers might pretend that in the South this phrase could translate to "heritage and the land of the Confederacy," it originated and rose in popularity just before the Nazis came to power, and the idea of blood and soil, with its inherent racist xenophobia, fueled many of their most heinous laws.[2] When my high-school friend texted me that Spencer's torch-bearing marchers were chanting those words, they rang through my ears in German, *"Blut und Boden."* I heard in them the nineteenth-century ideologies that bound German land to German blood, ideologies that I first heard when studying Wagner in music classes.

This essay listens to the events of August 11 and 12, as well as to those of a smaller and less publicized torch rally on October 7, as spectacles. It positions Charlottesville in the summer of 2017 as a major battle site and as a cross between a pilgrimage site and an epicenter. In this second decade of the twenty-first century, white supremacists are staging a culture war that transports toxic, violent imaginings of Western culture and apocalyptic nationalism, especially opera, to the former slave-holding South. Beneath the Confederate flags, Nazi symbols, and loud cries of white nationalism that filled the summer of hate were familiar refrains, rhythms, and narrative arcs. The events of August 11 and 12 were part of a year of spectacles designed to draw out and play on institutional legacies of white supremacy and especially its twentieth-century renditions, making copious use of burning torches, the singing of "Dixie," and Nazi slogans. This essay makes two primary interventions that push scholars to use their skills and knowledge. First, music scholars and practitioners, as well as scholars in other humanities fields, can use the language and history of our disciplines as a massive weapon against Spencer and his followers; they are not the only ones who know history and who understand production value. Second, we must listen and read between the lines of our world, not just the worlds of our scholarly inquiry. Artists should know firsthand the good and the bad work music can do, and we should know the dangers of any kind of nationalism. Music making and art are no more inherently good than anything else. Usually when I ask UVA students in my Introduction to Music class to name experiences where singing unifies, they mention church and football games; this year they talked about chanting Nazis and screaming white supremacists.

Richard Spencer is a harsh reminder that a liberal arts education does not necessarily defend against white supremacy, nor do efforts by the University of Virginia and other universities to memorialize enslaved workers.[3]

And the events he catalyzed bring to the fore the fact that it is not enough to get college students to see the grotesque potential of some of the music they love, especially if it includes sounds mobilized by the likes of Stalin and Hitler. Most undergraduates who take music classes learn about sonic performances of nationalism; it's a box or chapter in many textbooks. But these days it might be even more important to make sure they can hear the ways that racialized nationalism plays out politically and musically in their own contemporary spaces.

August 11 and 12 was the third major hate show in Charlottesville and at UVA in four months. This was not a surprise attack. The first tiki-torch rally occurred in May 2017, and then in July the KKK marched. And they were not done after August 12. The groups that had been loudly planning to come to Charlottesville, including the National Socialists, Traditional Workers Party, and Warlocks, brought anger at an increasingly diverse America; they want travel bans on Muslims and widespread immigration bans. They unapologetically hate Jewish, black, brown, and gay people. In the weeks leading up to the events, a guy called "Baked Alaska" got himself removed from Twitter for posting a cartoon with Trump in a Nazi uniform and Laura Loomer in a gas chamber. Internet sites with clear instructions on where to park and where to go if you wanted to carry a weapon made it clear that rally organizers planned to combine their First Amendment free speech rights with their Second Amendment rights to carry nearly any guns they wanted.

Despite the fact that these groups violently opposed the communities we at the university serve, official communications in the days leading up to August 11 and 12 and in the days after reminded community members that the right to assembly allows even Nazis to assemble; this is true. The University of Virginia loves the First Amendment and will go to great lengths, as it should, to defend reprehensible content. So if I were the president of the university or the university's general counsel, I might have taken a break from bowing before the First Amendment and learned about the university's policy on open flames in public spaces. On Monday, August 13, it took me three minutes on Google to figure out that, actually, the university has a robust policy on open flames: they are not allowed.

REFRAIN

Spencer's musical and theatrical experience rendered the August 11 torch rally on the Lawn as predictable as a Rossini opera or a *Law and Order* episode. In Trump Tower on Election Day, 2016, he said that if he couldn't be secretary of state he wanted to be minister of culture and "spend millions of dollars on Wagner."[4] He chooses words and props carefully: at an alt-right gathering in November 2016, Spencer lashed out against Jews and said that America belonged to "white people." He described Trump's election as a "victory of will," a phrase that nods to Leni Riefenstahl's 1935 *Triumph of the Will*, a film that iconically glorified Hitler's impossible ideal of ethnic purity.[5]

The torches came back on October 7 in a production Spencer called Charlottesville 3.0. During the weekend that UVA celebrated its bicentennial with, among other things, a one-million-dollar multimedia performance held on the night of the Charlottesville High School homecoming dance, Richard Spencer made a pilgrimage back to Charlottesville for his third torch-lit march—another stop on his operatic tour of hate. Like all of Spencer's productions, this one featured chanting, marching, racial slurs, and shouting. And like all of them it was broadcast live on YouTube, inviting viewers from all over the world and every corner of the internet to join. The poorly lit YouTube documentation begins in the manner of a cheap TV show, with "Okay, we're live." Spencer and his stagehands attempt to organize their troops into vocalizations and rhythmic marching toward the contested Robert E. Lee statue, which had been shrouded in giant trash bags and surrounded by orange fences. About twelve minutes into the production, Spencer leads an out-of-tune rendition of "Dixie." Spencer and his creepy choir might not sound good, but they don't have to in order to incite violence.

Spencer's favorite prop—the (supermarket) tiki torch—is carefully chosen from another of Riefenstahl's Nazi propaganda films. For the 1936 Olympic games, Joseph Goebbels and his Nazi propaganda machine organized a torch relay that would inaugurate an Olympic tradition that now reaches millions of viewers on prime-time TV and stands as an unquestioned tradition of the Olympic games. They did so in part to connect the Aryan nation to ancient Greece, imagined to be the seat of Western civilization. The Olympic Games all told performed a link between Nazi Germany and ancient Greece, positioning German civilization as the heir to classical antiquity. Credit for the torch idea seems to go to Carl Diem, the secretary general of the 1936 Olympics, a historian who based his rally on one supposedly run in Athens in 80 BCE. The torch played well, as it had already been widely used in parades to attract especially youthful followers. And the torches, made by the arms manufacturer that made machine guns for the Nazis, raced through Hungary, Czechoslovakia, Yugoslavia, and Bulgaria, countries the Nazis would invade just a few years later.[6] The Nazis filmed their relay, and Leni Riefenstahl made a film out of it called *Olympia,* which emerged as another key Nazi propaganda film. Riefenstahl's beautiful, technically innovative, and aesthetically rich movies used explicitly Wagnerian motifs to present views of ardent nationalism. Riefenstahl's movie was not about the Olympics or about glorifying ancient Greece; it was about glorifying Hitler's apocalyptic message and about delivering a message of ethnic purity.[7]

Like any decent music major, Spencer's choice of tunes comes with equally deliberate symbolic weight. Make no mistake: the singing of "Dixie" in front of the shrouded statue of Robert E. Lee is not a hymn to Southern heritage. Before Virginia even seceded, the *Richmond Daily Dispatch* published this: "Do you not know, questioner, that Dixie's Land has become the 'National Anthem of Secession?' That it is called for in Southern Theatres, and received with cheers and applause, while Hail Columbia and the Star Spangled Banner are hissed down?"[8] Written in 1859 as a blackface minstrel song by Ohio native Daniel Decatur Emmett, this song fits squarely in the tradition of people from outside the South writing and creating images that sustained the South. In the same year an opponent of the song wrote, "I make no objection to the tune—it is bold and even pleasing—yet it smells to [*sic*] strongly of the 'nigger'—to assume the dignified rank of National song." He went on in a manner that seems to explain in classic white supremacist logic that "our National melodies should possess a distinct character of their own; but, if we are to depend on any people for their caste, let it not be the untutored son of Africa—the distorter of old Scotch and Irish tunes given to the world in the balmy days of the bards and harpers. If the Confederate States require a National anthem, let them adopt one of pure origin—one that will not be ashamed of its parentage."[9] And as Tom Lehrer pointedly wrote in a 1953 song entitled "I Want to Go Back to Dixie," the idea and ideal of Dixie was deeply rooted in violence. In this year before *Brown v. Board of Education,* he used a satirical song to show the ways in which the fantasy of Dixie whitewashed the violence endemic to the perpetuation of a dying Southern culture.[10] These are Tom Lehrer's words:

I want to go back to Dixie,
Take me back to dear ol' Dixie,
That's the only li'l ol' place for li'l ol' me.
Old times there are not forgotten,

Whuppin' slaves and sellin' cotton,
And waitin' for the Robert E. Lee.
(It was never there on time.)
. . . .
I want to talk with Southern gentlemen
And put that white sheet on again,
I ain't seen one good lynchin' in years.

The timbre of deep, bad singing sonically marks violent masculinity. It has the sonic effect of cock rock, with brash, rhythmic shouts that eschew melody.[11] This music sonifies the misogyny and rape culture that are gateway drugs to the alt-right. The noise of mostly men singing "Dixie" oozes toxic white nationalist misogyny. In the video from October 7, Spencer used language to enhance the misogynist timbre. He identifies his group as "uncut men willing to stand for our future." "Let's sing a song," he says. Standing next to the shrouded statue, Spencer shouts to his enemies to "show that you have some balls." This almost Freudian obsession is no accident. The twenty-first-century white nationalists find fascinating the term "cuck," derived from "cuckold." It slams establishment conservatives who let social justice warriors and political correctness emasculate them. This aligns with racism and xenophobia. After the Civil War white supremacists used the image of black men raping white women to mobilize a movement. This imagined protection of Southern white women is as misogynist as it is racist, valuing women largely for their chastity, which depends on a violent heterosexual patriarchy. Dylann Roof shouted in his 2015 shooting rampage, "You rape our women, and you're taking over our country, and you have to go."[12] And Trump, the pussy-grabbing president himself, called Mexicans "rapists" as a way to get Americans behind his dystopian wall.

RESONANCES

To hurt the Negro and avoid the Jew
Is the curriculum. In mid-September
The entering boys, identified by hats,
Wander in a maze of mannered brick
Where boxwood and magnolia brood
And columns with imperious stance
Like rows of ante-bellum girls
Eye them, outlanders. [13]

During the 1932–33 academic year the Pulitzer Prize–winning poet Karl Shapiro, a Jew, enrolled in classes at UVA. In 1942 he wrote the poem "University" about his experience. Shapiro wasn't wrong about the curriculum. UVA's thriving eugenics program has been written about extensively.[14] Eugenics as a key part of the biology department and medical school curricula lasted at UVA into the 1950s. In addition to filling generations of Virginia men with this pseudoscience, UVA faculty shared ideas with the Nazis; ten years after the Virginia assembly passed its 1924 sterilization act, the *Richmond Times-Dispatch* wrote, "Dr. DeJarnette expressed admiration for the sterilization program now being carried out in Hitler's Germany. He said he was not familiar with the details of the German law, but said 'the Germans are beating us at our own game and are more progressive than we are.'"[15] Not surprisingly, almost none of those central European academics who came to the United States to flee Hitler's racism chose to come to UVA.

Eugenics was not just a scientific practice. There was an important cultural component to UVA's eugenics program, one that once again connected preservation of the Old South with racial purity and that shared with Nazi cultural programs an investment in an unadulterated folk.[16] UVA's curriculum and creative practice merged with eugenics logic and contributed to the construction of segregation. Music played a key role. Although UVA had always offered some form of music instruction, the music department was founded in the 1920s under the influence of John Powell.[17] Powell, an honorary member of the glee club, used the collection and production of folk music to position a superior white creative potential as part of segregationist logic. In 1922 he founded the first post of the Anglo-Saxon Clubs of America, whose goal was to preserve Anglo-American culture, which they did in part by cosponsoring the Virginia Sterilization Act.[18] Powell started a UVA chapter in 1924.[19] He and his colleagues first defined themselves as part of a broad national movement toward nativism but ultimately focused on the "Negro problem." He described achieving the white supremacist project "first, by the strengthening of Anglo-Saxon instincts, traditions, and principles among representatives of our original American stock; second, by intelligent selection and exclusion of immigrants; and third, by fundamental and final solutions of our racial problems in general, most especially of the negro problem."[20]

In 1923 he wrote:

We know that under Mendelian law the African strain is hereditarily predominant. In other words, one drop of negro blood makes the negro. We also know that no higher race has ever been able to preserve its culture, to prevent decay and eventual degeneracy when tainted, even slightly, with negro blood. Sixty centuries of history establish this rule. Since the first page of recorded fact, history can show no exception. Were the American people to become an octoroon race, it would mean their sinking to the level of Haiti and Santo Domingo.[21]

With the term "octoroon" Powell referred to a racial calculus that his colleague W. A. Plecker had denoted. As soon as the Virginia Assembly passed the Racial Integrity Act of 1924, Plecker sent instructions on the accurate reporting of racial composition to officials registering births and deaths. Powell tied this math to the preservation of culture and the potential for aesthetic judgment.

TO SING OR NOT TO SING

Music departments face a special challenge in the aftermath of any traumatic or violent event. There is a collective fantasy that making music necessarily heals and unifies, but that's simply not the case. For starters it's worth remembering that collective singing at UVA has not always been to the good. When Spencer returned chanting to UVA on August 11, he did what many UVA students do: he sang school songs on the Lawn. And when he led his creepy rendition of "Dixie" on October 7, he led a song from the UVA songbook, which was celebrated as part of the UVA bicentennial in 2017.[22] By the time the songbook was compiled in 1906, "Dixie" came with a familiar mix of nostalgia and militarism. And by the 1940s it served at UVA football games as the sonic backdrop to Confederate memorabilia. When UVA played Yale in 1941, both sets of fans sang the tune as a way to celebrate the invasion of the Confederacy.[23]

The UVA songbook also contains the song "Virginia's Banner." The words, by Graham Cootes (class of 1902), seem to be about college flags:

What would Old Virginia do
Without the Orange and the Blue?
Every college has a flag, but ours is best.

But the book goes on to instruct readers to sing the song to the tune of "Every Race Has a Flag but the Coon." The tune was famous in the South because merely whistling it could supposedly incite violence.[24] Written in

1901 by Fred Helf and Will A. Heelan, the song explicitly denies African Americans access to a flag and a nation. In it the "Blackville Club" bemoans the fact that it has no flag to march under.

> Every race has a flag but the coon
> He says, "Now I'll suggest a flag that ought to win a prize
> Just take a flannel shirt and paint it red
> They draw a chicken on it with two poker dice for eyes
> An' have it wavin' razors 'round its head
> To make it quaint, you've got to paint
> A possum with a pork chop in his teeth
> To give it tone, a big hambone
> You sketch upon a banjo underneath."

This tune fits squarely in the "coon song" genre, a song type popular from the 1890s through the 1920s. The lyrics portray blacks as lawless, comic, nationless, and uneducable, and the tunes have catchy ragtime rhythms familiar to singers from minstrel songs and vaudeville. Coon songs served as aural instruments of white supremacy. And, indeed, the years in which coon songs were the most popular were also the years in which white violence against African Americans reached a peak in the South. The 1890s saw an increase in lynchings; the ritualized murder of black bodies happened almost every two days. Coon songs made this violence manifest in song.[25]

Even setting aside examples of music making that directly fuel fascism, collective sound isn't the same as collective action. As the Reverend William Barber, a national civil rights leader who rose to prominence through the Moral Mondays campaign in North Carolina, said to a packed church in Charlottesville the week after August 12, "You can't heal by singing 'We Are the World.' Healing and social progress don't come until you understand the causes and structures of the problems."[26] There was a lot of "We Shall Overcome" at UVA in the aftermath of August 12. Too little, too late. "We Shall Overcome" says we shall overcome *someday*. August 2017 was apparently not someday.

Everyone is quoting James Baldwin these days, but it's worth doing again here because he identifies the variable that spells the difference between a healing song and a fascist chorus: "Sentimentality, the ostentatious parading of excessive and spurious emotion, is the mark of dishonesty. . . . The wet eyes of the sentimentalist betray his aversion to experience, his fear of life, his arid heart; and it is always, therefore, the signal of secret and violent inhumanity, the mark of cruelty."[27] To cultivate our students' and citizens' capacities for human decency, we need to remain vigilant about both the potential and the limits of music making and of critical reading. It is crucial to continue making creative work and to keep thinking and writing, though the regimes of violence and terror are crashing through the gates. But it's not enough. And the faux-harmonizing language of diversity won't be enough either. The only choice is to fight back.

Two songs compose the soundtrack of my August 11 memory and offer singing as a weapon in the current cultural war. In St. Paul's Church, when cell phones exploded with news of the alt-right torch parade, the Reverend Osagyefo Uhuru Sekou—who had trained locals in nonviolent direct action in preparation for the August 12 rally—led the entire congregation singing and stomping "This Little Light of Mine." It made the building shake. "We have some company," he called to us, as we were singing. "Let's show them love conquers hate." In that moment, the song became a weapon and training: it fueled the courage that would become our armor in the hard phase ahead. Nonviolent protest and staring down the face of evil are not peaceful or easy. There's a powerful myth out there about the 1960s, and it comes with a common time, consonant, and diatonic musical backdrop. Martin Luther King warned against moderates who worked to avert tension. If you went to Reverend Sekou's training you got trained in having your ass kicked sonically and physically just by sitting or standing there as a witness to hate.

The other song I remember so clearly from that Friday night church service was sung by the two rabbis from Congregation Beth Israel. The next morning that synagogue was surrounded by rifle-wielding right-wingers and was not protected by police, state troopers, or National Guard. The rabbis led the congregation in "Olam Chesed Yibaneh," which translates as "the world is built through love," although the translation that's used as a refrain in the song is more of a proclamation, a call to action: "We will build this world with love." The song's folksy sound feels familiar to Jews and non-Jews alike. It doesn't even have the chromatic markings of much Jewish and Israeli music. Our rabbis have beautiful voices, every Jewish kid who goes to religious school in this town knows the lyrics, and anyone can catch the tune. The interfaith crowd rocked it. It's melodious, but not sweet.

"Olam Chesed Yibaneh" has been embraced by the activist group IfNotNow, a Jewish antiracist group that opposes the Israeli occupation of the West Bank. The song's words come from David—the same David who slew the evil giant Goliath in the age-old story. Earlier that night at the church, the nationally renowned political organizer and spiritual leader Reverend Traci Blackmon had told the congregation that the small, young David did not just kill the enormous Goliath—whom she equated to the poison of white supremacy—with a small pebble from his slingshot. He didn't stop with the pebble. After David killed Goliath, he cut off his head and held it up for all to see. Now is the time, she reminded us: "Let's show them love conquers hate." She said, with a sound that crashed through the microphone, that it was time to take off the head of the white supremacy giant. David's refrain, sung to the chorus of "Olam Chesed Yibaneh," became a conviction and fierce weapon. And of course David first achieved fame as a musician.

The response to hate cannot be just performing smooth, perfectly-in-tune versions of folk tunes, and it can't be just saying we stand against white supremacy. Those of us who teach at universities will have to admit that we can graduate not only the Richard Spencers but also his followers. When real live white supremacists show up, implicit bias training, inclusive syllabi, and safe-space statements don't do any good without a willingness to use the musical and musicological toolkit to hear the current situation and speak or sing out against it. This is a good time to remind everyone not only of the white supremacist traditions that are built into the bricks and mortar of the University of Virginia but also of the traditions of progressive faculty and student activism.

I want to conclude with a self-indulgent story about playing music. In the days after August 11 and 12, a makeshift memorial went up on Fourth Street in Charlottesville. The street is now famous because it is where James Alex Fields rammed his car into a crowd, killing Heather Heyer and injuring several others. Community members lined the street with flowers and chalked messages on the concrete. A newly opened spa cleansed the area with sage every night. With full cooperation from the police, people started bringing larger and larger items: a little bookcase, potted plants. There were a few large vigils with speakers and collective singing. One night a shaman came with her dog and chanted. Small children drew colorful pictures and read books someone left there; a few kids played their instruments. People talked quietly in small groups. Sometimes they cried. My jazz colleague and I started a ritual of playing trumpet and viola there at odd hours, early in the morning or late at night. An anonymous party stole music stands from the UVA music department and put them at the site; they melded into the drying plants, and kids chalked on them too. Sometimes people stopped to listen. One night a group of students who had been injured by the white supremacist's car came and sat on the ground; one young woman cried uncontrollably. I listened as much as I played. I don't think this music did any real collective healing work.

I understand now that although many people truly loved our tunes, this music making was about me. Maybe I wanted to finish the tune I couldn't finish on August 12 when we played our duo at a designated safe space. On that day, I was grateful to have the viola as an appendage. My son and I had flunked out of direct-action training. And despite making many impassioned speeches about not engaging the hate, I failed at that, too. By noon on Friday, August 11, I had already yelled at a white supremacist who wrote nasty things on a giant chalkboard we call the Free Speech Wall. I used my bare hands to try and rub it out. On the morning of August 12, I did get through one song just fine: "It Could Happen to You," written in 1943. I plucked the bass line as my son described an antifa guy with multiple knives and white nationalists with automatic weapons. But just before the bridge of Duke Ellington's 1935 "In a Sentimental Mood," I heard through a friend's cell phone that "both sides are armed and ready to fire. There's a state of emergency." The helicopters that had been buzzing for days seemed to speed up, and the sounds of feet walking and marching got louder and faster. I lost my place in a tune I can play in my sleep. I suspect that I played at the Fourth Street memorial site because I wanted to get my place back. I think we're all trying to get our place back.

NOTES

1. Hunton and Williams, *Final Report: Independent Review of the 2017 Protest Events in Charlottesville, Virginia,* Dec. 1, 2017, www.hunton.com/images/content/3/4/v2/34613/final-report-ada-compliant-ready.pdf, accessed Feb. 23, 2018.
2. The literature on German Romantic nationalism and its ties to the land and folk is vast. For one recent account, see Anthony D. Smith, *Nationalism: Theory, Ideology, History* (Cambridge, MA: John Wiley & Sons, 2013).
3. On efforts at the UVA, see President's Commission on Slavery and the University, http://slavery.virginia.edu, accessed Feb. 23, 2016.
4. Julia Ioffe, "Scenes from the Trump Hotel," *Politico Magazine,* Nov. 9, 2016, www.politico.com/magazine/story/2016/11/scenes-from-the-trump-hotel-214441.
5. This is a famous propaganda film directed by Hitler's favorite filmmaker, Leni Riefenstahl. It features speeches by Hitler and other Nazi leaders. It also made new and radical use of music and cinematography. There is a vast literature on the film. For one good example, see Mary Devereaux, "Beauty and Evil: The

Case of Leni Riefenstahl's *Triumph of the Will*," in *Aesthetics and Ethics: Essays at the Intersection*, ed. Richard W. Miller et al., 227–56 (Cambridge: Cambridge University Press, 1998). On the music, see Ben Morgan, "Music in Nazi Film: How Different Is *Triumph of the Will?*," *Studies in European Cinema* 3, no. 1 (2006): 37–53.

6. David Clay Large, *Nazi Games: The Olympics of 1936* (New York: Norton, 2007).

7. This is much discussed by historians. For an account see Large, *Nazi Games;* and Synthia S. Slowikowski, "Burning Desire: Nostalgia, Ritual, and the Sport-Festival Flame Ceremony," *Sociology of Sport Journal* 8, no. 3 (1991): 239–57.

8. *Richmond Daily Dispatch*, March 25, 1861.

9. Ibid., May 11, 1861.

10. The song was released in 1953 on the album *Songs by Tom Lehrer*. He released it on his own label, called Lehrer Records.

11. On cock rock, see Steve Waksman, "Every Inch of My Love: Led Zeppelin and the Problem of Cock Rock," *Journal of Popular Music Studies* 8, no. 1 (March 1996): 5–25. On the aesthetic appeal of cock rock, see Daphne A. Brooks, "The Write to Rock: Racial Mythologies, Feminist Theory, and the Pleasures of Rock Music Criticism," *Women and Music: A Journal of Gender and Culture* 12, no. 1 (2008): 54–62.

12. Raf Sanchez and Peter Foster, *Telegraph*, June 18, 2015, www.telegraph.co.uk/news/worldnews/northamerica/usa/11684957/You-rape-our-women-and-are-taking-over-our-country-Charleston-church-gunman-told-black-victims.html.

13. Karl Shapiro, *Person, Place and Thing* (New York: Reynal and Hitchcock, 1942).

14. See especially Gregory Michael Dorr, *Segregation's Science: Eugenics and Society in Virginia* (Charlottesville: University of Virginia Press, 2008).

15. "Delegates Urge Wider Practice of Sterilization," *Richmond Times-Dispatch*, Jan. 16, 1934.

16. On the cultural manifestations of eugenics, see Ewa Barbara Luczak, *Breeding and Eugenics in the American Literary Imagination* (New York: Palgrave Macmillan, 2015); and Betsy Nies, *Eugenic Fantasies: Racial Ideology in the Literature and Popular Culture of the 1920s* (New York: Routledge, 2002).

17. The basics of John Powell's life are in his obituary. "Obituary of John Powell," (Newport News, VA) *Daily Press*, Jan. 23, 1963. His correspondence concerning eugenics is in Box 39 Folder 8, Papers of John Powell, 1888–1978, Albert and Shirley Small Special Collections Library, University of Virginia.

18. On the Anglo-Saxon Clubs, see Paul A. Lombardo, "Miscegenation, Eugenics, and Racism: Historical Footnotes to *Loving v. Virginia*," *University of California, Davis Law Review*, 21, no. 421 (1988): 429.

19. On the UVA chapter, see Lombardo, "Miscegenation, Eugenics, and Racism," 429.

20. *Richmond News Leader*, June 5, 1923. This article was titled "Post No. 1, Anglo-Saxon Clubs, Has 400 Members." It was reprinted in a pamphlet of the Anglo-Saxon Clubs of America. Similar ideas are discussed in "The Price of Pollution," *News Leader*, June 15, 1923.

21. John Powell, "Music and the Nation," *Rice Institute Pamphlet* 10 no. 3 (July 1923): 132.

22. *Songs of the University of Virginia*, compiled and edited by Alfred Frederick Wilson (New York: Hinds, Noble and Eldredge, 1906). See also *Songs of the University of Virginia* (1936–37) RG-30/13/4.091.

23. For more on the connections between the idea of the Confederacy and football, see Christopher C. Nehls, "Flag-Waving Wahoos: Confederate Symbols at the University of Virginia, 1941–51," *Virginia Magazine of History and Biography* 110, no. 4 (2002): 469, 482–83.

24. On the violence in art, see Bryan Wagner, *Disturbing the Peace: Black Culture and the Police Power after Slavery* (Cambridge, MA: Harvard University Press, 2010). For a discussion of this particular tune, see James H. Dormon, "Shaping the Popular Image of Post-Reconstruction American Blacks: The 'Coon Song' Phenomenon of the Gilded Age," *American Quarterly* 40, no. 4 (1988): 450–71.

25. On coon songs and lynchings, see Karl Hagstrom Miller, *Segregating Sound: Inventing Folk and Pop Music in the Age of Jim Crow* (Durham, NC: Duke University Press, 2010), 48–52. On lynching as spectacle, see Amy Louise Wood, *Lynching and Spectacle: Witnessing Racial Violence in America, 1890–1940* (Chapel Hill: University of North Carolina Press, 2011).

26. Lisa Rab, "Meet the Preacher behind Moral Mondays," *Mother Jones*, April 14, 2014.

27. James Baldwin, "Everybody's Protest Novel" (1973), in *Notes of a Native Son* (Boston: Beacon Press, 1984).

RESPONDING

Ethical Commitments

ETHICS UNDER PRESSURE

An Autoethnography of Moral Trauma

WILLIS JENKINS

By the time torch-bearing white supremacists reached the Jefferson statue at the Rotunda on the night of August 11, the residents of Charlottesville had already lived through a year of intensifying pressure. Already there had been torches lighting a tableau of white terrorism, and already a candle-lit vigil in response; already there had been neo-Confederate rallies around statues, and already defiant counterprotests in answer; already there had been months of tactical work by white nationalist groups to turn Charlottesville into a symbolic battleground, and already months of fraught organizing for community defense by antiracist civic groups to oppose them. The moral and political dynamics surrounding the public reemergence of white supremacy were by August 2017 concentrated acutely in Charlottesville, such that most residents could not easily escape their affective stress.

Such a crucible affords a scholar of ethics an arena in which to observe how moral agents negotiate intensifying moral pressure. Treating the city as a "moral laboratory," in the term of anthropologist Mary Mattingly, a researcher could investigate the ways in which Charlottesville residents negotiate the stresses of their context and how they may try to open new possibilities within it. Mattingly uses the lab metaphor to focus attention on the "moral work" undertaken by agents to "create experiences that are also experiments in how life might or should be lived" and thereby reshape the possibilities of their social spaces.[1] In the case of Charlottesville, the "experiments" would be various enactments of how life might or should be lived when under pressure from white nationalist intimidation. The ethics scholar could then observe how residents worked with their inherited repertoires of moral ideas and civic practices to reckon with white nationalism, how those repertoires were challenged by the rising pressure on Charlottesville, and what participants did to open new possibilities of interpretation and action.[2]

However, over the past year I have been not only observing the pressure but also feeling it myself. I cannot analyze with ethnographic distance how the moral repertoire of others was challenged because my own sense of available responses has been stressed. Because I am, in that sense, involved in this lab as part of its experiment, my method here must rather proceed as a kind of autoethnography. This essay critically reflects on moral work I have undertaken amidst many others attempting to find the possibilities for life in a city under white nationalist siege.

Autoethnography is controversial as a method. Critics charge that it trespasses conventions of academic objectivity, foregrounds the researcher's own experience as a source for knowledge, and relies on affective narrative as proxy for analysis.[3] I am in fact usually dubious of work presenting itself as autoethnography for just those reasons. As a scholar of religious ethics, I would prefer to read a normative argument conducted in conversation with other recognized authorities without personal experience entering as implicit warrant.

Yet in the case of confronting contemporary white nationalism in Charlottesville, autoethnography offers a suggestive model for developing critical reflections on moral reasoning under pressure. In this case, the first-person subjectivity of the experiment may possibly be more aid than impediment to clear interpretation of the moral landscape of life in this city over the past year. In fact, I first wrote a version of this essay for other members of the community who had, in some form, vigorously opposed white supremacy and yet were, like me, subsequently struggling to find language to narrate their experience or to give an account of themselves after the attacks of August 2017.[4] We were struggling, I supposed, because of a kind of trauma—what we might call "moral trauma." If I could name and describe that trauma, I saw, it might help others understand how particular stresses of responding to white supremacy increased pressure on some of the very moral commitments that motivated us to take action in the first place. First-person ethical inquiry might help in explaining why—especially for other agents acting confidently from robust commitments to concrete actions—moral interpretation of our involvement became less rather than more stable. What made it difficult to give an account of ourselves?

MORAL TRAUMA

By the time torches neared the Jefferson statue at the Rotunda on the night of August 11, I was already well into an uncomfortable, first-person moral experiment. I had for a while participated in racial justice initiatives in the city—not as a researcher or professional ethicist but just as a white-embodied citizen who felt obligated to show up as I could. After the 2016 U.S. presidential election, local antiracist coalitions were forced to confront overt white supremacy as Charlottesville became, for a variety of reasons, a target of white nationalist organizing. Showing up became more perilous.

So it was that late on Friday, August 11, as armed and torch-bearing white supremacists marched through the University of Virginia, I found myself standing guard at the front doors of the mass meeting at St. Paul's Memorial Church where Traci Blackmon, Cornel West, and other leaders were speaking to hundreds of people. How did a religious studies professor end up in that position, you might wonder; surely security arrangements were in the hands of some more competent authority?

That question opens onto a destabilizing shift in perspective required of me and a number of others. A few hours earlier, for reasons that remain unclear, Charlottesville police had pulled back the officers initially promised to the church where the meeting was held, so organizers had scrambled to ask some allies for security help. I was asked to come help, not because I was experienced in security, but because I was nearby and trusted. By then organizers knew (and UVA administrators had been alerted) that there would be a torch-lit rally at the Rotunda, which was across the street from the church. There was chatter on alt-right social media that intimated threats to specific people inside the meeting. About ten of us stood on watch outside, all unarmed.

As the torches came into view at the Rotunda, someone sprinted across the street with an urgent message: students were holding their ground at the Jefferson statue at the bottom of the Rotunda steps with no one to defend them. She pleaded with us to go assist them. The lead organizer instructed us to remain at our posts, for there were hundreds of people in the church and no police in sight; our duty was to protect the assembly. The messenger cursed us in frustration and ran back. As it turned out, of course, the torches stopped at the Jefferson statue and encircled students and staff, who were first threatened and then assaulted. Police interceded some long minutes later.

I am haunted by that moment. Of course we should not have relayed to the crowd of untrained people inside the building, many already fearful of the situation outside, an invitation to confront an armed mob, and of course all of us standing guard could not have abandoned our post. But I am a faculty member, and those were our students. I implicitly trusted that university police (who surely, I thought, must be monitoring the danger) would step in before any bodily harm came to our students. That trust of course turned out to be naïve.

I have talked with many others who participated in various actions of that weekend and who now feel conflicted about what they did or about what happened. Some wish that they had made different decisions in particular moments, or that they had acted with more courage, or more discipline, or more creativity. Some who spent weeks planning and training wish that they had prepared differently. Others wish they had not followed official guidance from city and university to stay away and had joined the public opposition. Some who saw police allow thugs to attack unarmed residents in public spaces, or who were themselves attacked, now find themselves rethinking their security. Some are painfully wondering—as does Lisa Woolfolk in this volume—why the university seemed more eager to discipline students protesting white supremacy than the armed outsiders promoting it. Others—who found unlikely allies in antifa, militias, or anarchic networks of care—find their trust in formal civic orders shaken. Many are reeling from seeing white supremacy assert itself so proudly in public and their public institutions so hapless to oppose it.

We are experiencing moral trauma.[5] The commitments that compelled us to oppose white supremacists and the ideas that informed the diverse ways in which we actually acted on that August weekend are now haunted by what happened. Events have bruised those commitments and ideas, and we may wonder if, beneath the contusions, fractures have opened in our moral worlds. For some, that Friday and Saturday refuse to settle into a consistent pattern of interpretation and so irritate us into reconsidering the implicit trusts that shape our sense of a world, the practices by which we engage it, and the lexicon we use to give an account of it. Those of us with this experience find ourselves haunted; it seems that memory cannot settle events into past story because our experience has destabilized ideas and language for doing so.

What is the task of the academic ethicist in the face of moral trauma? It is not, I think, to solve various dilemmas of decision making (e.g., to rule on what would have been the correct decision outside the mass meeting). The more helpful intellectual inquiry interprets how people reconsider and renegotiate their moral repertoires as they grapple with difficult events and unexpected problems. Three fissures of moral thought, in particular, seemed to create internal friction for myself and for a number of other participants.

FREE SPEECH AND WHITE TERRORISM

One stress on residents was created by the perceived absence of moral competence by police, university, and city to adequately see and address the threat of white terrorism. Each institution depicted itself as constrained in its capacities to protect students and residents from white terrorism due to its obligations to protect rights to free speech of "alt-right protesters." Indeed, each presented itself as constrained to privilege that which (leaders of each institution were quick to say) all decent people should actually abjure. It is our sober duty to give succor to this dread monster, they seemed to say; please stay in your homes while we do.

The position held by civic institutions in regard of free speech thus intensified moral pressure on those who felt threatened by white supremacist violence or morally obligated to prevent it from terrorizing others. In advance of the August 12 rally, UVA's president, Teresa Sullivan, sent a message to all students and staff warning us to stay away. Any administrator would rightfully emphasize safety in the face of a potentially dangerous event, but Sullivan went beyond precaution to instruct us that "to approach the rally and confront the activists would only satisfy their craving for spectacle."[6] She quoted a white nationalist relishing the prospect of their opponents revealing themselves to be insane enforcers of political correctness in order to declare to every student and employee of UVA that any form of confrontation would amount to complicity. "The organizers of the rally want confrontation; do not gratify their desire."

With firsthand knowledge of how long and carefully some counterorganizers had been planning for this rally, I wrote to Sullivan, pointing out that her message disparaged the multiple local groups—including a nonviolent collective of faith leaders—who had principled reasons to risk confrontation, tactical ideas about how to do so effectively, and were holding training sessions for their members to prepare for the dangers. Sullivan responded by acknowledging that some might have reasons of conscience to protest directly but went on to insist: "Protest in other venues, including preach-ins, teach-ins, prayer meetings, etc., are also constitutionally protected—and face much reduced risk of danger in other locations."[7]

But whether protest in another location would enjoy the same constitutional protection was hardly the question with which organizers were concerned. They were, of course, asking themselves what forms of protest would most effectively confront a deadly ideology and most likely protect others from its violence. I declined to participate in the university's diversionary teach-in for the same reason I did not follow the mayor's instructions to stay home: neither would prevent these people from transforming Charlottesville into the symbolic capitol of white nationalism.

The fundamental aim of the organizers of the August 11 and 12 Unite the Right rallies was to show the world that white power could openly assert itself in symbolically important spaces, thus setting the stage for a white nationalist renaissance. There would be, they promised, a new dawn "after Charlottesville." Richard Spencer issued an August 11 manifesto entitled "The Charlottesville Statement," anticipating a watershed political moment.[8] Every person who showed up in public to refuse to cede them political space sensed that far greater peril lay in staying home than in risking confrontation. The greatest peril that day, we supposed, was in letting white terrorism stalk the city unopposed.

Civic leaders disagreed with our perception, however, charging us with inept complicity and implicit disrespect for freedom of political expression. By focusing on the abstract category of constitutionally authorized speech, civic leaders were obtuse to the specific threat of white terrorism. President Sullivan, Mayor Mike Signer, and other leaders treated that threat in formal abstraction: white supremacy as a specimen of hate speech, itself a category in derivative relation to the category of free speech. Thinking abstractly and ahistorically like that occluded clear perception.

Formal respect for free speech had in fact made me hesitate to join previous confrontations with white nationalists in Charlottesville. I wondered if I might be wrongly silencing views simply because I found them objectionable, or if I might be playing into their tactical weaponization of free speech claims. I have since heard from a number of residents who followed the official guidance to respect free speech and to stay away from the August 12 rally they now wish that they had joined the defense of the city. What did we need to see differently? The historical particularity of the threat represented by white supremacy.

White supremacy is singular because of its massive historical role in making the world in which we live in Charlottesville, in Virginia, in the United States. Those men were not simply uttering "hate speech"; they were reenacting the history of white domination in a context still riven by racialized inequalities in matters basic to life, liberty, and the pursuit of happiness. Allying themselves with the symbols and chants of genocidal Aryanism, bristling with torches and guns, and declaring in advance their readiness to kill in order to protect assertions of white power, they did not present us with a case of objectionable political expression. They presented us with white terrorism, which must be confronted sui generis.[9]

Those who came out to publicly confront it recognized that threat for what it was and did not heed official instructions to divert our attention or register our disagreement elsewhere. In doing so, however, some of us felt tension with respect that we do, after all, hold for freedom of speech and for the democratic importance of listening to views with which we disagree.[10] How to maintain that respect and enact its democratic virtues while also maintaining an uncompromising opposition to white terrorism was a tension negotiated through many uneasy tactical choices about the specific forms of protest one would create or join: Teach-in or protest? Permitted march or civil disobedience? Silent witness or loud confrontation? These choices were often made by affiliating with those individuals whose moral perception of the situation we most trusted, which, in the concrete moments those choices were made, at once revealed and reconstructed political alignments.

Those of us who took actions in contravention of official directives implicitly withdrew trust from the moral competence of our leaders and from the formal lexicon they used to frame the situation. By withdrawing that trust and resolving to stand in the way of white terrorists, even at peril to other values, some of us found ourselves on the boundary of incivility.

THE CIVIC IMPORTANCE OF INCIVILITY

When, that Friday night, several hundred torch-bearing young men transformed UVA's historic Lawn and Rotunda into a glowing theater of white supremacy, it was not an alien visitation but rather an attempt to revivify a major tributary of the university's own history. The march was led by two UVA alums, who, by focusing their two rallies around the statues of Jefferson and Lee, aimed to enact the white nationalist interpretation of our founding ideals that has in fact governed the greater part of this university's existence. In doing so, they forced us to confront how vulnerable our present is to its "past." As John Mason and Lisa Woolfolk record in their essays for this volume, UVA has long been an incubator for white supremacist ideologies. Those torch-bearers enacted the way white supremacy haunts us still, ever ready to reclaim its territory.

Yet another tributary of our history includes ideals of equality and justice that now support a prevailing university ethos in which diversities are valued and cosmopolitan inquiry prized. As Claudrena Harold shows in her essay for this volume, the university has been ambivalent in progress toward fully vindicating those ideals. Sustaining and realizing the ethos of inquiry we want depends not on forgetting and suppressing our white supremacist past, but rather on actively repudiating it and reparatively addressing its legacies. The university's interpretation of those ideals and our repudiation of their white nationalist version were tested that Friday night. Except for a handful of brave students and staff who circled around the statue of Jefferson, we—the university—failed. Defense of the ideals through which the university's white supremacist past now seems repugnant was left, when faced with actual white supremacists, to a small band prepared to be "incivil" in their resistance.

The historian Annette Gordon-Reed, who understands more clearly than most the conflicts within Jefferson, wrote that "the menaced people standing around the statue, no doubt holding many different views about Jefferson the man, symbolize the fragility of . . . the ideals that animated Jefferson in the Declaration, his insistence on the separation of church and state, his belief in public education, religious tolerance, and science."[11] In failing to protect our menaced people, we also failed to protect those ideals. The interpretation of the university to which most of us are now committed is vulnerable to (re)capture by white nationalism—which was precisely the point of such theatrical invasion. On the front pages of papers everywhere, the world saw the image of a university caught in a caesura of commitment, momentarily powerless to avoid being routed by its past. Almost: we owe to those who stood up to them at the Jefferson statue a debt of gratitude for refusing to politely cede the symbolic center of the university. When, a month later, some of the same students shrouded the same Jefferson statue in protest of the university's failures, they tacitly proposed that defending the university's ideals may sometimes require giving offense to those negligent in joining the defense.

On August 12 the city was defended more successfully by people indisposed to extend civility to those whose mission attacks fundamental conditions of our civic life. Some in the defense seem to have been well accustomed to incivility and indeed enthusiastic in its exercise. For others, including me, incivility was more uncomfortable. Some came ready to use violence to defend the city. Some had trained in nonviolent civil disobedience. Others would show in legal, permitted ways how hostile they were to an ideology of violence. In each form, civic defense seemed to depend on incivil actions.

Many UVA students were among those who defended Charlottesville on Saturday, some by marching and holding public space, others by providing legal observation and medical care in the streets, still others by staffing safe areas. Everyone had to make decisions about their civic responsibilities without help from the university, which, again, had called members to a diversionary teach-in. A university in a city expecting siege might have offered more helpful education, both for its students and citizens. It might have, for example, helped people better understand the risks and their contexts by holding workshops on the historical range of ways people have defended civic order with organized incivility. If we take our mission to be "developing responsible citizen leaders," then we should want to train leaders who understand the purposes of freedom, not just how to respect its formal rules.[12] There may be times that civic order depends on it.

By instead emphasizing that its members should prioritize safety and avoid incivility, the university followed the city in normalizing white terrorism as civic action deserving due respect. Students and staff who refused its counsel may have felt compelled to sharpen their suspicion of institutionalized white privilege at work in the leadership. Some, in order to clearly break from these normalizing processes, may then have felt increased obligation to perform their willingness to break with civility. While some thrilled to this possibility, for others it was nauseatingly difficult.

Religious relations with civility were also stressed. The young, upstart clergy who led the most visible forms of holy incivility to white supremacy are now celebrated. Yet their calls to action were not wholeheartedly embraced by local faith leaders, many of whom found that they could not bear association with incivility, no matter how principled. Most religious communities in fact stayed aloof. The senior pastor of one downtown church, which had initially offered itself as an assembly area for faith leaders going out for nonviolent direct action, decided that the church would not admit anyone involved in civil disobedience—including fellow clergy. That church's resolve to keep itself pure from incivility broke down in the intensity of the day, as wounded protesters came to their medical station, traumatized people streamed in crying, and finally, at the end of the day, that holy incivility clergy group found exhausted refuge there.

Incivility is not a good in itself; it is rather, in the understanding of many participants, a provisional deviation from social norms precisely in order to defend moral principles on which those norms rest. Had the streets of Charlottesville been filled with tens of thousands of peaceable residents, as they were in Boston a week later when white supremacists attempted to rally there, the range of possibilities for defense of the city would have expanded—even without any better response from university, city, and state. But when polite people stay home for fear of appearing indecorous in their opposition to evil, then the options narrow for those not content to cede civic space to white supremacists. Indeed, that civic absence made it more difficult for people of conscience to resist in ways consistent with all that their consciences hold true. Because they were not joined by thousands of colleagues, those who did risk incivility to testify against white supremacy found themselves even more exposed—bodily and morally.

NONVIOLENCE RECONSIDERED

On Saturday, August 12, a line of nonviolent faith leaders stood defenseless against terrorists. In full view of police who were content to allow a line of nonviolent clergy be smashed by white supremacists, they were charged by men with clubs and shields, only to be rescued from serious assault through a last-moment intercession by antifascists with their own clubs and shields.[13] One nonviolent faith leader later described antifa "as angels" to her in that moment, a sentiment repeated publicly by Cornel West and others whose commitments have been steadfastly nonviolent up until this point.[14] I have heard from several people who were working without weapons to try to protect others, or who were themselves nonviolent protesters, that they are now reconsidering their commitments to nonviolence.

Charlottesville that Saturday offered a peculiar context to apply the received patterns of reflection on justified political violence. Government actors set the stage in a way that showed that they had rewritten the rules of engagement: they would protect white supremacists inside Emancipation Park, but the dozen city blocks around it were given over to whoever could take them by force. There were implicit limits to what combatants could do, for overhead a team of state police snipers surveilled the scene through rifle scopes while down below private militias offered their own on-the-ground policing. Yet no one really knew what would cause either force to open fire—the rules of engagement were hidden from the people they were supposed to protect.

That strange arena stressed settled commitments regarding use of political violence. Unauthorized interventions of force seemed necessary simply to protect those lawfully and nonviolently registering public opposition to marauding white supremacists. Since law enforcement agencies were not going to do that, nonviolent residents found themselves reliant on those who came prepared to intervene on their own authority, with their own weapons. In light of their dependence, some nonviolent protesters subsequently wondered about their implicit approval of deployments of force by others. Which raised for some another question: Was it also legitimate for residents not only to defend others from violence but also to forcibly repel the terrorists?

Deliberations over just use of political violence are of course ancient to a number of traditions. A range of plausible positions can authorize informal intercessions with violence for self-defense, for the sake of protecting others, and possibly even for repelling an unjust enemy. That is not novel; I just mean that people fluent with those traditions, who thought that they knew their place among them, now find themselves less sure because of what happened in Charlottesville. For example, some nonviolent protesters, having witnessed how reluctant city, university, and state police forces were to defend residents from white terrorism, have begun to train themselves to intervene with force the next time. Witnessing the appearance of racist asymmetry in deployments of police violence (the only intervention on August 12 was to protect a white nationalist), some even call for the abolition of police and an alternative organization for community defense.[15]

Let me hasten to say that, as one with a primary commitment to nonviolence, I worry about those renegotiations. Deploying violent force seems almost to require, as a kind of psychic defense mechanism, dehumanizing one's target. Violence makes it difficult to retain the humanity of one's enemies. The antifa banner condemning "fascist scum" on August 12 was just a half-step from the vermin epithets that often moralize exterminative or genocidal thinking—not dissimilar from the systemic dehumanization that antifa oppose.

For myself, I hold that we must keep faith with the humanity of terrorists, even while directly and uncompromisingly opposing their attempts to terrorize. Moreover, taking up arms in distrust of government competence to keep the peace places one in a frightening political world—one represented by those private militia—where violent actions can be justified by recursively reinforcing interpretations of corrupt government or inhuman enemies. I am not quite ready to live in that world. But I am much more uneasy with the one I am inhabiting.

CONCLUSION: RESILIENCE AND
TRAUMA RECONSIDERED

By the time the torches reached the Jefferson statue on August 11, Charlottesville had already lived through 255 years of white supremacy. That is our ongoing challenge. It should be easy to oppose Nazis when they oblige to identify themselves with actual Nazi flags and accessorize themselves with torches and guns. That it was so difficult for us sobers my view of the prospects for reckoning with the history to which they gave expression: the pathology of white supremacy that moralizes resentment and inequality through yearnings for meaning and identity.

The ideology that raised monuments to white power in the Jim Crow era—including Charlottesville's Lee statue—has been resilient. It continues to coil through U.S. politics, shaping moralizations and resentments to support policies that, in material consequence, continue to inscribe white supremacy into how we are housed, policed, governed, educated, and monied. I am, in a peculiar way, grateful for what those angry men made explicit, for I have now threatening faces that personify the ongoing reproduction of white supremacy that we must confront with still greater determination, creativity, and courage. For once in my white-embodied life, I viscerally experienced what others have known longer and more intimately: what it looks like for police, city, and university to protect that monster rather than those it threatens.

That has not left me unchanged. The moral trauma I experienced in opposing white terrorism in person shook me, but it has been also transformational; the experiments I undertook over the past year have realigned the ideas, trusts, and commitments through which I understand responsibilities for dismantling white supremacy and possibilities for repairing its legacies. Reflecting on those experiments is laying groundwork for better ones.

Neither should the experience leave the university unchanged. For anyone with a sense of the historical resilience of white power in U.S. history, what now menaces Charlottesville cannot be surprising. Yet the experience *should* continue to morally traumatize us, to shake our ideas and commitments, and to lead us into better experiments in how the life of the university we want to remember might take shape amidst the legacies of the university we have actually been.

NOTES

1. Mary Mattingly, *Moral Laboratories: Family Peril and the Struggle for a Good Life* (Berkeley: University of California Press, 2014), 27.

2. The cultural toolkit metaphor comes from Ann Swidler, "Culture in Action: Symbols and Strategies," *American Sociological Review* 2 (1986): 273–86. I have written about inventing new moral possibilities from inherited toolkits in Willis Jenkins, *The Future of Ethics: Sustainability, Social Justice, and Religious Creativity* (Washington, DC: Georgetown University Press, 2013).

3. On methodological controversies over ethnography, see the argument among the following three articles: Carolyn Ellis, Tony Adams, and Arthur Bochner, "Autoethnography: An Overview," *Forum: Qualitative Social Research* 12, no. 1 (2011); Paul Atkinson, "Rescuing Autoethnography," *Journal of Contemporary Autoethnography* 35, no. 4 (2006): 400–04; Sara Delamont, "Arguments against Autoethnography," *Qualitative Researcher* 4 (Feb. 2007): 2–4, www.cardiff.ac.uk/socsi/qualiti/QualitativeResearcher/QR_Issue4_Feb07.pdf.

4. See also John Edwin Mason's essay in this volume, "History, Mine and Ours: Charlottesville's Blue Ribbon Commission and the Terror Attacks of August 2017."

5. "Moral trauma," as I use the term here, differs from "moral injury," which presupposes an integrity that has been violated by being compelled to do something that the agent holds as immoral or compromised. Moral injury has begun to feature in diagnoses of PTSD for some war veterans, and a discourse has arisen to understand and treat it. Moral trauma may not necessarily be the result of a violation of some standing integrity. If the experience causes one to rethink one's initial commitments, to reconsider implicit trusts, to realign and reconstruct one's moral world with a different understanding of reality, then subsequent interpretation may narrate the trauma as revelatory or positively transformational. I call it "trauma" because it presents itself similarly: temporal intrusion, haunting recollections, and disruption of memory processes and narrative accounting.

6. Mass communication, "An Important Message from Teresa A. Sullivan Regarding August 12," Aug. 4, 2017.

7. Teresa Sullivan, personal communication with the author, Aug. 6, 2017.

8. Richard Spencer, "The Charlottesville Statement," Aug. 11, 2017, https://altright.com/2017/08/11/what-it-means-to-be-alt-right.

9. For a formal legal complaint asserting that white supremacists conspired to terrorize, see *Elizabeth Sines et al. v. Jason Kessler et al.,* www.integrityfirstforamerica.org/sites/default/files/Complaint.pdf, accessed Feb. 24, 2018.

10. See Risa Goluboff, "Where Do We Go from Here?," in this volume, on the deep constitutional tensions at issue, including the double bind for universities obligated by both the First Amendment and Title VI of the Civil Rights Act. I do not pretend to glibly solve those tensions here; I rather point out how obtuse and untrustworthy seemed official guidance, which left moral agents to negotiate those tensions on their own.

11. Annette Gordon-Reed, "Charlottesville: Why Jefferson Matters," *New York Review of Books,* Aug. 19, 2017.

12. University Code of Ethics and Mission Statement, www.virginia.edu/statement ofpurpose, accessed Feb. 24, 2018.

13. This moment is recounted in Hunton and Williams, *Independent Review of 2017 Protest Events in Charlottesville, Virginia,* 129, www.charlottesville.org/home/showdocument?id=59615, accessed Feb. 24, 2018.

14. Rebekah Menning, quoted in Dahlia Lithwick, "What the Alt-Left Was Actually Doing in Charlottesville," *Slate* Aug. 16, 2017, www.slate.com/articles/news_and_politics/politics/2017/08/what_the_alt_left_was_actually_doing_in_charlottesville.html.

15. Hunton and Williams, *Independent Review,* 128.

DIALOGUE IN BAD TIMES

RACHEL WAHL

THE WRITING ON THE WALL

There is a short, black wall on the downtown pedestrian mall in Charlottesville. It is familiar to residents as the "Free Speech Wall," or to many of the city's children, as, less ambitiously, the "Chalk Wall." Anyone can leave their ideas or drawings etched across its surface.

In less politically charged times, the speech on display might have disappointed those hoping for a robust and challenging exercise of the First Amendment, which is engraved on part of the wall's surface. The wall for a while served primarily as a site where one might root for a favored athletic team or try out an outré turn of the phrase. Such observers may have been increasingly relieved, and then, perhaps, increasingly alarmed, as the 2016 election neared. The wall became political.

Good, I thought, observing this shift. A public conversation.

Quickly, though, the missives on the wall turned to personal attacks on local politicians. It seemed a vehicle to scare those individuals rather than to persuade a public to adopt an ideal or policy. But no matter the content, then and now, it is all washed away every so often by hose or sponge, leaving a clean and open surface. With each washing, the possibility returns of that good public conversation.

The wall sits a few blocks from the site where Heather Heyer was killed. As the world now knows, she bravely protested the groups espousing hate that marched on our downtown on August 12, 2017. For a very short time afterward, the wall was transformed by two powerful murals. One showed soldiers defeating Nazis in a display that connected Charlottesville's struggle to a longer historical one, against not only foreign power but also, one felt at the time, against evil itself. The other was a drawing of Heather's face, lest we forget. These murals were washed away too soon.

Eventually, the wall again became a site of political contestation. In the days after August 12, it was a vehicle for a city in mourning to express its hope and outrage. Hope that love and resistance might together overcome hate and oppression. Outrage that, some felt, the city had failed to protect them.

Around October 2017, a message started to appear regularly. In large, bold letters that stood apart from the other missives, it proclaimed: "Final Exam: Did you learn to love?" The words appeared over and over. They were on different sides of the wall. The wall would be cleaned, and they would be back the next day. Similar messages were sometimes etched nearby. One read, "Kindness is free."

One day, another message appeared underneath this assertion. It argued, "You must have a lot of privilege. Justice > kindness." Justice is greater than kindness.

This chalked exchange encapsulates a central tension that has animated deep animosity in the months leading up to and following August 12, 2017. From concerts for unity to city hall meetings disrupted by protesters, what has divided the town is not only or even primarily the opposition between overt racism and those who fight against it; as city residents keep reminding ourselves as a kind of mantra to calm our frayed nerves, most of the rally attendees were, we still hope, from out of town. Rather, what has divided city-dwellers is precisely how such racism should be combatted.

One way that this divide reveals itself in Charlottesville is through the intense contestation regarding whether and how communities should engage with institutional authorities. Disruptions of city council meetings, for example, have given rise to deep disagreements over the value of "civility."[1] Does its value lie in the necessary respect for others and for order that allows the city to accomplish worthy public aims, or is civility the pretense that enables racist norms and policies to continue unabated? Should we try to talk to each other or focus on protest and lawsuits? What is a waste of time or even harmful?

Contributors to this volume reveal the stakes of this debate. Reflecting on the misplaced nostalgia for a civil rights movement defined by peaceful music and good feelings, for example, Bonnie Gordon notes that antiracist activism is often anything but calm. Dr. Martin Luther King, she states pointedly, warned us to beware moderates who hope only to ease tensions.

I have been studying dialogue across such divides for several years now, and I am as interested in the flaws of dialogue as in its benefits. Yet I have also helped to organize these conversations. So when I hear this warning about moderates, I stop breathing for a moment. For dialogue between city officials and activists in Charlottesville might be understood as precisely such a misstep. While uncomfortable, though, such potential critiques can draw needed attention to the question of what—if any—good might be derived from dialogue between particular people, at some particular time.

It is on this question that I have focused my research.[2] Yet it must remain precisely that—a question—in each new endeavor. In any proposed meeting, is the aim to diffuse tension, and if so, for what purpose? Is ameliorating tension the only aim, and if not, what are the others? Are these worthy aspirations? No solution is complete or appropriate for every circumstance.

In what follows, then, I will not suggest that dialogue alone can secure a just society: city officials and community activists would be united in their laughter at that idea. It is not my intention that anyone should abandon the many tools of democracy to build a good society through talk alone. And as I will say throughout this piece, I do not "recommend" dialogue. By this I mean that nobody should be asked to take on the burden of personal exposure. Especially in the aftermath of what Willis Jenkins in this volume rightly refers to as "moral trauma," such exchanges can sometimes do more harm than good. What I offer here aims to open up possibilities for those who feel called to dialogue. This is meant to be reassurance that there may still be reasons to engage in dialogue, as uncertain and troubled an endeavor as it most certainly is.

DIALOGUE

On August 12 I spoke to a small gathering of people about the possibility of dialogue. At the time we met, the day had not yet revealed the suffering it would contain. The discussion ended at noon, just before the state of emergency was called and we dispersed. We discussed the meaning of dialogue between many different kinds of groups that on that day seemed poised to deepen in their animosity toward each other, but because of the nature of my research, we particularly wondered whether and how it might unfold between police and community activists.

In the weeks leading up to August 12, antiracist activists and police had planned to meet to discuss how to avoid violence on that already-dreaded day. Ultimately, the police could not come, due to a rally-related emergency city council meeting that they were compelled to attend.

Months later, kindness to those on the other side of any line seems a luxury lost, even in times when one might have a good reason to trust that other side. Justice must be pursued because trust in others' decency has failed.

Yet even in the worst of times, some feel drawn to try. For some community members as well as police, this effort may be rooted in a personal desire to understand people who seem so distant from oneself. For others, it may be a burning need to tell one's story to a person who, one feels, has not fully recognized the particularities of one's circumstances or even one's humanity. Still others may feel committed, due to their professional roles or their stake in the community, to more productive relationships between groups who are divided, which they may see as involving cooperative problem solving or even just decreased animosity. Many pursue dialogue for all of these reasons, hoping they can all transpire through human contact.

I have seen local police officers and community members sit down with each other with these aims. I have seen civilians who are no less opposed to each other due to deep political divides gather together with the same aspirations. All come knowing that dialogue is no panacea. Indeed, people who participate in dialogue are more likely to harbor fears that it is worthless than to err on the side of wild optimism about its potential.

This essay addresses that fear. As I will reiterate and elaborate on below, I do not intend to suggest that people *should* engage in dialogue with their opponents when they do not already feel drawn to it; nor do I suggest that dialogue should displace other methods of building a good and just society. People want many things from dialogue, but dialogue can never be a prescription. Even in more stable times, in times marked more by their tedium than their trauma, I would not "recommend" dialogue. Human understanding can be borne of neither force nor edification.

Instead of recommending dialogue, then, I will offer some reflections on what I have observed in attempts between divided groups to speak with each other and the possibilities for its unfolding in the wake of public trauma such as has occurred in Charlottesville. I consider a countercase: What unfolds between public officials and community activists in the absence of attempts at mutual understanding? I examine this to consider what is at stake, and what might be gained and lost, in attempts to speak with others.

I take up this inquiry in a setting far removed from the statue of Robert E. Lee. I do so in the tradition of peace educators, who often begin an analysis of social cleavages using a distant setting that is less likely to trigger the deep wellspring of emotion in one's own context. Such distance allows us to examine what has unfolded without the proximity that makes such initial investigation so painful. This case, then, is located in North India, where I spent twelve months interviewing law enforcement officers enrolled in a human rights education program. I wanted to understand how police respond to antitorture efforts and so conducted sixty in-depth interviews with thirty-three police officers as well as thirty-five human rights activists and educators in the states of Delhi, Haryana, Uttar Pradesh, and Punjab.

A DIFFERENT SETTING

"When people see us coming, they say, 'There are a police officer and two people.' They don't say, 'There are three people.'"

"The human rights activists do not understand that the police officer is also a man."

These are the kinds of comments I heard often during the year I spent interviewing police officers in North India. Over and over, police told me that they felt dehumanized by human rights activism. It also made them angry. Activists have no idea what police work entails, police lamented, yet they tell us that we are bad and incompetent and try to ruin our lives. To make matters worse, these activists, the police believed, live far easier lives than they do, yet condemn police for abuses of power. They hated activists. At best, they thought them a joke.

What were these activists doing that was so offensive? In India torture and extrajudicial killing are pervasive, even commonplace. This violence has many sources, including criminal gangs and corrupt politicians. But many human rights groups point to local police who at times use violence not in disobedience of superiors but in fact at their behest and under the direction of elected officials.[3] Human rights activists use every tool at their disposal to try to stop it. This typically involves public-shaming campaigns, such as publishing reports and sharing stories with the media that call out perpetrators for specific instances of wrongdoing. This also involves bringing cases to the national or state human rights commissions and sometimes involves lawsuits, though in India it is not possible to bring a state official to court without prior permission of the government.

I did not interview criminal gangs or politicians, but police in India told me that this activism limits somewhat their use of violence. Knowing that they could be publically shamed or dragged through a lengthy court case may make it less worthwhile to use extrajudicial violence, even if it is demanded by other sections of society. I wish to emphasize: *even one life protected by such restraint is worth everything.*

However, these tactics do not persuade police in India that such violence is wrong or that there is any reason to use nonviolent methods at times when they are less likely to be caught. To be sure, some officers are opposed to violence such as torture, but not because they have been shamed by activists. One officer I interviewed, for example, spoke passionately of his opposition to torture due to his Hindu religious commitments. But many officers see this violence as the only way to uphold justice in an atmosphere of pervasive lawlessness and corruption, where the formal legal system functions badly. Given that police understand themselves as doing their best in a bad system, activism that shames them does little to inspire their desire to protect rights. As one officer put it, due to human rights campaigns, the police "operate less."

There are vast differences between policing in India and the United States. Yet one similarity is the distrust and suspicion between some activists and police officers. There is the assumption of bad faith on both sides, with similar consequences here and abroad.

Why does this matter? Who cares how police and activists feel about each other? one might ask. What matters is whether the right laws are passed, that the right people are held accountable, the right people are punished.

In fact, Indian police and human rights activists might find common ground in this view. Both orient their work to a conception of justice premised in accountability and punishment for the guilty. Police in India concede that they cannot know that every person they suspect is guilty, but believe that they must sometimes use violence to find out. They do know that this is against *the law* in the sense of actual legislation. But they believe that given a context of pervasive corruption and judicial inefficiency, using violence that violates the law is, however ironically, the only way to uphold *the law* in the sense of social order.

Human rights activists are appalled at this compromise. Many police in countries with different constraints and incentives may be similarly distressed. But they may share the premise that discipline is the key ingredient in justice. Human rights activists, for example, acknowledge that low-ranking police in India are themselves abused by supervisors, work in abysmal conditions, and have little autonomy. They aver, however, that excusing torture on these grounds would give carte blanche to the practice. In other words, people who are not fully culpable must be held accountable if justice is to be attained.

I do not mean to equivocate. Bringing someone to court or firing them from their job is not comparable to torture. What is similar though is the orientation to punitive measures as the surest means to transform society. This orientation—the belief that only coercion brings progress in regard to the people one views as causing the problem—makes dialogue, to say the least, a challenge.

PROBLEMS AND POSSIBILITIES

Laws matter. But continued antipathy can sometimes limit how much they matter. For there will always be enough discretion so that what is in people's hearts shapes what they do in this world. And deepened polarization can constrain the extent to which efforts to reform our society can feel like projects on behalf of the common good. It erases the idea that such a thing could exist. Whatever the other side does then becomes something worth fighting.

This does not mean that we stop fighting for justice. Many people, in fact, engage in protest *and* try to build relationships with people they oppose. They may put their bodies on the line at a rally one day and sit down to have a careful conversation with police the next. Many police, too, seek to do their part in upholding justice, such as through assuring the punishment of people who have broken the law, while also working to build relationships with people in the communities they serve. Indeed, many people are simply trying to do everything possible to create a good and just society.

Yet as many frustrated participants in formal or informal dialogues know, it is not enough for people to sit in a room together and talk. Words must be received by people who listen. A great deal of scholarship has been devoted to the barriers to good listening. As is often noted, the inequality that exists outside the room rarely remains outside of it. For one, people who speak in accordance with the norms of the dominant culture may be considered more rational and credible, even if they are not.[4] The voices of the less powerful may not truly be heard, even if they speak.[5]

Moreover, when activists walk into a room to dialogue, they walk in as activists. When police enter, they enter as police. How could it be otherwise? Yet nobody wants to be in conversation with people who view them with suspicion. Neither activists nor police wish to open themselves to those who see them as the problem. They may talk to them. But receptivity is harder.

Is it possible, then, to suspend suspicion? Is it possible to engage the issues that divide us, to address that which lies at the center of our rifts, yet at the same time remain receptive to the person before us?

One reason it does not feel possible is because sometimes it does not feel ethical. Suspending suspicion and remaining receptive often feels like a betrayal of what is true, of justice itself. But I *do* know who this person is, or what this institution does, one might object. Receptivity may undermine my capacity to deal with them as their past actions have proved they require.

These fears are heightened in dialogue between state officials and people who have been oppressed. It is one thing to ask for such consideration between groups who share roughly equal status. But it is a different matter when there is significant inequality between groups—and when one group holds direct power over another. Long histories of legal and societal racism are a striking example. Moreover, people may legitimately worry that if state officials believe that they can ameliorate critiques by talking, this could undermine the pressure exerted by lawsuits and public shaming. Even if it doesn't have that effect, some worry, it might simply be a waste of energy that could be better used elsewhere.

Furthermore, contemporary liberal common sense is that we must think systemically. We must reform or transform institutions. We must understand that racism is structural and systemic. We must work against these structures and systems.

These concerns are important. I would never recommend as a general rule that people engage in dialogue rather than engage in explicitly political and legal processes to secure justice. Indeed, scholars have attempted to determine when deliberation between state officials (such as police) and communities is appropriate and when communities should rely on protest and lawsuits to pursue change.[6] I do not believe that such an assessment can be made outside of the particularities of each situation and the people involved.

Indeed, although it may be unsatisfying as a suggestion, the appropriate time for dialogue can only be sensed by particular people in particular situations. Which is why what I suggest is not a formula for determining when to talk and when to fight, but rather the cultivation of a sensitivity to assess when there might be an opening to do the former. These openings may occur within or totally outside of formal dialogues. And they may have little to do with consensus on policies, though they may help build up to this in the long run. Rather, the opening may simply be to see the persons in our midst as persons who suffer as we do.

For if we see individuals as synonymous with the systems, structures, and groups of which they are a part, this is dehumanizing. People feel it, and as a result they resent those who are trying to do good work. Rhetoric against reformers then starts to feel satisfying, because it reassures people that those who hate them are wrong. And polarization deepens. Reform is met with greater resistance.

It is not only to avoid deepening resistance, though, that dialogue might be valuable. It might contain the potential to change the hearts and minds of those with whom we speak. But here is the rub: we cannot aim for that directly. For when people perceive themselves as appreciated for their own sake, they are receptive. When we feel that we are a means to someone else's ends, we resist.

I will offer examples from a second distant setting that exemplifies a no less divisive dynamic: dialogues between university students who voted for Donald Trump or Hillary Clinton. These dialogues began in the weeks following Trump's inauguration between students at the University of Pennsylvania and Cairn University, an evangelical Christian school. They have since expanded to include many universities in Pennsylvania. I have been observing these sessions and conducting in-depth interviews with the students who participate.

These students are not haunted by the long history of distrust that characterizes relations between police and communities. Yet they are deeply opposed to each other's ideas and see each other's views—if not each other—as the cause of the country's problems. As such, many wondered if the only meaningful form of dialogue would be that in which they succeed in changing how the other side votes. Mutual understanding may feel good, some worried, but accomplish little.

Yet the deepest changes occurred when people experienced others as not trying to change them at all. A young man I interviewed, for example, recalled:

> There's one moment where I had to sort of catch myself moving towards the defensive position. . . . Once everyone's political stance and vote had been made known to everyone, and I realized that I was . . . outnumbered, in terms of Trump to Hillary. And there was a question concerning Donald Trump. . . . I just sort of noticed in myself, "Oh, I'm all alone in this now?" And for a moment, feeling like I have to defend myself and defend Donald Trump as well. But I was able to catch it, and say no. . . . Having seen how they were interacting in the conversations already, they weren't seeking to attack or tear down anybody. So I was able to relax and say no, I don't necessarily need to respond in that way. I can continue to respond honestly.

In this case, it was the sense that he did not need to defend his position that allowed him to soften it. He did not need to defend Trump, because the people he was speaking with did not attack him for voting for Trump. Hence, he could be honest about the ways in which he, like all people, harbors doubts and questions about his own position. Another student went even further, explaining that at the end of the evening, "I [was] not sure if we all agreed with each other," but that he "definitely came away thinking differently about certain things that I thought were pretty clear to me." Among the issues on which he had shifted in his opinion were public funding for education and the admission of refugees into the United States. He came to a new understanding of how educational inequality deepens social inequality. He was persuaded that while American security remains important, there may be reason to balance it with humanitarian concern for people escaping war. When I asked him what made those changes possible, he replied, "We were all pretty relaxed . . . and it was just a good conversation. *Nobody really tried to bend anybody.* People were very respectful."

Such clear-cut shifts in perspective were not common. More frequent was the sense that the "other side" is more reasonable—and more human—than one had previously realized and an opening to the *possibility* of being moved by their ideas. But in the rare moments when people did discuss a changed perspective, it was in a setting in which they had relaxed their guard.

Even in the hardest of settings, in dialogues I observed between police and communities, it was during similar moments in which suspicion was suspended that shifts seemed possible. One white police officer remarked of an African American woman who was present at the dialogue, "She says, 'I understand.' Do you know how disarming that is?" This woman's willingness to acknowledge his experience "disarmed" this officer. Although this moment's relationship to actual disarming is unknown, it creates an opening in which the attempt at understanding might be reciprocated. Indeed, this same officer praised an African American attorney who attended the dialogue. Recalling how much he valued her efforts to work with the police to discuss ways of deescalating stops of youth, he then felt moved to imagine what it might be like if his own son were stopped regularly by the police after having done nothing wrong. He imagined in particular how angry he might feel. I do not know whether this officer's willingness to put himself in another's position was inspired by the recollection of this attorney's spirit of collaboration, but it might have helped him to feel less defensive.

None of this suggests that people should be inhibited from expressing anger and pain borne of oppression. As I argue at length elsewhere, democracies thrive on the assertion of rights and the freedom of expression, not polite goodwill alone.[7] Moreover, I do not offer these few examples as proof that dialogue "works" or any such nebulous claim.

The many tools of democracy and the law should not be abandoned to rely only on goodwill and the humanization of others. Nor should oppression or criminal acts be ignored. Yet there is a possibility that within and around other work, something between persons might transpire that opens up new avenues for moving forward. Nobody should be tasked with what can be a too-heavy burden of first-person interaction. But for those who feel drawn to it but fear it is in vain, this essay is meant to provide the suggestion that the uncertainty of these endeavors should not detract from their potential importance.

CONCLUSION

Over a year before August 12, a local police officer remarked on the need for relationships between police and the community. For if we don't have relationships, he concluded, "We are going to have an intifada."

Is it appropriate to speak of building relationships between the police and communities in the wake of August 12? There are few things that are clear about this question. But there are three points that emerge as more reliable than the rest.

The first is that any attempt at kindness cannot neglect questions of justice. Neither the police nor communities will hold much love in their hearts if they feel the one aims to bypass the latter. Views of who should be held accountable, and for what, differ wildly, and avoiding these conflicts will provide only the thinnest of veneers over what everyone knows divides them. In other contexts in which intifada is a reality, programs to bring opposing sides together have been criticized on precisely these grounds. Peace educators have had great success, for example, in forming connections between Palestinians and Israelis when they are removed from the active conflict. Programs that take people to another country, or even to a neutral space in their own backyards, have made lasting impressions on countless participants. Yet what occurs when they return to a setting of inequality and violence? Moreover, critics point out, when these programs encourage participants to recognize each other's humanity but obscure the ways in which political and economic inequality erodes their wellbeing, they may do great harm.

Yet at the same time, it is likely that starting with justice will leave both sides unmoved and even deepen divides. If politics is war by other means, then dialogue that begins from politics is protest by other means. My own research has shown that possibilities emerge when people first humanize each other and then move on to the substantive issues that divide them.[8] This humanization involves both understanding each other as people beyond the positions each occupies and recognizing the experiences that have formed the way they feel, think, and act in those positions. Humanization is a necessary but insufficient condition of good dialogue; it is necessary for later discussions of divisive issues to be productive, but on its own would likely be viewed as a distraction from what matters. In other words, kindness should never replace justice, but it may sometimes precede it.

Second, dialogue can never be a prescription. I have asked myself countless times whether I could be in dialogue with someone who I believe threatens the life of those I love. I doubt it. I might collapse from the burden of proving my humanity. I am in awe of people like Daryl Davis, an African American musician who befriended Ku Klux Klan members and through his goodness transformed many of their lives. I do not know if I could be so strong. Hence, I do not "recommend" dialogue as a blanket "solution" to every divide. It is rather what one does when one feels called to understand, when one is moved to mending.

Third, it may be that dialogue cannot begin between institutions and groups. Eventually, forums between police and communities might restart and be productive. But the opposition now may be too dense. It may instead begin between people, who are always easier to speak with than organizations.

In the weeks after August 12, a local police officer deeply troubled by how the day had unfolded reached out to me with the desire to repair relationships with the community. I contacted a local community organizer, who relayed that people were grieving but still eager to talk. Complications regarding the lawsuit against the city and the ongoing investigation led the officer to believe that the meeting should be postponed, a judgment that disappointed and saddened the officer.

When I relayed this to the local activist who had been organizing with other community members, the activist replied with a counteroffer: "How about if we meet as people, instead of representatives of organizations? How about if we just have lunch?"

I conveyed this message to the police officer, who responded, "That is just about the nicest offer I have had in some time." The relief was palpable, even in the stale medium of the text message.

This lunch hasn't happened quite yet, though not due to any lack of willingness on the part of the officer. We are not humans alone, untethered from our web of professional, political, and personal commitments. But the possibility floats before me, giving me hope that there is a way forward. This is not because such a meeting will solve the complex problems of this town, but because it is a reminder that there are many people with this intention. This is a place not to end, but to begin.

NOTES

1. See, for example, "Incivility at City Council Meetings Defended," *Charlottesville Tomorrow*, Jan. 14, 2018, www.cvilletomorrow.org/news/article/29570-incivility -at-council-meetings-defended.

2. For more on my research, see Rachel Wahl, "Learning from Our Enemies: Human Nature, Democratic Conflict, and the Risks of Dialogue," in *Philosophy of Education 2017* (Urbana: University of Illinois Press, 2018); Wahl, "No Justice, No Peace: The Police, People of Color, and the Paradox of Protecting Human Rights," *Human Rights Quarterly* 39, no. 4 (2017): 811–31; and Wahl and S. White, "Deliberation, Accountability, and Legitimacy: A Case Study of Police-Community Forums," *Polity* 49, no. 4 (2017): 489–517.

3. Commonwealth Human Rights Initiative: *Police Reform Debates in India* (2011), www.humanrightsinitiative.org/index.php?option=com_content&view =article&id= 182&Itemid=511, accessed Feb. 24, 2018; *Feudal Forces: Reform Delayed (Moving from Force to Service in South Asian Policing)* (2010); *Police Accountability: Too Important to Neglect, Too Urgent to Delay* (2005), www.humanrights initiative.org/publications/chogm/chogm_2005/default.htm, accessed Feb. 24, 2018. See also personal interviews with the staff of the Human Rights Law Network (2012); personal interviews with the staff of the Commonwealth Human Rights Initiative (2012); and personal interviews with the Asian Centre for Human Rights (2012).

4. Jane Mansbridge et al., "The Place of Self-Interest and the Role of Power in a Deliberative Democracy," *Journal of Political Philosophy* 18, no. 1 (March 2010): 64–100; Daniel S. Allen, *Talking to Strangers: Anxieties of Citizenship since Brown v. Board of Education* (Chicago: University of Chicago Press, 2004); Iris Marion Young, *Inclusion and Democracy* (Oxford: Oxford University Press, 2000).

5. Barbara Applebaum, "Bridging Divides or Deepening Them? Dialogue under Conditions of Social Injustice," *Philosophy of Education 2017* (Urbana: University of Illinois Press, 2018).

6. Archon Fung, "Deliberation before the Revolution: Toward an Ethics of Deliberative Democracy in an Unjust World," *Political Theory* 33, no. 3 (2005): 397–419.

7. Wahl, "No Justice, No Peace."

8. Rachel Wahl, "The Inner Life of Democracy: Learning in Deliberation between the Police and Communities of Color," *Educational Theory* 68, no. 1 (forthcoming 2018); and Wahl, "Dispelling the Burden of Agency: Receptive Learning during Political Crisis" (under review).

HOW I LEARNED THAT DIVERSITY DOES NOT EQUAL INTEGRATION

GREGORY B. FAIRCHILD

I am a product of the civil rights movement. I suggest anyone of my age must acknowledge that fact. I have lived through marked change in institutions, especially in the entry of women, racial and ethnic minorities, and immigrants into formerly segregated enclaves. I've seen these as encouraging developments.

It was raining in Martha's Vineyard on the morning of Saturday, August 12, 2017, so my family didn't head to the beach on what would be our last day of vacation. As we turned on the television in our bungalow, major networks were showing the disturbing photos from Charlottesville the night prior—men with torches surrounding Jefferson's statue, chanting about being *replaced*. As the day continued, there were more images of escalating threat culminating in eventual violence in downtown. The action onscreen was happening very close to our home, but we were miles away. I caught glimpses of friends, school police officers, and neighbors participating in what was becoming a melee. I remember the image of a banner stretched across Market Street proclaiming that "Diversity Makes Us Stronger." I was reminded that I've never been convinced that the mere fact of diversity, as a condition, leads to strength. My life and work have shown me that America is increasingly diverse yet remains very segregated. Because of the persistence of segregation, latent distrust percolates and, eventually, explodes into events like those of August 12. Integration requires intentionality. And I've also learned that it isn't only far-right protesters who find integration challenging.

Well before my birth. The scaffolding that led to the racially integrated experiences I've had was put in place well before I was born. I cite two key federal policy decisions (among others) that altered the trajectory of what otherwise would have been a much more segregated upbringing for me.

I would have lived amid the racial segregation that characterizes the lives of most Americans.

In 1948 President Truman signed Executive Order 9981, declaring, "There shall be equality of treatment and opportunity for all persons in the armed forces without regard to race, color, religion, or national origin."[1] At the time, my father was a teenager attending a segregated high school in North Tulsa, Oklahoma. Soon thereafter, he entered Hampton Institute, a historically black institution, and would select to pursue a math major and courses in Military Science (ROTC).

When he began ROTC my father's expectations about command on the field would be that he would serve in a segregated unit. At that time black officers commanded all-black units (and a few otherwise black units were commanded by white officers). This is the reason that many of the World War II films I've enjoyed—*Saving Private Ryan, The Thin Red Line*—have a number of white ethnic characters—Jews, Italians, Irish, Greeks—and are devoid of black characters. As a child I was nagged by the sense that something was missing from these films. Many blacks, like my grandfather, Robert Fairchild Sr., served in the "Great War." Years later I accepted a segregated truth: my grandfather couldn't have been there with them.

While my father was in college, the Korean War began. As the conflict progressed, there was an operations problem: racially segregated training facilities created a bottleneck in bringing troops to the field, slowing the speed of needed replacements.[2] A few officers began to experiment with integration in small ways, and Truman's order crystallized action. In 1954 my father graduated from college and took his commission. He was facing a novel challenge: he was being asked to do something that he hadn't seen modeled—be a black officer leading integrated troops into battle.

Through the historical sweep of all wars in which U.S. troops participated, from the American Revolution through World War II, the Unites States Army had been diverse. Now, with the Korean War, it was mandating racial integration. As a result, there was a model of leadership that was being endorsed and normalized—blacks could work with and even command whites.

The second noted policy decision that influenced the integration in my life came in 1963. Robert S. McNamara, Secretary of Defense, issued Directive 5120.36 just a few months before I was born:

> The military departments shall . . . issue appropriate instructions, manuals and regulations in connection with the leadership responsibility

for equal opportunity, on and off-base, and containing guidance for its discharge. (para. II.B.1)

Every military commander has the responsibility to oppose discriminatory practices affecting his *men and their dependents* and to foster equal
opportunity for them, not only in areas under his immediate control, but
also in nearby communities where they may live or gather in off-duty
hours. (para. II.C) [emphasis added][3]

This statement recognized that after operating successfully within integrated units, many servicemen remained segregated by the housing,
schools, and facilities in the communities in which they and their families
lived. After McNamara's directive the military began to use its economic
purchasing power, in the form of housing subsidies, to integrate surrounding communities. There were also initiatives to force integration in public
schools located near their bases. Fully fifteen years after Truman's integration order, the communities in which U.S. Army bases were located were
diverse, but they were not integrated. Personally, McNamara's order meant
I could attend schools with nonblack children.

Lessons from mothers. During the 1970s my family moved to Germany. As
a preteenager living "on base," I would drop by the homes of classmates
after school. Friends would announce our arrival to their mothers in German, Japanese, Spanish, or Filipino (what I would later learn was Tagalog).
Years later when I spoke with my father about the frequency of interethnic,
international, interracial marriage in the military, he gave a simple explanation: "Where there are troops, there will be mothers." I was growing up
in a world composed of those who were fighting to defend America and,
supposedly, its values. In that environment integration was the norm and
not the anomaly. We lived in base housing next to white, Asian, and Latino
neighbors; I attended schools and played and fought with kids from across a
broad demographic. I didn't make much of the fact that my friends' mothers didn't speak English. And then we returned to America . . .

Almost segregated schools. In the mid-seventies, amid the nation's bicentennial celebration, my father was stationed at Fort Monroe, in Hampton,
Virginia. My sister and I were enrolled in our first local, "off-base" public
school. One of my initial observations was that this school was demograph-
ically different—the majority of my classmates were black. I also recall having my first real crush. (Renee Jones had a huge Afro and wore bell-bottom
jeans.) In 2013 I did a search on the demography of the school and found it

was closed. At the time of closure, the student body was 70 percent black. (For comparison, 50.5 percent of Hampton's residents are black.)[4]

When my father eventually retired from service, he took on a new career: he became a loan officer with Central Fidelity Bank, and we moved to Campbell County, Virginia (a suburb of Lynchburg). My sister and I matriculated at Brookville High School. (Jerry Fallwell is one the school's prominent alums.) I was surprised again. Racially, this new school was a mirrored opposite of Hampton. There were perhaps thirty black students in a school of approximately six hundred. My return to the states had revealed that America wasn't as integrated as I'd experienced overseas. Few, if any, mothers spoke a foreign language, and you could attend either a predominantly white or black school—but not one that was integrated to match the country's composition.

Included, not accepted. My high school was racially segregated. However, this didn't mean I experienced aversive, crushing discrimination. As I progressed through the grades, I was eventually elected the student body president, captain of the track team, and held a number of other leadership positions.

Looking back, two experiences remind me that presence is not the same as integration. In my senior year, I was elected to the school's homecoming court. This required me to escort Liz Zecchini onto the football field at half-time. I learned the next day that a ten-minute, arm-in-arm walk with Liz onto the field was objectionable to some of my classmates' parents (many of them alums of the school). An interracial homecoming court was too much for them.

The second was an evening that was embarrassment, mainly for my parents. My parents decided to throw a birthday party for me at our house. (We are a family that cooks elaborate meals and relishes hosting parties.) In the days leading up to the event, I invited everyone I knew. We were expecting over fifty people, given indications from classmates.

On the night of the party, a half-dozen people eventually trickled in. As the night wore on, I remember being confused and seeing the uncomfortable expressions my parents were valiantly masking (as were my classmates who had come to the party). I didn't understand. I wondered whether some disaster, like a massive traffic accident, had occurred. When I arrived at school the following Monday, there were many pained explanations throughout the day. It became clear that my classmates' parents were afraid to have them visit our house for a party, and especially after dark. I couldn't fathom why. What about our family was unsafe? At this point my father was the local branch's commercial and mortgage loan officer, which meant that many of my classmates' parents had visited with my father seeking loans, many that he eventually approved.

These were two real lessons for me: First, back home in America there were limits to the acceptance of integration. You could be elected by your peers but shouldn't publicly escort one of them at a football game. Second, social position didn't guarantee protection from stereotyping. Being student body president or loan officer didn't mean peers didn't harbor fears about you. Nevertheless, I left high school with hope. Many of my classmates had been embarrassed by these events. The generation ahead would indeed integrate society as we became adults and took the reins of the leading institutions. My white friends told me so.

Becoming a scholar. Some years later, when I was a PhD student, I became formally interested in integration as a social science research arena. In the work of a broad body of scholars, I found the data and language that captured what I observed. *Diversity* was a measurable indicator of difference in a set of people. As a state, diversity didn't necessarily require action. On the other hand, *integration* was a process that involved intentionality. Integration might mean some people would be uncomfortable, but it was important for progress.

As I began to formally study integration, I consumed a stew of related social science articles. For example, one early influence was Gordon Allport's "Intergroup Contact Hypothesis," developed and presented in his book *The Nature of Prejudice* (1954).[5] Allport's proposition was that an ingroup member's level of prejudice toward outgroup members is inversely correlated with the degree of contact that someone has with that group (i.e., whites will have lower prejudice if they have more contact with blacks of similar social status). Increased opportunities for interaction would allow individuals to test their stereotypes, and over time they would find their stereotypes hollow. I saw echoes in the arguments being forwarded around that same time (mid-fifties) by the *Brown* plaintiffs regarding educational segregation. Enforced and rigid barriers to intergroup relations, they argued, were demonstrably damaging to black children. Continued segregation would sustain existing negative black prejudices and stall the social progress of black children.

As I read the many papers replicating, debating, and testing Allport's theories, I recognized what a "natural experiment" my experience on military bases had been: First, I had attended integrated schools and lived in integrated neighborhoods from my earliest years. Second, I'd lived in communities where there was integration across social status levels. Unlike what I'd found when I left the confines of bases, there were black, Asian, and Latino leaders in the upper reaches of the military. My father was an officer, commanding a racially integrated Howitzer battalion (approximately four hundred troops) on a German base. Third, I had grown up with an expectation of racial equality. I didn't worry that my behavior—say, questioning white authority figures—would be viewed as a violation of norms, or "uppity." I hadn't received messages from my parents about the importance of appearing racially deferential to avoid sanction or even worse. If you'd asked me then, as a young scholar, I would have shared the stark racial differences I'd noted between my experiences on military bases and back in everyday America. I would've told you that I assumed that these differences were really an artifact of my parents' decision to take employment in the American South. I would learn that was a misimpression.

As I continued my research, I learned that even with passage of the Fair Housing Act of 1968, residential segregation continued to characterize our neighborhoods. This reconsideration came when I read Doug Massey and Nancy Denton's *American Apartheid: Segregation and the Making of the Underclass* (1993).[6] They presented a comprehensive, disturbing case that residential segregation was not only durable across the United States, but that it played a deterministic role in calcifying inequality and gaps in educational attainment, wealth accumulation, and access to employment. One big surprise was that, in fact, the South was one of the *least segregated* regions of the country. This, however, was a dubious distinction. Massey and Denton termed America's major cities "hypersegregated." They shared that American levels of segregation were only comparable to one nation in modern history: South Africa under Apartheid.

Understanding segregation's variants. As I dove deeper into my studies, I also learned that segregation could be measured in multiple ways that could represent different patterns of behavior and distributions of groups across space. I began to use various segregation indices in my own research work. To illustrate some of these revelations, allow me to provide three visuals.

In these illustrations, grey circles represent the majority group, white the minority. Figure 1 shows a pattern with the minority group members clustered at the bottom. Figure 2 shows a centralized minority cluster, not unlike what are commonly called "inner cities." Figure 3 shows a few minority group members at the top and most clustered at the bottom.

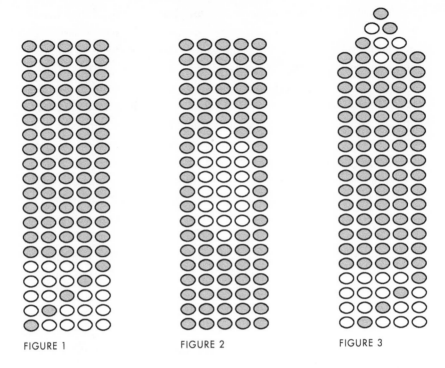

FIGURE 1   FIGURE 2   FIGURE 3

It should be immediately clear that each figure presents a different type of social relationship. Yet, all represent the same level of diversity (20 percent minority, white circles).

If we consider that vertical space in these visuals can represent a scaling of social status, class, power, or economic resources, then circles near the top have more access to power than those nearer the bottom. The pattern shown in Figure 1 has all minority, white circles clustered together at the bottom. Figure 2 shows a middle status group of white circles that is bookended above and below. Figure 3 shows a pattern common to many U.S. corporations in which I've worked. There are a few white circles at the top, none in the middle, and a cluster at the bottom. And, I am sorry to acknowledge, this pattern reminds me of many workplaces here at UVA.

Understanding segregated schools. If the research on segregation in housing left me disappointed about American progress, studies on America's public schools were no more comforting. Gary Orfield and Chungmei Lee released *"Brown* at 50" in 2004, with the subtitle "King's Dream or *Plessy's* Nightmare?"

A half-century after the Supreme Court found that segregated schools are "inherently unequal," there is growing evidence that the Court was correct. Desegregated schools offer tangible advantages for students of each racial group. Our new work, however, shows that U.S. schools are becoming more segregated in all regions for both African American and Latino students. We are celebrating a victory over segregation at a time when schools across the nation are becoming increasingly segregated.[7]

Orfield and Lee comprehensively reviewed the state of segregation in America's public schools. The differences between diversity and segregation were clear in two statements: "American public schools are now only 60 percent white nationwide and nearly one fourth of U.S. students are in states with a majority of nonwhite students."[8] So, public schools were more diverse than ever. And, a few sentences later, the authors added: "However, most white students have little contact with minority students."[9] Schools weren't integrated. A later paper illustrated that the pace of educational integration was slow, rather than proceeding "with all deliberate speed" as has been recommended by Chief Justice Earl Warren at the time of the *Brown* decision: "Contrary to many claims, the South has not gone back to the level of segregation before *Brown*. It has lost all of the additional progress made after 1967 but is still the least segregated region for black students. . . . Segregation is typically segregation by both race and poverty. Black and Latino students tend to be in schools with a substantial majority of poor children, but white and Asian students are typically in middle-class schools."[10]

It turns out that the public schools in the Charlottesville Metropolitan Statistical Area (MSA), composed of Albemarle, Greene, and Nelson Counties, as well as the City of Charlottesville, show signs of racial and economic segregation. For example, although in 2010 the schools had an overall white composition of 66.4 percent, the average white student went to a school that was 75.4 percent white.[11] Further, the average white student attended a school in which 30.3 percent of students came from low-income households.[12] For comparison, black students composed 16.2 percent of all students, and the typical black student attended a school that was 30 percent black and in which 47.6 percent of students were low income. These skews are of course related to the housing patterns in the area.

Decisions about geographic space, educational and residential, are informed by the realities of race and class. In her essay in this volume, Preston Reynolds tells the story of Paul Brandon Barringer, former chair of UVA faculty from 1897 to 1903, who explicitly worked to reify segregation at the university. We learn from Reynolds that Barringer believed that "the 'Negro problem' was more than a political problem. Blacks, simply by living in proximity to whites, created a massive public health threat for white persons." In her essay Lisa Woolfork draws us to recall that the original decision to place UVA in Albemarle County was because of its ease of access by the white population, and Willis Jenkins asserts that "white supremacy is singular because of its massive historical role in making the world in which we live in Charlottesville, in Virginia, in the United States." In his essay, Guian Mckee strongly suggests that UVA has not only ignored the role it has played in exacerbating displacement of low-income workers but has also abdicated responsibility for rising inequality. As the leading economic engine in our area, this is quite an indictment.

Segregated workplaces. I began to research segregation across American life and came across a report titled *Workforce 2000,* published in 1987 by the Hudson Institute and Department of Labor. In a chapter titled "Demographics as Destiny," the report mentioned that although the aggregate growth of the U.S. workforce would slow in the coming decades, three subgroups would grow, and thus American workplaces would become more diverse: women, minorities, and immigrants.[13]

Over twenty years later, the *Review of Economics and Statistics* published a careful study of segregation in the American workplace, finding "considerable segregation by race, ethnicity, education, and language in the workplace. Only a tiny portion of racial segregation in the workplace is driven by education differences between blacks and whites."[14] If this wasn't discouraging enough to me, the *American Sociological Review* published a paper documenting workplace desegregation trends since 1966, which concludes: "Most strikingly, black-white workplace desegregation essentially stops after 1980. The observation in the occupation-based literature that equal opportunity progress stalls at about 1980 is generally supported, although there is also some disturbing evidence of resegregation after 1995 in old economy sectors."[15] My workplace here at UVA is considerably more racially segregated than any I've worked in prior to moving to Charlottesville. (I had a considerable corporate career prior to becoming a scholar.)

Taken together, the body of research indicated that segregation was pervasive in American daily life. However, I had to interrogate my feeling that segregation is necessarily a bad thing. Melvin Oliver and Thomas Shapiro's *Black Wealth, White Wealth* helped shape my understanding. They chart how housing policy, including zoning and access to mortgage loans, limited minority families' ability to accumulate assets.[16] Since home equity is typically the single largest asset in the average American's household, segmentation and closure of housing markets perpetuates wealth inequality, reifying segregation in other institutions.

My review of a broad set of social science literatures and my own burgeoning research revealed that the prevailing rhetoric that America was becoming an integrated society was simply inaccurate. Hypersegregation across the lived spectrum in America—schools, neighborhoods, workplaces—means that Americans have few opportunities to interact across racial groups in ways that would allow them to experience each other as equals. Closed housing markets would sustain differences in wealth accumulation. Absent an intentionality to integrate, many otherwise well-meaning Americans would experience the benefits of the status quo without feeling complicit, enjoying the perpetuation of segregated systems that support racial inequality without intending harm. When I was leaving high school, I hoped for a generation that would go beyond rejecting aversive racism, but I didn't understand that America needed a leadership that would engage proactively and intentionally to upend segregation. Truman and McNamara, men scarcely regarded as civil rights activists, had shown such leadership. Where are these nudges by our leadership today? I've wondered if perhaps this is due to a lack of awareness of the status of segregation. Integration in daily life is less common than many Americans may realize. The preponderance of discourse about diversity has unintentionally contributed to what I now term the "illusion of inclusion."

Beyond protests and hashtags. In the weeks and months following August 11 and 12, there has been considerable thought and discussion about what happened that weekend. For many, the word "Charlottesville" is now synonymous with white supremacist uprisings, which causes considerable hand-wringing in our community. The university's Center for Politics released a poll fielded in response to the events in our town.[17] The findings suggest what social theorists like Allport proposed decades ago would be one of the continuing costs of segregation—an inability to understand the perspectives of outgroup members:

> Nearly one-third of respondents (31%) strongly or somewhat agreed that the country needs to "protect and preserve its White European heritage." Another third (34%) strongly or somewhat disagreed with the statement, and 29% neither agreed nor disagreed. . . . Fifty years after the United States Supreme Court struck down bans on mixed-race marriage in *Loving v. Virginia*, about one-sixth of respondents (16%) agreed with the statement that "marriage should only be allowed between two people

of the same race" and an additional 14% neither agreed nor disagreed with the statement, while 4% said they didn't know. In total, about a third failed to express tolerance of interracial marriage. . . . Within this poll a sizable number of respondents selected the "neither agree nor disagree" option. Given the racially charged and controversial nature of some of the statements polled, these "middling" answers seemed remarkable, particularly given the fact that a "Don't know" option was also presented and was available if, for example, one wished to express uncertainty or a lack of knowledge.

Reading this passage, you can nearly hear the surprise in the study's authors. For me, I see the ignored prescriptive suggestions of so many from long ago—that segregation harms the segregator and segregated, that prejudice and stereotypes solidify under segregation. It is difficult for me to see how our expressed intent to have a civil society characterized by mutual respect will not be blunted by the many ways that we are separated by race and class. Because we are so diverse, and yet so segregated, opportunities for intergroup contact are, and will continue to be, precious and few.

Making sense of the senseless. A healthy dose of the things that university faculty can influence—teach-ins, history lectures, sensitivity training, privilege walks—cannot alter the fact that we continue to have an increasingly diverse yet starkly segregated society. As the perceived pool of available resources shrinks and inequality rises—in jobs, assets, power—distrust across groups will fester without intentional redress. A growing underclass will worry about what they see as a diminishing share of the pie—along with worries about immigration, miscegenation, new religions, and foreign languages. In short, they will give voice to worries of *replacement,* as we heard from the men and women that surrounded Jefferson's statue on August 11.

I see my colleagues struggling with whether, when, and how to talk personally and openly about race in the classroom—and being fearful that their phrasing will offend. I should add that this is my observation about my colleagues of many races and nationalities and not just those in the majority. Without shared experience, they are at a loss for words. Our collective struggle to provide leadership after events like those of Charlottesville in August 2017 is blunted by our inability to find voices that can connect the distances between us.

Many of my colleagues have posted flyers on their doors that attest to their support for the ideals of diversity. My encouragement is that they become intentional about integration. This could be relatively easy—say, sharing a meal with someone that isn't of their own racial or ethnic group. And these efforts could be difficult. I know as a parent that choosing the neighborhood in which we live, the clubs or religious institutions that we join, or the schools that our children attend are challenging and complicated decisions. I can personally attest that those difficult directives of the U.S. military decades ago have paid dividends in terms of my comfort across racial groups, as they have for many others who grew up like me. It is obvious to me that without those directives, segregation would pertain. Rachel Wahl, in her essay in this volume, reminds us that dialogue is not a panacea and that finding common ground is not necessarily possible if there isn't underlying trust.

We should keep in mind that diversity and integration are not the same things. We should recognize that we may make pronouncements promoting diversity, but we are failing to be intentional about integration. We should acknowledge that our uncertainty around race stems from our lack of practice. We should take time in our daily lives to be intentional about opening spaces and creating opportunities that allow us to face what may be uncomfortable. Risa Goluboff, in her essay, notes that parents encourage their children to share, not hoard, their favorite toys when they enter the sandbox. I've seen parents give this advice and have given it myself. The uncomfortable truth is that our sandboxes—our schools, neighborhoods, workplaces, and social gatherings—are starkly segregated.

Intentional, regular, integrated experiences can help leaders—contemporary and future—build the "muscle" to speak with resonance and authenticity when there are fractures in our community. Segregation provides the sustenance for leaders hoping to foment racial animus and violence. If there is trepidation on talking in these ways—even in a cordial setting like a meal—how difficult it must be to provide language that lifts us up when times are uncertain.

NOTES

1. Executive Order 9981, Harry S. Truman Presidential Library and Museum, www .trumanlibrary.org/9981a.htm, accessed Dec. 7, 2017.
2. C. C. Moskos Jr., "The American Dilemma in Uniform: Race in the Armed Forces," *Annals of the American Academy of Political and Social Science* 406, no. 1 (1973): 94–106, quote p. 97.
3. M. J. MacGregor, *Integration of the Armed Forces, 1940–1965* (Washington, DC: Government Printing Office, 1981), 1:547–51.
4. Merrimack Elementary School, Public School Review, www.publicschoolreview

.com/merrimack-elementary-school-profile, accessed Dec. 7, 2017. Comparison data on the demography of Virginia schools is from Quick Facts, www.census .gov/quickfacts/fact/table/hamptoncityvirginiacounty/RHI225216#viewtop, accessed Dec. 7, 2017.

5. G. W. Allport, "The Effects of Contact," in *The Nature of Prejudice* (New York: Basic Books, 1954), chap. 16.

6. D. S. Massey and N. A. Denton, *American Apartheid: Segregation and the Making of the Underclass* (Cambridge, MA: Harvard University Press, 1993).

7. Gary Orfield and Chungmai Lee, "*Brown* at 50: King's Dream or *Plessy*'s Nightmare?," Civil Rights Project at Harvard University, 2004, p. 1, https://civilrights project.ucla.edu/research/k-12-education/integration-and-diversity/brown-at-50 -king2019s-dream-or-plessy2019s-nightmare/orfield-brown-50-2004.pdf, accessed Feb. 25, 2018.

8. Ibid., 2.

9. Ibid., 3.

10. G. Orfield and E. Frankenberg, "Increasingly Segregated and Unequal Schools as Courts Reverse Policy," *Educational Administration Quarterly* 50, no. 5 (2014): 718–34.

11. The source for all of the quoted school segregation indices is https://s4.ad .brown.edu/Projects/usschools/DataMain.aspx, accessed Feb. 25, 2018. Interested readers can review more about these data and analyses in J. R. Logan and J. Burdick-Will, "School Segregation, Charter Schools, and Access to Quality Education," *Journal of Urban Affairs* 38, no. 3 (2016): 323–43.

12. In these analyses low-income is defined as less than $32,000 in household income for a family of four.

13. W. B. Johnston, *Workforce 2000: Work and Workers for the Twenty-First Century* (Washington, DC: Government Printing Office, 1987), 75–104.

14. J. K. Hellerstein and D. Neumark, "Workplace Segregation in the United States: Race, Ethnicity, and Skill," *Review of Economics and Statistics* 90, no. 3 (2008): 459–77.

15. D. Tomaskovic-Devey et al., "Documenting Desegregation: Segregation in American Workplaces by Race, Ethnicity, and Sex, 1966–2003," *American Sociological Review* 71, no. 4 (2006): 565–88.

16. M. L. Oliver and T. M. Shapiro, *Black Wealth, White Wealth: A New Perspective on Racial Inequality* (Hoboken, NJ: Taylor & Francis, 2006).

17. UVA Center for Politics, "New Poll: Some Americans Express Troubling Racial Attitudes Even as Majority Oppose White Supremacists," www.centerforpolitics .org/crystalball/articles/new-poll-some-americans-express-troubling-racial -attitudes-even-as-majority-oppose-white-supremacists, accessed Nov. 8, 2017.

RACE, PLACE, AND THE SOCIAL RESPONSIBILITIES OF UVA IN THE AFTERMATH OF AUGUST 11 AND 12

GUIAN MCKEE

In the months since August 11 and 12, 2017, both the University of Virginia and the wider Charlottesville-Albemarle community have undergone an extended period of reflection and debate. Local politics have been rocked with recriminations about the management of the rally and counter-protest, and the university has wrestled with its own failures of planning in regard to the invasion of torch-bearing alt-right marchers on the evening of August 11. More broadly, the events of August 11 and 12 have extended and intensified an ongoing conversation about race, poverty, and inequality, both historical and current, in Charlottesville and at the university. UVA had already been engaged in an effort to acknowledge the history of slavery at the university, as well as the consequences and memorialization of the Civil War and segregation. (It had done much less to address the long history of white supremacy at the university, which Lisa Woolfork traces in this volume.) These discussions, both before and after August 11 and 12, have not yet addressed the full scope of the university's role in the wider community and the effects, positive and negative, that it has on nearby neighborhoods. Nor have these conversations pushed into the potentially uncomfortable terrain of what the relationship between UVA and the community could and should be: How does the university interact with the communities in which it is located, and with the people who live there and often work at the university? What are the mutual responsibilities between the university and these communities? How do race and inequality shape these connections? These relationships, both existing and potential, are not simple and include nuances that neither activists nor local leaders nor university administrators have fully confronted. Without engagement of such issues, there is a danger that the opportunity of the post–August 2017 period will be missed. For

UVA, as one of the nation's leading public universities, this moment offers something of particular importance: a chance to create a new national model of institutional responsibility and community commitment—if resources can be found and if old ways of thinking about such relationships can be discarded.

These questions arise at a time of heightened national attention to the critical economic, social, and political significance of universities and academic medical centers (AMCs) in the life of American communities. As traditionally conceived, such institutions have a clearly defined mission to society: teaching students, conducting advanced research, and providing patient care. In pursuing these ends, however, AMCs have become a massive, even dominating presence in many communities around the United States. As a result, the so-called eds and meds sector has increasingly taken on outsize importance in areas of activity that extend far beyond the traditional mission. Universities and AMCs are dominant regional employers, they control real estate, they offer community health services, they lead urban redevelopment projects, they provide policing services, they build housing, and they attempt to address local poverty. In some cases, they have adopted what is in effect a quasi-governmental role in their immediate communities.[1]

In the Charlottesville area, the UVA Medical Center is the largest private employer in the city, and UVA is the largest employer in the wider region. The university, however, has not fully considered whether it can do more for the community than provide such jobs. For example, UVA has not explored whether, or how, it might contribute to solving such issues as workforce housing, transportation, skill development, local wage growth, regional planning, or the formation of partnerships both with and among surrounding local governments.

Baltimore's Johns Hopkins Hospital provides a useful illustration of the expanding social role of universities and academic medical centers. Hopkins has long had a difficult relationship with the low-income, heavily minority community of East Baltimore in which it is located. Issues of contention have included basic ethical standards for research on human subjects (most famously, the case of Henrietta Lacks and the HELA cell line created from her tissues), an urban renewal project adjoining the hospital that displaced nearly fourteen hundred households in the early 1960s, hostile relations with labor unions, and, most recently, the controversial East Baltimore Development Initiative, a $1.8-billion, eighty-eight-acre redevelopment project that has cleared and rebuilt large portions of the low-income, predominantly minority neighborhood that adjoins the hospital.[2] Yet in the aftermath of the April 2015 death of Freddie Gray while in police custody and the ensuing protests and confrontations with police and city leaders, Johns Hopkins Hospital accepted a strikingly new conception of its community responsibilities. In September 2015, in direct response to the upheavals, Hopkins led a coalition of community activists and Baltimore hospitals that proposed a $40-million Health Employment Program to create one thousand entry-level hospital jobs for inner city residents, including former prisoners. Funded by an increase in the rates that hospitals charge the state's insurers, the jobs would range from community health workers and Obamacare enrollment assistors to dietary staff, nursing assistants, and security guards. The program explicitly sought to address the absence of opportunity and hope in Baltimore's most desperate neighborhoods.[3] Opposition from the insurance industry and Maryland's hospital rate-setting agency eventually scaled the Health Employment Program back to 375 jobs, funded jointly by a partial rate increase and a reallocation of preexisting hospital resources. The program went into operation in 2016.[4]

Despite the reduced number of total jobs, the Baltimore Health Employment Program captures a remarkable moment: a major academic medical center, affiliated with a leading private research university, asking a public regulatory agency for access to the financial capacity to undertake a direct job-creation program, not for any specific health-care purpose but to meet a pressing social need in the community. As such, it offers a powerful example of an unresolved debate in American society about whether, and how, universities and AMCs should be instruments for addressing critical public problems.

Johns Hopkins's response to the Baltimore uprising is relevant to UVA in the aftermath of August 11 and 12 because it raises a series of critical questions: What can, and should, society expect from institutions of higher education? Have those responsibilities changed? Does a crisis such as the Freddie Gray protests in Baltimore or the alt-right invasion of Charlottesville alter those relationships and responsibilities, or does it simply make them impossible to ignore?

TAX EXEMPTIONS AND LOCAL GOVERNMENT: THE CONTEXT OF UNIVERSITY SOCIAL RESPONSIBILITY

In order to address such questions, specific components of UVA's relationship with surrounding communities must be considered. One of the most significant of these is UVA's effect on the local tax revenues that largely determine the capacity of city and county governments to redress inequalities. As a result of their not-for-profit status and ostensible public purpose, land acquired by universities and medical centers is exempt from local and state tax rolls. In a few cases, cities and academic institutions have created payment-in-lieu-of-taxes (PILOT) programs, under which the institution makes a payment equal to a percentage of the taxable value of its exempt land. Only Boston has really made this work; other cities such as Philadelphia ended PILOT programs because of political difficulties.[5]

In recent years Charlottesville has not had an active conversation about PILOTs. At least in part, this silence is a product of the institutional structures and practices of the university. A portion of UVA's land holdings are officially owned by the UVA Foundation. According to its 2015 tax filings, the UVA Foundation held more than $67 million in land, along with nearly $114 million in buildings (after depreciation).[6] In most cases the foundation holds the land for possible future university uses. As long as ownership remains with the foundation, the land generally continues to be taxable (with some exceptions). Given the extent of the university's land holdings in the Greater Charlottesville region, this structure is significant in terms of local tax revenue: the foundation's property tax payments in 2015 totaled just over $1.33 million.[7] When land is transferred to the university or health system for institutional development, however, it almost always becomes tax-exempt. If the medical center builds a new facility on land previously held by the foundation, for example, the property goes off the tax rolls.[8]

The consequences of such property-tax exemptions are real and significant. A review of city property records undertaken for this study reveals that in the City of Charlottesville alone, the Rector and Board of Visitors, the university itself, and the UVA Foundation own at least ninety-two tax-exempt properties. In 2017 these properties have a total assessed value of more than $1.02 billion dollars. The properties range from Madison Hall (location of the university president's office; assessed value of $4.77 million) to the medical center's Lee Street and 11th Street parking garages (assessed values of $18.7 million and $22.6 million, respectively) to a block of cleared land (formerly housing) in the Fifeville neighborhood just west of Roosevelt Brown Boulevard across the railroad tracks from the medical center (assessed value of $1.4 million). Perhaps most notable is that UVA owns a series of student apartment buildings, many of them in the Jefferson Park Avenue–Brandon Avenue corridor south of the university, which appear very similar to commercial rental properties. Because they have a tax exemption for educational purposes, however, these apartment buildings constitute a kind of shadow dormitory system.[9] Holding such questions of classification aside, at the city's current tax rate of $0.95 per $100 of assessed value, the ninety-two properties would generate approximately $9.7 million in revenue if they were not tax-exempt. This is equal to a small but not insignificant portion of the city's $162 million fiscal year 2017 budget; put differently, it would fund about 12 percent of the city school system's operating budget, and it is nearly four times larger than the city's fiscal 2018 contribution to its affordable housing fund.[10] This foregone revenue would not change the city's fiscal capacity, but it would make a meaningful difference.

UVA, though, does not make such tax payments. It does pay "service charges" and "property maintenance charges" on a number of tax-exempt city properties not used for educational purposes and also provides funds for fire protection services. In 2017–18, these totaled $38,000 in service charges, $55,000 in property maintenance charges, and $305,416 in fire protection charges, for a total of $398,416 (compared to the estimated foregone taxes of $9.7 million).[11] Albemarle County's fiscal year 2018 budget includes a $138,259 payment "from the State for service charges incurred by the University of Virginia in lieu of property taxes."[12] Together, these payments are a fraction of the potential taxable value of UVA's exempt holdings. Neither activists nor local leaders have challenged this system, but at least in theory, a PILOT program like the one in Boston could represent an important source of revenue for local government. Such payments would support local services from schools to housing to job training for the local community. They would thus represent an indirect way for UVA to meet pressing needs near Grounds.

Such payments, though, would come out of the rest of UVA's budget, potentially undermining programs in the university's traditional mission areas. UVA has assertively—and proactively—countered arguments that it should make a greater local financial contribution. In its most recent economic impact statement, the university maintains that a focus on tax exemption is too narrow and emphasizes instead the broader economic effect of its operations: "It is a common misperception that public universities and non-profit health systems do not generate tax revenue. . . . [But] through its local spending, as well as direct and indirect support of jobs, the presence of UVA stabilizes and strengthens the local and statewide tax base." UVA finds that in 2016, the academic division of the university generated $600 million in direct economic impact and $1 billion in indirect and induced economic impact in the region, along with 11,391 directly created jobs and 9,179 indirect and induced jobs (through UVA-related spending), as well as $87.6 million in "state and local government revenues" in the Charlottesville region alone. The UVA health division has an even greater economic presence: $1.8 billion in direct economic impact and $1.4 billion in indirect and induced economic impact in the region, along with 12,776 direct jobs and 11,255 indirect and induced jobs and $111.6 million in regional government revenues. The university also highlights the value of employee and student volunteer time: $29.9 million for the academic division and $16.8 million for the health system.[13] The numbers are impressive, and the overall point is not without merit. UVA *does* generate substantial economic benefits, including local tax revenue, for the Charlottesville area and the commonwealth. Both the region and the state would be poorer and less dynamic without the university presence.

Yet the structure of the economic impact report itself highlights a key limiting characteristic of UVA's conception of its social responsibilities, particularly in relation to the events of August 11 and 12 and their aftermath. The impact numbers cited above are for the *entire* Thomas Jefferson Planning District Commission area, which includes Fluvanna, Greene, Louisa, and Nelson Counties in addition to the communities in which the university is immediately located: the City of Charlottesville and Albemarle County. Additional economic statistics in the report underscore the university's statewide impact. The approach highlights a contradiction: because of its status as a state university with national and global ambitions, UVA views itself as acting in relation to regional, state-wide, and, increasingly, national and international contexts. As such, it does not accept special responsibility or concern for the poverty and racial inequality on its own doorstep. Instead, such issues are addressed at UVA through a combination of broad overall economic impact and student volunteerism (which, technically, is mostly accomplished through the independent entity of Madison House). While the former is the keystone of the local economy *as it exists,* and the latter is well-intentioned and perhaps even effective at building empathy and a sense of social responsibility among students, the reality remains that neither has been sufficient to redress the historical chasms of race and poverty in the *immediate* Charlottesville community. Deeply rooted, racially linked poverty continues to exist in neighborhoods located just blocks from the university. Economic impact and student volunteer projects have not and will not be enough to resolve these nearby problems.

THE COSTS OF GROWTH: LAND, NEIGHBORHOODS, AND UNIVERSITY EXPANSION

Tax exemption aside, the economic impact of the university and the growth that it creates may not always be an unmitigated good. For many urban universities and academic medical centers (Johns Hopkins Hospital, discussed above, offers a prime example), the need for land to facilitate expansion and new construction has created a deep tension with surrounding communities. Displacement of residents by university- and hospital-driven expansion has generated resentment and anger dating back at least to the era of urban renewal. In Charlottesville the university's role in shaping land use has generally been a subtler one. The university did not directly participate in Charlottesville's two official urban renewal projects, Vinegar Hill and Garrett Square, both of which displaced minority and lower-income residents and businesses in the downtown area between the 1950s and 1970s. The city and university did discuss a possible third urban renewal project in the largely African American Gospel Hill neighborhood near the UVA hospital in the late 1960s. The city eventually decided not to pursue the project, largely because the project did not fit easily with federal guidelines.[14] UVA, however, ultimately acquired the homes and businesses in Gospel Hill and cleared them to make way for Jordan (now Pivin) and McLeod Halls and the Claude Moore Health Sciences Library during the 1970s and the new hospital building during the 1980s (along with parking garages to accommodate the cars of staff and patients).[15] Community discussions led by Charlottesville's recent Blue-Ribbon Commission on Race, Memorials, and Public Spaces (which John Mason explores in his contribution to the volume) clearly demonstrated that Gospel Hill, although relatively small compared to Vinegar Hill or Garrett Square, is part of the historical memory of neighborhood destruction among African Americans in the city.[16]

Such direct cases of displacement are not the only way that the university's size and growth can create conflicts over urban space. As post–August 12 activism has shifted from the alt-right to a broader focus on race and inequality, affordable housing has emerged as a critical and pressing issue. In this area the university has a complex effect. While university employees live throughout the Charlottesville region, a significant percentage live in the city itself or in nearby areas of Albemarle County. This trend has been driven by the resurgence of interest in urban living among younger adults, as well as by the widely noted amenities and appeal of Charlottesville itself.

This trend has led to the restoration of older housing stock and has helped to maintain the economic and cultural vitality of the Downtown Mall and other commercial spaces through the recession of 2008–09 (not to mention the city's property-tax base). All of these are significant contributions that are too often dismissed by critics of university-driven gentrification. Yet it is nonetheless true that housing demand among people affiliated with the university has increased housing costs for middle- and lower-income residents in the city and in nearby areas of the county. Such effects have exacerbated an existing shortage of affordable housing, an issue that (along with repercussions from August 11 and 12) dominated the 2017 city council campaign.[17]

Student housing needs also shape the local housing market. Due to limited on-grounds housing, a high percentage of students live in neighborhoods near the university, often occupying houses that would otherwise enter the wider rental or for-sale market.[18] The recent construction of large, privately built, student-oriented apartment complexes on West Main Street and Jefferson Park Avenue has significantly increased the supply of student housing. Although widely criticized for their architectural failings and for a supposed (although economically illogical) effect of driving up rents in the city as a whole, these complexes should alleviate student pressure on the wider rental market, which over time will at least slow the rate of rent increase in the remaining housing supply. Such construction does not, however, significantly reduce the absolute shortage of low-income units in the city.[19] The combined effect of employee and student housing needs thus creates both practical and theoretical questions: Should the university build more on-grounds dormitories to house students and reduce pressure on the off-grounds local market? Does the university, as the dominant institutional presence in the city and region, have an obligation to address housing needs for its workers or for others in the surrounding community? Private universities such as Johns Hopkins and the University of Pennsylvania have undertaken initiatives both to house more undergraduates on campus and to provide mortgage guarantees and other housing support for employees and in some cases, community members.[20] Should UVA's mission now extend beyond the traditional areas of teaching, research, and patient care and into areas like affordable housing? What are the implications of assigning such a role to a higher education institution or academic medical center?

JOBS, BUT NOT A LIVING WAGE: THE LIMITS OF
THE ACADEMIC GROWTH ENGINE

The jobs that UVA generates illustrate a related but far more specific and immediate dimension of these difficult questions. While many faculty, administrative, and staff positions offer good-to-excellent salaries and benefits, service-level positions at the university are frequently low wage, and in some cases, contingent. Many such workers at UVA are actually employed by outside contractors who are not obligated to meet the university's wage and benefit standards.[21] Nor is this a new issue: as early as 1971 students, faculty, and community activists marched on the Rotunda to demand improved wages and equal employment opportunities for university employees. In 1996 the UVA Office of Equal Opportunity Programs released the *Muddy Floor Report,* which highlighted the links between race, gender, and poverty among the university's employees. As discussed in Claudrena Harold's essay in this volume, the *Muddy Floor Report* found that minority and female workers made up a vastly disproportionate share of the lowest paid employees, especially in the service workforce. As a later summary noted, "The numbers were especially staggering for the university's housekeeping staff: about a third were eligible for food stamps; their starting wage was $12,756 per year, or a little over $6.13 per hour (nearly $3,700 below the federal poverty line); roughly half were African American, and a majority were women."[22] The report led to the formation of a labor action group, which campaigned for an $8 living wage at the university. In 2000 the Board of Visitors increased the lowest starting salary from $6.10 to $8.19, although it made no acknowledgement of the living-wage campaign, did not index the wage to future cost of living increases, and did not apply the wage standard to outside contractors.[23]

The lack of such a formal living-wage policy at the university has led to a recurring cycle of activism. A campaign in 2005–06 culminated in a four-day student occupation of President John Casteen's office, which ended only when university police arrested the students and forcibly removed them from the building. As a new round of mobilization began in 2010, the Charlottesville City Council reaffirmed its own commitment to a living wage and urged the university to accept living-wage principles as well. This wave of student activism culminated in a "lie-in" at a Board of Visitors meeting in 2011 and a fourteen-day hunger strike in 2012, which received national media attention.[24]

Throughout the multidecade living-wage effort, the university has maintained a consistent position, emphasizing the limitations on its resources, the steps that it has taken to improve wages and benefits, and its overall economic impact. It also focuses on market wage rates in the region, rather than on a wage calculated on the cost of living, thus challenging the economic assumptions and analysis underlying living-wage demands.[25] A December 2017 report to the Board of Visitors noted that UVA's current lowest wage is $12.38 per hour (plus benefits equal to $4.82), which it claimed is higher than an MIT calculated living wage for the area of $11.86 cents. It neglected to note, however, that the MIT figure was for a single person; for an adult with two children, the MIT study calculates that a living wage would be $30.06.[26]

Ultimately, UVA's response to living-wage demands relies on turnover and exhaustion among student and employee activists. Since 2015 the living-wage campaign at UVA appears to have lost momentum. Although a living-wage organization still exists at the university, the issue has not remerged as a priority in the wave of post–August 11 and 12 activism.

UVA'S SOCIAL RESPONSIBILITIES

How much should UVA do for nearby neighborhoods and communities in Charlottesville and Albemarle? The post-uprising employment program sponsored by Johns Hopkins Hospital, as well as the problematic redevelopment effort that Hopkins has implemented over the last fifteen years, is suggestive of one model. In undertaking large-scale redevelopment and employment programs in Baltimore, Johns Hopkins accepted and tacitly acknowledged a quasi-governmental level of responsibility commensurate with its status as a core institution of the local and national economy. This reflects the reality that postindustrial cities such as Baltimore have been devastated by the erosion of their tax base through loss of jobs and population, leaving city governments unable to fulfill many basic functions. As a result, institutions such as Hopkins take on roles that would once have been the sole responsibility of government: managing redevelopment, overseeing the use of urban space, creating new schools, building housing, and organizing programs of direct job creation to meet community need.

In theory UVA might do something similar to address inequality in Charlottesville. Given the role of slavery, segregation, and eugenic science (see Preston Reynolds's essay in this volume on the latter) in the university's history, racial justice might be a particular focus. Neither the city nor the wider region, of course, suffers with the levels of poverty and desperation experienced by cities like Baltimore, but a case can be made that UVA nonetheless actually has a greater capacity than local government to address deeply rooted poverty and racial inequality. Possible actions might include the following:

1. Programs to develop affordable or even low-income housing targeted at UVA employees but potentially open to community members as well; specific strategies could be developed by a housing task force of community members, UVA employees, and faculty with expertise in a range of related fields; such a task force could also provide meaningful opportunities for student engagement;

2. Programs to provide mortgage or rental support for UVA employees; such efforts could be part of the charge to the housing task force described above;

3. Creation of a development review board, consisting of community members, local and university officials, faculty, and students, that would assess the economic, social, and ethical implications of university expansion projects for the surrounding community; such an entity would parallel the institutional review boards that assess the ethics of human and animal research proposals, and would be vested with similar powers to approve or reject projects;[27]

4. Commitment to a true living wage, including for contract employees;

5. Expanded initiatives to support workforce development among UVA employees, such as skill upgrading and professional pathway facilitation, potentially in collaboration with the Virginia Community College System;[28]

6. Commitment to expanded higher education access for low-income and nontraditional college students, especially in the local community; this should include a more cooperative approach to accepting transfer credits from community colleges; another approach might include free or discounted tuition for the children of lower-income employees.[29]

Wherever possible, student involvement in such efforts should be encouraged and facilitated in order to make them an integral part of the education experience offered by the university. Many of these steps would represent significant, even radical, departures from the status quo at the University of Virginia. Yet they offer the university a chance to be a true innovator, to set a national standard for the behavior, practices, and responsibilities of a public university in the twenty-first century. More broadly still, they suggest that the university must consider, at a far deeper level than it has to this point, whether it truly wants to be a good neighbor in its immediate community by recognizing key points of interconnection, engaging in honest dialogue, and working for mutual benefit. A further point is worth noting: such actions, in whatever specific form they ultimately take, would begin to address the complex and problematic legacy of Jefferson and the stain of the university's founding in slavery.

In doing so, UVA would be acting within a long-standing tradition of American political development, going back to the early years of the republic, of complex relationships between private actors and the state under which government assigns public responsibilities, powers, and resources to voluntary, private actors. This pattern of political development is so pervasive that many historians of the state now question the utility of a bright-line distinction between public and private in the United States.[30] It already applies to universities and medical centers such as Johns Hopkins, and it could apply at UVA as well.

Some caution, however, should be exercised in regard to such an approach, whether at the university or in the community. UVA's traditional mission remains and must be fulfilled. As such, the resources available to the university are large but not unlimited—and demands are many. More general still is the point that with the adoption of such a model, whether in Charlottesville or around the United States, academic institutions are being asked to undertake huge governing tasks that in many respects go far beyond the precedents in historical patterns of U.S. state development. These responsibilities are often outside their traditional mission and expertise, and it may simply be too much to expect that they will act for interests beyond their own. Such institutions may be agents of government, but they are not the government. What is needed is more open discussion about the nature and extent of UVA's current responsibilities to the wider community, and, more generally, about whether universities are the appropriate vehicles for the pursuit of such public purposes. The issue and ensuing debate, though, must be joined.

NOTES

1. Davarian Baldwin, "When Universities Swallow Cities," *Chronicle of Higher Education,* July 30, 2017. See also Ira Harkavy and Harmon Zuckerman, "Eds and Meds:

Cities' Hidden Assets," Brookings Institution (Center on Urban and Metropolitan Policy), Survey Series, August 1999; Timothy J. Bartik and George Erickcek, "The Local Economic Impact of 'Eds and Meds': How Policies to Expand Universities and Hospitals Affect Metropolitan Economies," Brookings Institution (Metropolitan Policy Program), Metro Economy Series, December 2008; Marla Nelson, "Are Hospitals an Export Industry? Empirical Evidence from Five Lagging Regions," *Economic Development Quarterly* 23, no. 3 (August 2009): 242–53.

2. Marisela Gomez, *Race, Class, Power, and Organizing in East Baltimore: Rebuilding Abandoned Communities in America* (Lanham, MD: Lexington Books, 2013). For an institutional perspective, see Greg Rienzi, "The Changing Face of East Baltimore," *Johns Hopkins Gazette*, Jan. 2013.

3. "Overview of Health Employment Program Proposal," in Health Services Cost Review Commission (HSCRC) Pre-Meeting Packet, Sept. 9, 2015, http://hscrc .maryland.gov/Documents/commission-meeting/2015/09–09/HSCRC-Public -Pre-Meeting-Packet-2015-09-03.pdf, accessed Feb. 26, 2018; Maryland Hospital Association, "Health Jobs Opportunity Program," in HSCRC Post-Meeting Packet, Sept. 9, 2015, http://hscrc.maryland.gov/Documents/commission -meeting/2015/09–09/HSCRC-Post-Meeting-Packet-2015-09-09-v2.pdf, accessed Feb. 26, 2018.

4. Chet Burrell to John Colmers, Oct. 21, 2015, in HSCRC Post-Meeting Packet, Nov. 18, 2015, and Kimberly Robinson to Colmers, Nov. 13, 2015, both at http:// hscrc.maryland.gov/Documents/commission-meeting/2015/11–18/HSCRC -Post-Meeting-Packet-2015-11-23.pdf, accessed Feb. 26, 2018; Maryland HSCRC, *Preliminary Staff Report for Commission Consideration Regarding Health Job Opportunity Program*, Nov. 18, 2015, quotations on pp. 1, 5, http://hscrc.maryland.gov/ documents/commission-meeting/2015/11–18/HSCRC-Public-Pre-Meeting -Packet-2015-11-10.pdf, accessed Feb. 26, 2018; *Final Report of Health Services Cost Review Commission Regarding Population Health Work Force Support for Disadvantaged Areas, as Approved by the Commission on December 9, 2015*, http://hscrc .maryland.gov/Documents/commission-meeting/2015/12–09/HSCRC-Post -Meeting-Packet-2015-12-16.pdf, accessed Feb. 26, 2018; Meredith Cohn, "Hospitals to Create up to 375 Jobs for Disadvantaged City Residents," *Baltimore Sun*, Dec. 9, 2015.

5. Maryland Department of Legislative Analysis, Office of Policy Analysis, *Property Tax Exemptions and Payments in Lieu of Taxes in Maryland*, Jan. 2014; Pamela Leland, "PILOTS: The Large-City Experience," in *Property Tax Exemption for Charities*, ed. Evelyn Brody, 193–210 (Washington, DC: Urban Institute Press, 2002).

6. UVA Foundation, "Form 990: Return of Organization Exempt from Income Tax" (2015), Schedule D, Part VI, ProPublica Nonprofit Explorer, Nov. 4, 2017, https://projects.propublica.org/nonprofits/organizations/541682176/ 201701093493000131/IRS990ScheduleD, accessed Nov. 4, 2017.

7. UVA Foundation, "Form 990: Return of Organization Exempt from Income Tax" (2015), Part IX, ProPublica Nonprofit Explorer, https://projects.propublica .org/nonprofits/organizations/541682176/201701093493000131/IRS990, accessed Nov. 4, 2017.

8. Bill Chapman, "Property Tax Arrangement between UVA and City Is Unclear, Unexamined," *C-Ville Weekly*, March 6, 2012, www.c-ville.com/Property_ tax_arrangement_between_UVA_and_city_is_unclear_unexamined/# .WgEn37aZPNJ.

9. Specific properties were identified on the city's GIS viewer through searches using terms such as "University of Virginia," "University of Virginia Foundation," and variations on UVA "Rectors and Visitors." The city is not consistent in its coding of owner names, so the results may undercount total tax-exempt property ownership. City of Charlottesville, Charlottesville GIS Viewer, http:// gisweb.charlottesville.org/GisViewer, accessed Feb. 26, 2018.

10. The City of Charlottesville currently has a tax rate of $0.95 per $100 of assessed value, which is higher than Albemarle County ($0.799) and the cities of Bedford ($0.530), Fredericksburg ($0.790), Waynesboro ($0.800), and Williamsburg ($0.570), but lower than other midsize Virginia cities including Alexandria ($1.043), Bristol, ($1.070), Chesapeake ($1.050), Fairfax ($1.040), Martinsville ($1.062), Petersburg ($1.350), Roanoke ($1.190), and Salem ($1.180), and identical to the rates of Staunton and Winchester (all as of 2014). City of Charlottesville, *Operating and Capital Improvement Budget, Adopted Fiscal Year 2017–2018*, ii, L-9, K-3, www .charlottesville.org/home/showdocument?id=54331, accessed Feb. 26, 2018; Virginia Department of Taxation, "Local Tax Rates 2014," www.tax.virginia .gov/sites/default/files/inline-files/Local%20Tax%20Rates%20TY%202014_ March%2024th%202016.pdf, accessed Jan. 29, 2018.

11. UVA also contributed funds to the construction of a new firehouse on Fontaine Avenue near Central Grounds; City of Charlottesville, *Operating and Capital Improvement Budget, Adopted Fiscal Year 2017–2018*, General Fund Revenues, C-1.

12. County of Albemarle, Virginia, *FY 2018 Adopted Budget*, General Fund Revenues, 72, www.albemarle.org/upload/images/Forms_Center/Departments/Budget/ Forms/FY18/FY18_Adopted_Budget_S-FY18-Budget_Complete_Document.pdf, accessed Feb. 26, 2018.

13. Madison House, the primary vehicle for UVA student volunteer work, which is discussed extensively in the report, is an independent 501c3 organization. UVA, "The University of Virginia Academic Division, UVA Health System, and UVA-Wise: Economic Impact Study FY15," (Tripp Umbach, Nov. 2016), 10, 26–30, 34–37.

14. Werner Sensbach, Memorandum to Messrs. Shea, Stacey, Drs. Wood, Hunter, Nov. 21, 1968; A. E. Arrington, "National Goals and the Proposed Gospel Hill Renewal Area," March 20, 1969; and A. E. Arrington to Vincent Shea et al., Aug. 14, 1969, all in Claude Moore Health Sciences Library, Historical Collections, Hospital Executive Director's Office (HEDO) Collection, Box 10, Folder 36: Urban Renewal: Correspondence and Miscellaneous Ms. 1968–1969.

15. Claude Moore Health Sciences Library, Historical Collections, UVA Hospital Celebrating 100 Years—Part 3—History of the University of Virginia Hospital from the 1970s to the Millennium, online exhibit, http://exhibits.hsl.virginia .edu/centennial/growth_part3, accessed Feb. 26, 2018.

16. City of Charlottesville, Blue Ribbon Commission on Race, Memorials, and

Public Spaces, *Report to City Council*, Dec. 19, 2016, pp. 15, 18; and Charlottesville Inventory of African American Historic Sites.

17. Sean Tubbs, "Two City Panels Meet to Further Discuss Affordable Housing Policies," *Charlottesville Tomorrow*, Sept. 18, 2017, www.cvilletomorrow.org/news/article/28596-hac-meeting-with-planners; Brian Wheeler and Sean Tubbs, "At Local Forum, Experts Talk Mixed-Income Housing," *Charlottesville Tomorrow*, Nov. 12, 2017, www.cvilletomorrow.org/news/article/29156-at-local-forum-experts-talk-mixed-income-housing.

18. According to *U.S. News and World Report*, "39 percent of the [undergraduate] students live in college-owned, -operated or -affiliated housing and 61 percent of students live off campus." UVA's on-campus percentage is actually higher than either Berkeley (26 percent) or the University of Michigan (33 percent), www.usnews.com/best-colleges/uva-6968/student-life, accessed Feb. 26, 2018.

19. Chris Suarez, "Despite New Habitat Development, Affordable Housing in Area Still Scarce," *Daily Progress*, Nov. 25, 2017.

20. Judith Rodin, *The University and Urban Revival: Out of the Ivory Tower and into the Streets* (Philadelphia: University of Pennsylvania Press, 2007), 81–106; Sarah Gantz, "Baltimore Housing Program That Partners with Employers Eyes Growth," *Baltimore Business Journal*, Dec. 2, 2015.

21. This has the unfortunate effect of paralleling the early university practice of renting out the Hotels on the range to hotelkeepers who often owned the slaves who served faculty and students; Julia Munro, "Hotelkeepers of the Academical Village," *Jefferson's University . . . the Early Life*, June 9, 2017, http://juel.iath.virginia.edu/node/326.

22. University of Virginia, Office of Equal Opportunity Programs, *An Examination of the University's Minority Classified Staff (The Muddy Floor Report)*, June 1996, available from Vice President and Chief Officer for Diversity and Equity, Resources, https://vpdiversity.virginia.edu/sites/vpdiversity.virginia.edu/files/1996%20the-muddy-floor-report.pdf, accessed Feb. 26, 2018. The quotation is from Workers and Students United for a Living Wage, *Keeping Our Promises: Toward a Living Wage at the University of Virginia in 2012*, p. 10, "Living Wage at UVA," http://livingwageatuva.wixsite.com/lwc-uva/keeping-our-promises, accessed Feb. 26, 2018.

23. Workers and Students United, *Keeping Our Promises*, 10–11.

24. Ibid., 11–12, 67.

25. See, for example, Remarks by UVA President Teresa Sullivan at the Preliminary Meeting of the Board of Visitors, Feb. 23, 2012; Statement from Michael Strine, University of Virginia Executive Vice President and Chief Operating Officer, Feb. 29, 2012; and other documents on UVA's Competitive Compensation Issues website, www.virginia.edu/wages/strine120229.html, accessed Feb. 26, 2018.

26. Caroline Newman, "Board of Visitors Reviews UVA Minimum Wage, Well above Federal Levels," *UVA Today*, Dec. 7, 2017; Amy Glasmeier and Massachusetts Institute of Technology, "Living Wage Calculation for Charlottesville City, Virginia," *Living Wage Calculator*, http://livingwage.mit.edu, accessed Feb. 26, 2018.

27. Lawrence T. Brown et al., "The Rise of Anchor Institutions and the Threat to Community Health: Protecting Community Wealth, Building Community Power," *Kalfou* 3, no. 1 (Fall 2016): 79–100.

28. For a pilot program offering tuition assistance for university employees, see Education Benefit Pilot, www.hr.virginia.edu/hr-for-you/university-staff/university-staff-benefits/education-benefits, accessed Feb. 26, 2018.

29. The Virginia General Assembly considered a bill creating such a program in 2012. At the time UVA argued that it would cost $6 million to cover free tuition for 10 percent of the university's employees; Amanda Iacone, "Bill Would Discount Tuition for Professors' Children," *Daily Progress,* Jan. 22, 2012.

30. Brian Balogh, *The Associational State: American Governance in the Twentieth Century* (Philadelphia: University of Pennsylvania Press, 2015); James Sparrow, William Novak, and Stephen Sawyer, eds., *Boundaries of the State in US History* (Chicago: University of Chicago Press, 2015).

CONTRIBUTORS

ASHER D. BIEMANN is Professor of Religious Studies at the University of Virginia. He is the author, most recently, of *Dreaming of Michelangelo: Jewish Variations on a Modern Theme*.

GREGORY B. FAIRCHILD is the Isidore Horween Research Professor of Business Administration at the University of Virginia's Darden School of Business and Associate Dean for Washington DC Area Initiatives and Academic Director of Public Policy and Entrepreneurship. His work has appeared in such publications as the *Journal of Business Venturing* and *Small Business Publications*.

RISA GOLUBOFF is Dean of the University of Virginia School of Law, the Arnold H. Leon Professor of Law, and Professor of History at the University of Virginia. She is the author, most recently, of *Vagrant Nation: Police Power, Constitutional Change, and the Making of the 1960s*.

BONNIE GORDON is Associate Professor of Music at the University of Virginia. Her articles have appeared in publications such as the *Washington Post* and *Slate*.

CLAUDRENA N. HAROLD is Professor of African American and African Studies and History at the University of Virginia. She is the author, most recently, of *New Negro Politics in the Jim Crow South*.

WILLIS JENKINS is Professor of Religious Studies at the University of Virginia. He is the author, most recently, of *The Future of Ethics: Sustainability, Social Justice, and Religious Creativity*.

LESLIE KENDRICK is Vice Dean and Professor of Law at the University of Virginia School of Law. Her work has appeared in the *Harvard Law Review, Columbia Law Review, Michigan Law Review, Virginia Law Review*, and *Legal Theory*.

JOHN EDWIN MASON is Associate Professor of History at the University of Virginia. He is the author, most recently, of *One Love, Ghoema Beat: Inside the Cape Town Carnival*.

GUIAN MCKEE is Associate Professor of Presidential Studies at the University of Virginia's Miller Center. He is the author of *The Problem of Jobs: Liberalism, Race, and Deindustrialization in Philadelphia* and an editor of the *Presidential Recordings of Lyndon B. Johnson.*

LOUIS P. NELSON is Professor of Architectural History and the Vice Provost for Academic Outreach in the Office of the Provost at the University of Virginia. He is coeditor, with Maurie D. McInnis, of *Shaping the Body Politic: Art and Political Formation in Early America* as well as of a forthcoming volume on the spaces of slavery at Thomas Jefferson's Academical Village.

P. PRESTON REYNOLDS is Professor of Medicine and Nursing in the Division of General Medicine, Geriatrics, and Palliative Care at the University of Virginia. She is the author, most recently, of *Durham's Lincoln Hospital.*

FREDERICK SCHAUER is the David and Mary Harrison Distinguished Professor of Law at the University of Virginia. Prior to joining the Virginia faculty in 2008, he spent nineteen years as the Frank Stanton Professor of the First Amendment at Harvard University. He is the author, most recently, of *The Force of Law.*

ELIZABETH R. VARON is the Langbourne M. Williams Professor of American History and Associate Director of the John L. Nau III Center for Civil War History at the University of Virginia. She is the author of *Appomattox: Victory, Defeat, and Freedom at the End of the Civil War,* among other works.

RACHEL WAHL is Assistant Professor in the Curry School of Education at the University of Virginia and the author of *Just Violence: Torture and Human Rights in the Eyes of the Police.*

LISA WOOLFORK is Associate Professor of English at the University of Virginia and the author of *Embodying American Slavery in Contemporary Culture.*

INDEX